THE SECRETS OF

MASTER

BREWERS

—— • I • ——

TECHNIQUES, TRADITIONS, AND
HOMEBREW RECIPES
for 26 of the World's Classic
Beer Styles

JEFF ALWORTH

Storey Publishing

The mission of Storey Publishing is to serve our customers by publishing practical information that encourages personal independence in harmony with the environment.

Edited by Margaret Sutherland and Lisa Hiley
Art direction and book design by Jeff Stiefel
Text production by Kristy L. MacWilliams
Indexed by Christine R. Lindemer, Boston Road Communications
Cover and interior illustrations by © Kendrick Kidd

Storey books are available for special premium and promotional uses and for customized editions. For further information, please call 800-793-9396.

Storey Publishing
210 MASS MoCA Way
North Adams, MA 01247
storey.com

Printed in the United States by Versa Press
10 9 8 7 6 5 4 3 2 1

Library of Congress Cataloging-in-Publication Data on file

FOR PATRICK AND JOE

FOR GREASED PIG,
PARLIAMENT HOPADELIC,
AND ALL THE TASTY
BEERS WE'VE BREWED

CONTENTS

FOREWORD

Ted Rice, at the time a pub brewer at Blue Corn Café & Brewery in Albuquerque, had never tasted a German-made kölsch before he brewed one in 2003 that won gold at the Great American Beer Festival. A few years later, after he had visited Köln, he shook his head when I asked him to compare their beer with the one he'd made himself. "I can see some similarities," he said, smiling broadly.

Drinking kölsch in Köln or helles in the south of Germany put those traditional beers in perspective. "You see how delicate and refined they are. What happens when a number of breweries around a town or region all focus on one style is they elevate it," Rice told me. "Even a simple . . . ," he paused to consider his choice of words, "everyday beer gets better."

In these pages, Jeff Alworth explains how these styles are a result of regional and national ways of thinking about beer. His premise is basic: "To really understand the beers brewed in other countries, you have to put yourself in the mind of those brewers, to see how they came to their own basic assumptions and how they shape their beer." He also provides a definition of national tradition, writing, "It is a cultural institution, invisible, yet strangely powerful. Like other cultural institutions, it is created and perpetuated by interaction and familiarity."

When Jeff shares the secrets he's learned, he is not referring only to a list of ingredients or even brewing instructions. Brewers have learned directly from each other for millennia. "That's still the way people learn to brew craft beer," according to John Isenhour, a former pub brewer himself and now an instructor at Kennesaw State University whose classes focus on both the scientific and cultural aspects of brewing. His doctoral thesis dealt with the social history of brewing. Before the Industrial Revolution and widespread use of scientific tools such as the thermometer, some knowledge could only be passed directly from brewer to brewer. "You had to experience it with him," Isenhour said. "He'd say you do this when a mash bites smartly on your finger. You had to be there the first time to know what that meant."

Today, head brewer Jason Thompson can start the first brew of the day at Urban Chestnut Brewing Company in St. Louis from a tablet at home. The sparkling stainless steel 60-barrel brewhouse looms behind a 75-foot-long bar in the brewery's massive beer hall, with all its automation on display. Standing on the brew deck as a batch nears completion in one kettle while another starts to his left, he says, "We've got some action now. This is when it starts to get fun." He doesn't really need to be monitoring the system; he's programmed what ingredients will be added and when, and tweaked the process based on the raw materials.

Those are the essentials Thompson learned during more than a dozen years of brewer-to-brewer education. He began brewing in the Gordon Biersch Restaurant and Brewery chain in 2004. Cofounder Dan Gordon was the first American in more than 40 years to graduate from the five-year brewing program at the Technical University of Munich in Weihenstephan, Germany. "There was never a decision [to focus on German-inspired beers]," Thompson says. "I was going to brew beer and I was hired by a lager brewery."

He went to work for German-born and -trained Florian Kuplent (page 72) not long after Urban Chestnut opened in 2011. "It's hard to put into words," Thompson says, describing what he has learned from Kuplent. "I think we put a lot of emphasis on sourcing good ingredients. Florian comes from a place, our beer here comes from a place, where ingredients are important."

It's easy to visualize the invisible hand Jeff writes about when Thompson talks about adjusting the process to accommodate the raw materials. "We can do that because their understanding of what the beer should be is so sound," says Kurt Driesner, Urban Chestnut's quality assurance manager.

Ted Rice's 2003 medal illustrates that good ingredients and brewing practices can produce awards, but, as he discovered, the beer itself may not represent the place it comes from. Rice later helped found Marble Brewery, which in 2014 won Small Brewery of the Year at the GABF. Many of his beers have captured medals, including Marble Pilsner, the Kellerbier gold medalist at WBC in 2014 and bronze medalist in 2016. All the other Kellerbier winners were from European breweries.

"Are we trying to make a German pilsner?" Rice asks. "No. We are making an American beer. I never want to make a knockoff." And he comes back to the everyday beers he discovered in Germany. "We [American brewers] try to make a broad range for everybody. That's what we excel at. The things we make every day we do better," he says.

To that end, Jeff Alworth offers us a book full of out-of-the-ordinary *everyday* beers. Beers that brewers make every day, day after day. Beers that consumers drink every day, day after day.

Pick a style, any style, and begin learning from the best in the business.

— STAN HIERONYMUS
AUTHOR OF *BREWING LOCAL: AMERICAN-GROWN BEER* AND OTHERS

PREFACE: REVEALING THE INVISIBLE HAND

If you've ever had a chance to speak to a professional brewer about his approach, I bet you noticed something: he wasn't uncertain. Over the course of two decades, I've interviewed hundreds of brewers and I'm always taken by their level of conviction — even when a brewer says something that directly contradicts what I heard from another brewer a week before. In the process of making a beer, a brewer has to consider innumerable issues, like how soft the brewing water should be; what temperature(s) the grain should be mashed at and for how long; and whether filtration should be used and, if so, which type. A brewery is no place for the indecisive.

But how do they arrive at those decisions in the first place? A few years ago, I had the great good fortune to be selected by Workman Publishing to write *The Beer Bible*. In order to credibly write about the world's great beer styles, I had to visit breweries and talk to the people who made them. I drew up a list of the dream team of world brewing and asked if I could come and take a tour. Over 50 said yes, and just 2 didn't get back to me in time for the trip. None said no. So off I toddled to places like Fuller's and Samuel Smith's, Dupont and Rodenbach, Schlenkerla and Schneider, Budvar and Urquell. It was every bit the fantasy I'd hoped for — it actually *exceeded* my hopes — but what I took away from the collective experience was an unexpected revelation.

Let's go back to those brewery decision points. Before my world tour, I assumed they would have all been individual, that each brewery would have come to their system through an in-house process of trial and error. Instead, I found something more interesting. It turns out there's a national (or sometimes regional) way of thinking about beer. In some cases it's a profound influence, like brewing to Reinheitsgebot in Germany or bottle-conditioning in warm rooms in Belgium. But sometimes it was small and picayune, like how the English would never consider using the sugar made from beets, or how the Czechs use first-wort hopping.

But in all cases, there's a more pervasive cultural orientation to brewing, a kind of invisible hand that seems to guide breweries. English-ale brewing, for example, is heavily influenced by the pub, where half the country's beer is consumed. It's why so many of the styles are (still, even in the exploding era of craft beer) brewed to under 5% ABV. British drinkers don't go to the pub for one pint; they go for four. Belgian brewing, by contrast, is a product of history. None of the ales brewed there has a lineage of less than several decades, and most go back centuries. Even when Belgians try to brew a beer in a "new" style — as they did with stouts and Scottish ales — it goes through a cultural distortion field that makes it look like something that was originally brewed in the 1820s.

If you want to take this point to its most florid example, look to the twin German cities of Cologne and Düsseldorf, ultramodern western cities where local pubs could sell any style of beer in the world. Instead, the locals make only one beer style in each town, and they would never, ever dream of brewing the beer of the other town just a few minutes down the Rhine River. How, except by the dictates of that invisible hand of culture, could you describe *that*?

To really understand the beers brewed in other countries, you have to put yourself in the mind of those brewers, to see how they came to their own basic assumptions and how they shape the beer. As an American journalist asking a German weissbier maker questions about his brewing process, I got a quick lesson in where my assumptions lay. Every time I traveled to a new country, I received a new lesson in how brewers there thought about and brewed beer.

The last time I was perusing homebrew books on Amazon, I counted 497 or thereabouts. It is certainly not unreasonable to ask: couldn't we get by with just, say, a top 10? Do we really need a 498th homebrewing book?

If we need a new homebrew book — and obviously I think we do — it's because these methods and approaches haven't been transmitted to American homebrewers. I realized this when I started talking to homebrewers back home — and when I brewed a batch of beer in one of the styles I'd seen in Europe. (Although I'm still not a great brewer, I've been doing it 22 years, longer even than I've been writing about beer.) There's just no single resource out there that tells you how the Irish make stout, the English make cask ale, the Germans make weissbier, and the Czechs make pilsner.

I thought it would be a wonderful thing to contact those brewers I interviewed for *The Beer Bible* and have them translate their approaches to American homebrewers directly, the way I heard about them. There are recipes in each chapter of this book, but more important is the discussion of the invisible hand that guides each style's creation. The chapters were designed not to teach you how to clone a particular famous beer but to understand an entire approach to brewing in that beer's tradition. I've had a chance to have dozens of incredible brewers give me the secrets to the beers they brew, and I don't want to keep it all to myself.

I hope you find the information in this book as fascinating as I did.

Cheers — Jeff Alworth

HOW TO USE THIS BOOK

When I first had the idea to write this book, I was thinking I'd include a chapter for every beer style, much like they appear in *The Beer Bible*. As I began to get down to writing it, though, I realized that this would create quite a bit of redundancy. Because while it's true that brewers approach things very differently in, say Germany and Belgium, *within* a country they don't necessarily mix things up too much when brewing different styles. The difference between a strong Belgian golden ale and a dubbel basically comes down to a slightly different malt (and sugar) bill. And while brewing traditions have critical deviations from one another in some ways, in others — aging inside wooden tuns, for example — they share some features. It didn't make a lot of sense to keep repeating these practices over and over again, either.

So, what you'll find in the book is a country-by-country collection of chapters. Each section begins with a discussion of the country at hand and what makes its national tradition distinctive. It may not seem immediately evident how Berliner weisse and helles lagers are alike, but they have more in common than you might imagine. Beyond that, the basic techniques shared among the traditions, things like open fermentation, barrel aging, kettle souring, spicing, decoction mashing, lagering, are described in detail only once. If one of these practices is relevant to a particular style but detailed elsewhere, I've mentioned where you can learn more.

By the way, this book isn't a great starting place for those of you who have never brewed a batch of beer in your life, but it absolutely doesn't require you to be a master, either. It's for the almost-beginner. If you have never brewed beer, I recommend buying a basic how-to book and making a couple of practice batches before you start putting this book to use after about your third batch. Following are a few more specific points worth addressing.

BASIC ASSUMPTIONS ABOUT THESE RECIPES

The recipes in this book will make a 5-gallon (19 L) batch of beer. As I was working with brewers and putting together the ingredients list, I assumed a brewery efficiency of 75 percent. However, I also included values for both the percentages of the grain bill and the IBU contribution of each hop addition. If you want to make a 3- or 6.5-gallon batch, you can easily adapt the recipes to suit your batch size.

If you've found your efficiency is better or worse than 75 percent, adjust recipes accordingly. Each section on ingredients and formulation has a header for the malt bill, the type of mash (infusion, step, decoction), the length of the boil, fermentation and conditioning, and finally the package type.

GUIDELINES, NOT RULES

These recipes were created as basic blueprints. They describe the process commercial breweries use, and in some cases, it's going to be a serious challenge for homebrewers to follow the prescription precisely. Schneider & Sohn's Hans-Peter Drexler uses *seven* temperature rests to make his classic weissbier. If you were to do, say, three or four of these, would you end up with a tasty weissbier? Yes. The detail is given so that you can see the complete version, not to make you crazy. Beyond that, each recipe is offered with the knowledge that you will tweak it to your preferences. The chapters describe the orthodox approach to brewing the style, but they don't demand that you use it. (I'm an American, so I *would* say that, wouldn't I?)

EQUIPMENT VARIABLES

Every brewery is different; this applies to homebrew setups as well as professional breweries. The ingredients and formulations in this book don't tell you *how* to do some very important things. If you're doing single-infusion mashing inside a cooler and don't have any way to raise the temperature of your mash, step-mashing is going to be a challenge. Lagering is not easy. Post–kettle hopping may not be a snap. Since every setup is different, you are going to have to figure out how to implement these methods if you want to use them.

Another thing I've learned from poking around so many breweries is that this is precisely the situation professionals find themselves in all the time. They have breweries designed to do one thing, and they decide they want to do another. Just like homebrewers, they rig something up. And just like homebrewers, it *usually* works. Fiddling with equipment is part of brewing.

ASSUMED INFORMATION

Going into every recipe, there is a ton of detail that could be added — but in trying to keep the book to a manageable size, I'll let you address these on your own.

WATER. Tap water differs in every town (or well). These recipes assume your brewing water, or liquor, is basically neutral and salt/mineral-free. Many homebrewers with hard tap water buy reverse-osmosis or distilled water to brew with. If water amendments are necessary, that information is mentioned in the recipe. Additionally, many homebrewers adjust the pH of their liquor for brewing, which is up to you. For more on pH, see chapter 20, Italian Lagers.

MASH THICKNESS. Mash thickness is expressed as a ratio of quarts of water to pounds of grain, typically in the range of 1.25 to 2 quarts per pound. Use the thickness you're used to using and that works on your system.

RECIRCULATION. This is a process of filtering the wort of cloudy proteins and grain particles by running out wort and sprinkling it back on the grain bed (sometimes called "vorlauf"). You can recirculate for as little or as much as you normally do.

SPARGING. Sparging is the process of rinsing the grain with warm water (usually 170°F [77°C]) at the end of the mash. It is assumed every mash will end with sparging except when parti-gyle brewing.

BOIL VOLUME. Boil rates vary by kettle size. Note that specified boil lengths range from one to two hours and longer boils will need to begin with greater wort volume. You will have to calculate your own boil-off rate and adjust your system to end up with 5 gallons of pitchable wort.

WHOLE HOPS. All recipes were designed based on whole hop additions. Pellet hops result in greater utilization than whole hops, so adjust recipes accordingly.

HOP SCHEDULE. Just for clarity, the minutes given for the hop schedule refer to the amount of time each hop addition should be boiled. So in a recipe that calls for "XX hops, 60 minutes, and XX hops, 30 minutes," the first addition should boil for 60 minutes and the second should be added after half an hour to boil for the remaining 30 minutes. An addition calling for a 10-minute boil should be added 50 minutes into the hour.

PACKAGING. Homebrewers tend to prefer bottle conditioning or kegging, and in most cases your preference is fine. Note that in cases where there's a reason to choose one over the other, I have mentioned it.

RECIPE SOFTWARE

Most homebrewers have a preferred software program to calculate recipes. They all seem to use slightly different algorithms to produce their numbers. I don't know that any of these are necessarily better than others, but take note of how your beer turns out and compare it to the program you're using. If you're consistently getting more or less efficiency than you expect (a higher or lower starting gravity), you can adjust them in advance. In translating the recipes from the pros to a 5-gallon batch, I relied on Brewer's Friend, but there are many others available online. If you're using a different program, you might plug in the numbers in this book to see how close they are to your program and adjust if necessary.

HAVE FUN

That's the whole point! And you end up with tasty beer and more knowledge in the end. What could be better?

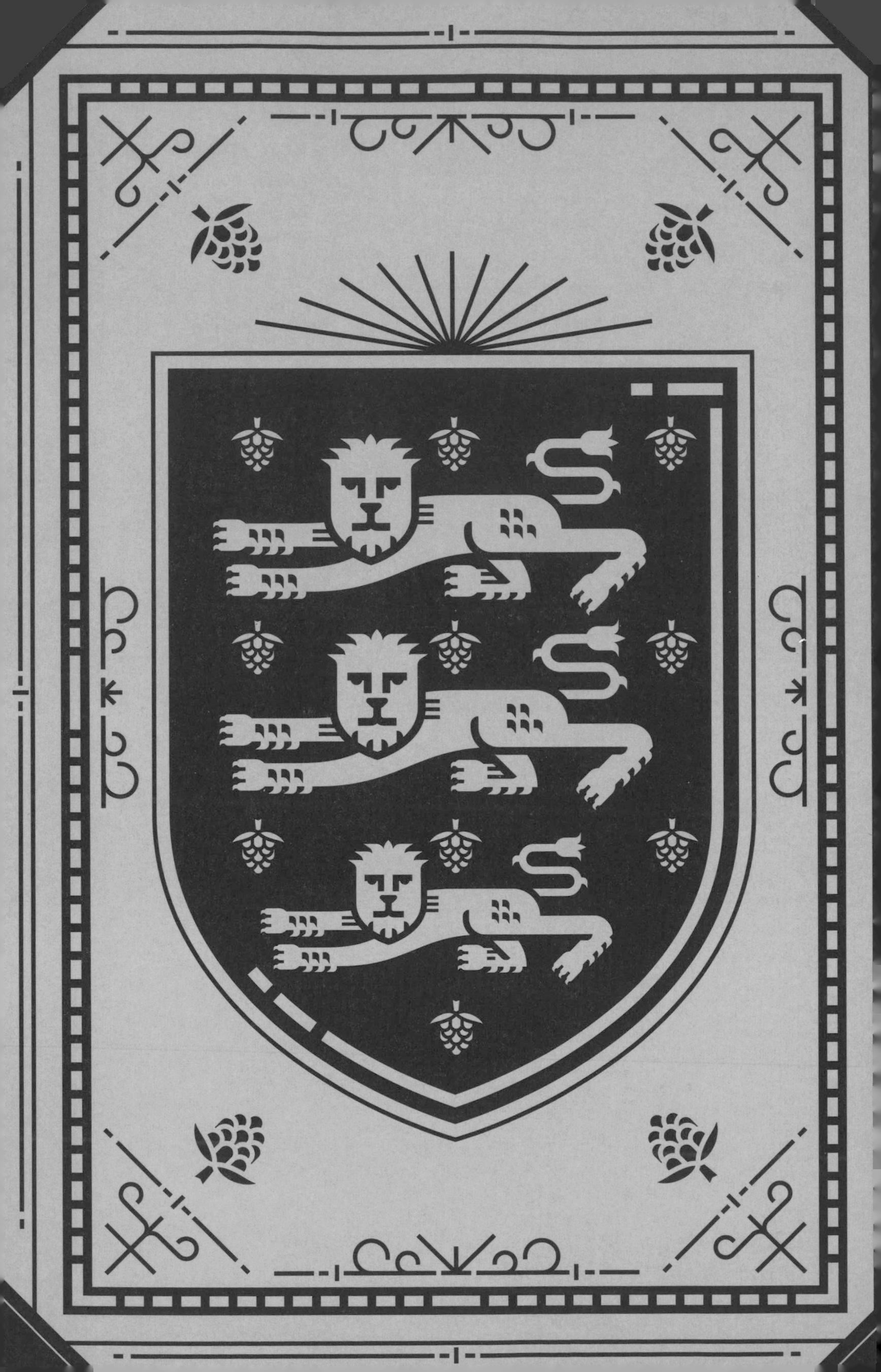

Part 1

British

TRADITION

—

Brewing is an ancient art on the island of Great Britain, and a number of practices in modern brewing have very deep roots. But the lineage does not run in a straight line, and there are also many paradoxes. The slender water channel that separates the island from continental Europe isolated brewers who were at times far ahead or far behind their contemporaries on the mainland.

Hops, for example, traveled throughout Europe before arriving last in Britain, and hop-free or low-hop brews (called "ales" locally — as opposed to the stronger, hoppy cousins known as "beer") were produced until relatively recently. On the other hand, British brewers advanced the science of brewing light-years ahead of mainland brewers during the Industrial Revolution. They used attemperation (a method of controlling temperature), steam power, sparging (rinsing the grain), and advanced malting techniques in ways the rest of Europe could only marvel at. (It's why the famous Austrian and Bavarian brewers Anton Dreher and Gabriel Sedlmayr traveled there to conduct "research" — some might call it industrial espionage — in 1833 and why the burghers of Pilsen outfitted their new brewery with a maltings, also known as a malt house, and kiln "equipped in the English manner" a decade later.)

But then everything slowed during the reign of Queen Victoria in the 1800s and has remained largely static ever since. If you have a chance to travel around to any of the old breweries now — Greene King, Samuel Smith's, Hook Norton — you find "Victorian tower breweries" still in use that were state of the art in 1860. They use gravity to send the beer on its journey from the mill down to the mash tun, then farther down to the kettle, and finally down to the fermenters. Greene King, in fact, felt the old design was so important that it recently spent £14 million to *restore* the Victorian elements. ("We could have gone mash-filter, we could have gone lauter, but no, we said we're staying with what we know," brewer John Bexon told me. "Okay, we could have gotten a bit more efficiency by doing it, but I think you lose the authenticity.")

This not only has created remarkable continuity in British brewing but goes a long way toward defining the contours of British ales. Made from single-infusion mashes on imprecise, manual equipment; boiled over open flames; and fermented in open, square fermenters, British ales have noticeable batch-by-batch variation (something that should hearten rustic homebrewers like me). Served on cask, the living beer evolves by the hour, so that drinkers develop a relationship with the mutability of their favorite pint.

John Keeling, the longtime head brewer at Fuller's, says this is a feature of British brewing, not a flaw. "You can never make batches of beer that are exactly the same no matter how good you are, and in fact, to try to make them exactly the same, that means taking flavors out because they're so hard to manage on that consistent basis. And that's really what we call character."

> You have a dialogue with [each] beer. To me, it's like walking into a bar and noticing your friend at the bar has had a haircut. He's still your friend, he just looks a little bit different. It's the same as going up to the bar, ordering London Pride and going, "Oh, can you pick out some orange notes in there?"
>
> — JOHN KEELING, FULLER'S

Since the turn of the new millennium, a strain of brewing in Britain has developed that takes its cues from the United States — stronger beer made with bales of hops. The older tradition is still dominant, however, and the new one has not lost a sight-line connection with cask ale. The British tradition, though evolving, remains very much intact. When you sit down in front of a pint of British ale or seek to brew one, these are the elements to keep in mind.

BASE MALT BARLEY VARIETIES. The key foundation to a British cask ale is the base malt, which provides the beer with the warm, comforting character that defines these beers. Americans have occasionally heard of one of these base malts, called Maris Otter, but this is in fact the barley variety, and there are a number of different ones in regular use: Pearl, Tipple, Halcyon, Golden Promise, and Optic. Each one gives a slightly different flavor. Some are nuttier and others more bready; some are sweeter and others drier; some have notes of toffee, figs, or Malt-O-Meal. Finding the base malt that exhibits the character the brewer wants is no less important on the flavor profile than finding the right yeast strain or hop variety.

ENGLISH HOPS. English hops are less assertive than American strains, a virtue that helps them harmonize with the rich, aromatic malts. Even in beers where stiffer hopping is called for, English varieties tend toward sweeter, more marmalade-like flavors. It's not always easy to source high-quality hops from England, but many American cultivars descend from English strains. Willamette descends from Fuggle stock and is a mainstay (because Fuggles are dying out in England, British brewers are replacing them with Willamette).

FRUITY YEASTS. Many old British breweries continue to use the same yeast strains they've used for decades, and they develop distinctive house character. This is another important way British ales are different from their American descendants, which commonly use neutral yeasts. English yeasts may accentuate the mineral quality of the water and often add jammy esters that taste like apricot, quince, and plum. They may also produce diacetyl, a flavor not out of place — in modest amounts — in a pint of cask ale.

HARD WATER. Everyone knows about the famously hard water of Burton upon Trent (which gives beer the sulfurous aroma locals call "Burton snatch"), but there's more nuance here than is usually appreciated. Most old breweries get their water from wells. And while it's true that most British water is hard, it's not possible to generalize about "Burton water" or "London water." One well dug at 25 meters will draw waters different from another well a few miles away dug at 50 meters. The unique water of each brewery is yet another element in the house character. Homebrewers trying to inject a bit of Britishness into their beer would do well to experiment to find which water amendments work best.

BREWING SUGAR. It is very common for British brewers to dose their grists with sugar to lighten the body and add a crisp finish to their beers. American palates favor fuller ales, but judicious use of sugar helps brewers achieve that famous "moreishness" in beers meant for being drunk in groups of twos and threes. Darker sugars may also be required in such low-alcohol beers as brown ales and milds.

CASK CONDITIONING. Traditional British beer was made to be drunk from the cask. This is not a romantic comment but a scientific one. British ale goes from the brewery to the pub literally in days, sometimes even before it has completely fermented. It finishes out in the pub's cellar, lightly carbonating inside the cask. This has a dramatic effect on the beer. Those flavors we've talked about — the rich malts, fruity yeasts, delicate hops, and minerally water — all blossom in the relatively warm environment (roughly 55°F [13°C]) of the cellar. When they're served fresh, pints of cask ale taste more vivid, fuller, and livelier than anything from a bottle. The homebrewer can achieve some of the effect with bottle conditioning, but rigging up a home cask (see chapter 1, Cask Ales) is the way to enjoy the real thing.

There are, of course, many more subtleties to the wonderfully understated beers of Britain, so let's dig and explore.

· CHAPTER 1 ·

CASK ALES

ask ale is a presentation, not a style. It is separated out here for special treatment because of the import of that presentation. Although not widely popular in the United States, cask ales still represent the spine of the British brewing tradition. In an English pub you will always find a local bitter on cask, possibly more than one, possibly in differing strengths; it might be accompanied by other styles — a mild, stout, strong ale or even a hoppy, American-style ale. (Scottish pubs have less fealty to cask, and local ales are sometimes served on keg.) What knits these beers together is the way they're prepared and served — alive, with fizz coming from fermentation just concluded, with low levels of carbonation, and at cellar temperatures.

Not all beer displays its qualities best in this environment. Cask ales are usually weak by American standards (3 to 5% is typical) and beguilingly simple. That's important, because on cask the flavors of beer are more naked, more accessible. Flavors that would otherwise be washed out by stiffer carbonation and colder temperatures have a chance to blossom. The example offered here is a standard English bitter, but the process would work with a mild, a brown, a porter, or even a lighter, less insistently hopped American-style ale. This is the beer presentation most overlooked by Americans (or sometimes used with inappropriately strong, hoppy styles), which is a real shame. Although cask ales yield their accomplishment more slowly, they are the equal to any beer in the world. Brew up a cask or four and spend time with the results; see if you don't discover their allure, too.

EST **Greene King** 1799
BURY ST EDMUNDS, ENGLAND

Greene King's estate — and it does feel like an estate — is one of the grandest of any brewery's. Sprawling across 44 acres, it combines the architectural splendor of a Georgian-era building with industrial Victorian steampunk touches. Giant steel tanks stand sentinel while pipes carry beer underneath the brewery — underneath the city streets, in fact — or sometimes soar aboveground, exposed, for hundreds of feet. The brewery itself overlooks the much shorter town structures like a benevolent lord surveying his domain.

The most fascinating part of the Greene King story is not its physical or corporate size. (With three thousand pubs and several important brands such as Morland and Belhaven in its portfolio, Greene King is the largest ale brewery in

Great Britain.) The intriguing part is that, with all the resources at its disposal, Greene King continues to make beer the way it has since the nineteenth century. The brewery has the classic design, with grain sacks and mill at the top floor following gravity's course toward fermentation several floors down.

A decade ago, as the brewery's old copper equipment creaked toward its inevitable end, Greene King had to decide whether to patch things up or modernize. Amazingly, the brewery chose to spend £14 million, not to build a state-of-the-art facility optimized for industrial, high-gravity brewing but to *restore* all the copper. The brewery still looks much the same as it did 40 years ago, but the equipment is back to its original nineteenth-century condition. Whatever else you might say about Greene King — and people always have lots to say about a country's biggest brewery — the beer is traditional from top to bottom.

Greene King's flagship brew is called IPA, but it's actually a light bitter, and a perfect cask ale. With just 3.6 percent alcohol (see? — not an IPA), it nevertheless has a toasty, caramel body and lively English hopping. It's the kind of beer that absolutely was designed to be served on cask, where the flavors bloom, and enjoyed in triplicate down at the pub. Prodded by the excitement British craft breweries have generated, Greene King expanded the IPA line to three other offerings, but they too are typical English bitters. The brewery doesn't ignore the march of time, but it has a characteristically traditional approach to addressing it.

BREWMASTER CRAIG BENNETT

Greene King has a difficult, almost contradictory charge: chart a course into the uncertain future while holding firmly to tradition. When outgoing head brewer John Bexon left in 2015, Greene King replaced him with a man who personifies change and continuity. Craig Bennett began homebrewing while he was at the University of Dundee, but his roots extend back even further than that — his uncle was also a brewer. After he received a degree in microbiology, he went on to get his brewing qualifications from Heriot-Watt University brewing school and then brewed for nearly a decade at McMullen & Sons. He joined Greene King 15 years ago and was recently involved in developing a line of experimental beers for Greene King under the Metropolitan label. So while he will guard beers such as Greene King IPA, Morland Old Speckled Hen, and the legendary Greene King Strong Suffolk, he has also developed green tea and whiskey beers. The future seems safe with Bennett.

Understanding Cask Ales

Americans who have only ever tasted English ales from the bottle (especially bottles shipped from the UK and aged for God knows how long) may wonder what all the fuss is about, but the point is these ales were not meant to be served from a bottle. No other beer falls nearly as far from its ideal state as cask ale when bottled, and I wonder why breweries even bother. Proponents often say it's a "living" thing that gets its character from the just-active yeast that settles inside the cask, but this isn't quite right. Any unfiltered beer is "living" in that sense. What actually gives it the character is the beer's freshness and the way it's served.

Cask ale is extremely young beer. Traditional breweries package their beer after a few days, even while primary fermentation is still under way. It is sent to pubs, where the fermentation finishes out, carbonating the beer naturally. Very often, breweries add a sachet of whole hops inside the cask. When the publican taps the beer, it is vibrantly fresh, right in the middle of the process of dry hopping. Freshness is key.

Pouring it from the cask — or pulling it via an engine — is also critical. The fresh beer is only lightly carbonated. When you're dealing with beers that largely fall below 5% ABV — and are sometimes just 3% — low carbonation helps create the sense of thicker body. Low carbonation and somewhat warmer temperatures encourage the flavors to emerge. This is particularly true with the flavorful base malts, which taste lush and full at the pub but fall away in the bottle. Serving these beers on cask is like creating a flavor magnifier. The malts, hops, and yeast all express themselves, but the beer is light and moreish, so you can sit back and drink two or three full pints without feeling tipsy or bloated. Even in Britain, cask ale is underappreciated — the fault of familiarity, probably — but a good cask bitter is one of the most impressive beers in the world.

Brewing a Cask Ale

For American homebrewers, brewing a cask ale is a snap. Traditional breweries like Greene King are imprecise (by modern standards) and simple — very much like home breweries. They employ single-infusion mashes, have straightforward boils and ferments, and are even packaged in a way that is, at least conceptually, wholly familiar to the homebrewer.

The thing to keep your eye on is the malt-hop balance and, particularly, on the importance of flavorful base malts. These are incredibly simple beers, but simplicity can be a trap. To hang flavor on such slender scaffolding, you have to begin with a classic English malt. Americans generally have access to Maris Otter, a winter variety, but there are so many other options. Optic, Tipple, Concerto (spring varieties) and Pearl and Halcyon (winter) are just a few examples of the different barleys used to make malt. We don't get all of these in the United States, but we do get more than Maris Otter, so consider experimenting. In Britain brewers have their own preferences, choosing barleys with flavors that will harmonize with the brewery's yeast and favored hops. In a good cask ale, malt flavors should not only be evident but distinctive.

These are incredibly simple beers, but simplicity can be a trap. To hang flavor on such slender scaffolding, you have to begin with a classic English malt.

A corollary to the focus on malt is a de-emphasis (from the American perspective) of hops. Even bitter, a style that depends on hop assertiveness, is not very bitter. In this case "balance" means that the hops should be of roughly the same intensity as the combined flavors contributed by malt and yeast and no more. It's hard for Americans to stay their hands when they reach for the hop sack, but if you try, you'll be rewarded when you pour your third pint and realize why that balance is prized in Britain.

BOTTLE CONDITIONING

In commercial brewing, conditioning a beer in the bottle or can is rare, at least outside of Belgium. Most homebrewers will have experience with it. The process is very simple. Just before bottling, you'll boil 2 cups of water and add dextrose, then add the solution to the carboy. Many sources give a defined amount of dextrose to use — usually around ¾ cup. This is a decent average, but it's much more reliable to go to an online calculator and find out exactly how much to add based on the level of effervescence you hope to achieve. Just type "priming calculator" into your search browser and follow the instructions.

CASK ALE

CRAIG BENNETT

GREENE KING

MALT BILL

6 pounds English pale malt (87%)

9 ounces medium crystal malt (8%)

5 ounces invert sugar (5%)

SINGLE-INFUSION MASH

147°F (64°C) for 60 minutes

Sparge at 169°F (76°C)

60-MINUTE BOIL

0.5 ounce First Gold, 60 minutes (8.0% AA, contribution of 15 IBU)

0.5 ounce Challenger, 60 minutes (8.0% AA, contribution of 15 IBU)

2 ounces East Kent Goldings, end of boil (5.0% AA, contribution of 4 IBU)

FERMENTATION AND CONDITIONING

Ferment with an English ale strain at 66 to 70°F (16–21°C). Cool to 46°F (8°C) for 24 to 48 hours.

PACKAGE

Cask condition (see Cask Conditioning at Home, page 16). If you want to make a standard English bitter and bottle it, increase the gravity to 11° P (1.044).

- Expected OG: 9.5° P/1.038

- Expected TG: 2.2° P/1.009

- Expected ABV: 3.8%

- Expected bitterness: 30–35 IBU

Notes: Bennett suggests a malt bill of 92 percent pale and 8 percent crystal for all-malt bitters, with an option to substitute up to 10 percent of the grist with sugar. Add the Goldings "at end of boil, in copper, whirlpool, or hop back."

NEXT STEPS

Bennett's recipe creates a classic bitter, similar to a slightly souped-up version of Greene King IPA. It will deliver the balance and drinkability you want from a cask ale, but there are almost innumerable permutations. Not only can you tinker with the basics of a bitter recipe — changing the grist ratios slightly, using all-malt grists, or using different hops, base malt, or yeast — but you can create a stronger bitter, mild, brown, or porter to be served on cask (examples of which follow). Cask ales are simple to make, but they require real craft and attention to dial in. Beers such as Timothy Taylor Landlord, Fuller's London Pride, or Greene King IPA didn't happen by accident but were instead refined over years.

USING SUGAR

Bill Schneller is a beer educator, an award-winning homebrewer, and a Beer Judge Certification Program Master Judge — and one of the people I turn to when I have homebrewing questions. He's also a big fan of using brewing sugar, particularly invert sugar (more on that in chapter 3).

"Increasingly, I make more and more bitters using dark sugar either instead of or in addition to crystal malt. I think most homebrewers, especially newer brewers, use way too much crystal malt. But if you use invert, you can drop the crystal altogether or you can drop it by half. Then you have a beer with 7 pounds of pale malt, a ¼-pound crystal, and a ½-pound Invert 2 (90 percent pale, 3.5 percent crystal, and 6.5 percent sugar). Richer color, different dried fruit flavors than from crystal alone, plus a drier, easier-drinking beer than if you use all crystal malt.

"I even have started to use No. 3 and No. 4 in stouts and porters. It gives raisin notes without lending too much residual sugar the way a dark crystal would. You just can't get the flavors of invert from crystal malts. Since I brew almost exclusively UK-style beers these days, I use it in almost every style of beer I make except for some of the bigger stock ales, which tend to be 100 percent pale malt. It adds complexity and flavors you just can't get anywhere else."

Cask Conditioning at Home

For a number of reasons, it's hard to make cask-conditioned beer for the home. The biggest challenge is freshness. In the traditional setup, the cask is prepared so that it must be served within a day or two. As the beer is served, the empty space in the cask is replaced by the ambient air in the cellar. Within hours the flavor begins to change, and it will sour and stale after a couple of days. A homebrewer might prepare a 5-gallon cask for a party, but if it isn't all used, she confronts the prospect of seeing a lot of good beer go to waste. That said, home-casking beer, even for special occasions, can be a real treat.

You can actually buy small English-style casks now. The little ones are called "pins" and hold 5.4 gallons — just about perfect for homebrewers. They're somewhat expensive, and you need to buy the various accoutrements needed for serving — keystones, shives, and spiles — but the casks will be with you for a lifetime and they are mighty cool. If you want to improvise a home cask and you're already using a Cornelius-style keg, you're in luck. Here's what you do.

MAKE A BATCH OF BEER as you normally would. If you're familiar with your yeast strain and confident you know when it will reach terminal gravity, transfer the fermenting beer when it is 1 degree Plato (.004) from terminal. (The recipe in this chapter calls for a terminal gravity of 1.009, so you'd transfer at 1.013.) Alternatively, let it go to dry, and then prime with sugar, calculating to add around 1.5 volumes of carbon dioxide. I highly recommend dry-hopping with an ounce or two in a hop sack at this point — it adds a wonderful layer of aroma to the freshly served beer.

GIVE THE KEG SEVERAL DAYS to finish fermenting. Before serving, situate the keg horizontally, *in the place from which you intend to dispense it*, with the bottom propped up about 4 inches and the gas valve at the bottom. Your cask is now full of yeast, and you want it to settle before serving. Buy some sacks of ice the night before you plan to serve the beer and drape them over and around the cask to chill the night before serving, or a minimum of 12 hours.

DISPENSING IS STRAIGHTFORWARD, except that in this cask arrangement you reverse the gas and beer dip tubes, so the gas dip tube is positioned at the bottom and the beer dip tube is at the top. Attach a short hose to the top (the gas) post and poke a cotton ball gently in the end. Attach a regular serving line with picnic tap to the bottom (the beer) post and serve.

CO₂ Option

Here's a not-traditional but important variation that will buy you more time: Proceed as above, but instead of attaching a serving-line-cum-cotton-ball to the air inlet, attach it to your regular CO_2 tank and set it to 1 to 2 psi while you serve it. Instead of oxygen filling up the cask, you'll be filling it with sanitary CO_2. When you're not using the cask, disconnect the gas so that it doesn't absorb into the beer. The idea here is to put a blanket of gas over the beer, not further carbonate it. (As a commercial practice, this is frowned upon by certain advocacy groups in England for arcane political reasons. As purely a matter of beer, it's completely respectable.)

There are elaborations to this basic system. You can create a container for the cask that is easier to keep iced. You can add a beer engine to the system and pump the beer. (A cheap alternative to a pub engine are hand pumps used in RVs that you can buy for 30 bucks online.) People tinker with the dip tubes and gas posts to pull less yeasty beer out. Once you have mastered the basic system, making incremental improvements is easy enough over time.

CHAPTER 2

STRONG BITTERS

trong ales were until recently not at all common in the UK. On a 10-day brewery tour in 2011, I got so used to 3.8% beers that when I encountered a "strong" ale in Yorkshire on about day 7 — it was all of 5% — I caught myself murmuring to the barkeep, "Wow, that *is* strong." In other words, strength is relative. Regular bitters start out around 3.5%, and by the time they're a percentage higher, they creep into a middle netherworld. Strong bitters fall in the 5 to 6% range and are not especially common. This confuses some Americans, who equate bitter and in some cases all of English beer with ESB — and here we need to do some unpacking.

There is no ESB "style" in Britain. Breweries try to signal to their customers when they're making stronger-than-usual versions with names like "best," "special," "strong," or "premium." In London one brewery styled their strong bitter "Extra Special." Fuller's ESB was (and is) such a good beer that it came to represent not only strong bitter in the minds of Americans but all bitters.

I can't actually blame my countrymen. If you haven't had a bottle recently, track one down. Fuller's ESB is a surprisingly powerful beer (and therefore a poor candidate to represent a common English bitter), with a boatload of hops and quite a decent alcohol punch (5.9% in the bottle). Its stats suggest something closer to the American lineage, but on the palate it's purely British. A toffeeish malt base is accented by marmalade hops fading into pepper and a twist of lemon, all wrapped up in lovely, fruity esters. If it is not the quintessential bitter, it may well be the quintessential *strong* bitter.

EST Fuller, Smith & Turner 1845
LONDON, ENGLAND

Fuller, Smith & Turner — Fuller's, to most people — has been making beer in London since 1845. As is often the case in Europe, brewing on the site pre-dated Fuller's, going back at least to the late 1600s. The name of the building itself — the Griffin Brewery — dates back to a previous owner and hints at the site's long lineage. The modern Fuller's we know — festooned with awards and famous around the world — was not always so. John Keeling, the head brewer, described the brewery in the decade before he arrived. "In the sixties, Fuller's was really a company not going anywhere — like a lot of regional breweries in the UK. Seventies come along, [and it was] still just pottering along, not really thinking about the future." The owners decided to make a change in the late 1970s and put Fuller's on its current course. Between 1978 and 1989 its three core bitters, ESB, London Pride, and Chiswick Bitter, each won a medal as Champion Beer of Britain, the country's most prestigious cask ale award — and ESB won it three times.

London was once the seat of British brewing, but over the centuries the number of breweries dwindled. By the time Young's closed down in 2006, Fuller's was the one remaining traditional London brewery. Now when people visit the capital and stop in for a pint, they often find themselves in a Fuller's pub. All three of the brewery's flagship bitters are made using the very old parti-gyle method of brewing (see Parti-Gyle Brewing, page 26), making Fuller's one of the most traditional breweries in the world.

And yet when visitors pop in they'll have a range of choices from dozens of beers Fuller's makes each year. As craft beer has flourished in the city (there are now more than 60 local breweries), Fuller's has embraced hoppy, strong, and dark ales. Their approach has created a blueprint for other traditional breweries for adapting to the changes in twenty-first-century tastes.

BREWMASTER JOHN KEELING

John Keeling arrived at Fuller's in 1981, but three and a half decades haven't dulled his drawn-out, rounded Manchester accent in the least. His arrival coincided with the brewery's illustrious revival, but Keeling's greatest contribution has been guiding Fuller's through Britain's craft beer era — during which London has seen its number of breweries jump to over five dozen. Unlike some traditional breweries that refuse to evolve, Keeling has reveled in experimentation and collaboration, exploring what tradition looks like when it's given a bit of air to breathe.

That willingness has paradoxically allowed many people to rediscover Fuller's traditional offerings. Because of Keeling's willingness to embrace the new, he has become an eloquent spokesman for the old and traditional. "Yes, I want it to occasionally surprise you," he says, of London Pride — though he could have been talking about any of Fuller's offerings. "Today it's a little bit more malty or caramelly or hoppy or fragrant or whatever — so that you are having a dialogue with that beer. And that's really what we call character."

Understanding Strong Bitters

Given how much strong bitters (ESBs, as Americans think of them) superficially resemble IPAs, it's surprising how different they are — and the differences are instructive. Modern American IPAs are built to highlight hops. Yeast and water play almost no role, and malt, to the extent breweries want its presence known, contributes only a dollop of sweetening caramel. Strong bitters rely on a balance of all these elements. The malts may contain a note of caramel or toffee, but the rich base malts have more aromas and tastes to create textures of flavor — you might get hazelnut or toffee or biscuit and the scent of warm bread.

It's typical for English strong bitters to begin with stiff, minerally water, and this in turn helps the hops, which are less assertive than in IPAs, pop. Finally, English breweries use ester-producing yeasts that fill out the palette of flavors with distinctive fruitiness that comes from house strains.

In the world of English brewing, strong bitters are a decided minority — their smaller kin are much, much more common in pubs around the island. That niche status allows brewers a little leeway in accentuating one element over another — Adnams Broadside is a velvety, sweet version, while Wells Bombardier is a rich, fruity ale. Others focus on nuts or hops, or highlight their flavors with a strong mineral profile. Homebrewers may be tempted to drive a strong bitter in the direction of an American IPA, but by finding one of these other elements to highlight, you'll produce a wonderful beer that impresses on its own merits.

Brewing a Strong Bitter

Much as with the regular bitter, there are no special tricks to brewing strong bitters. They go through single-infusion mashes and typical hopping schedules (though many breweries use hop backs after the boil). This is one of the few styles for which you might want to consider treating your water. Many breweries fully Burtonize their water, but that might be overkill. Burton water, depending on the well from which it's drawn, may have tons of minerals (magnesium, sodium, calcium, bicarbonate, sulfate, and chloride). I'd recommend starting with just a modest gypsum (calcium sulfate) addition — say, a tablespoon per batch.

JOHN KEELING
AND
GEORGINA YOUNG

—

FULLER'S

MALT BILL

10.75 pounds English pale malt (96%)

0.4 pound wheat malt (4%)

SINGLE-INFUSION MASH

149°F (65°C) for 50 minutes

Recirculate through the grain bed for the final 10 minutes until wort is clear.

60-MINUTE BOIL

1 ounce Target, 60 minutes (11.0% AA, contribution of 32 IBU)

0.25 ounce East Kent Goldings, 60 minutes (5.0% AA, contribution of 4 IBU)

Add for last 5 minutes:

0.5 ounce East Kent Goldings (5.0% AA, contribution of 2 IBU)

0.25 ounce Northdown (8.5% AA, contribution of 2 IBU)

0.25 ounce Challenger (7.0% AA, contribution of 1 IBU)

1 ounce Target at the start of fermentation

0.5 ounce East Kent Goldings for dry hopping (see notes)

FERMENTATION AND CONDITIONING

Ferment with Wyeast 1968 or White Labs WLP002 at 65°F (18°C). Transfer to secondary after 1 week, and let condition for an additional 2 weeks.

PACKAGE

Bottle or cask conditioning are ideal (see Cast Conditioning at Home, page 16). If kegging, carbonate mildly, and chill only to 50°F (10°C).

- Expected OG: 14° P/1.058
- Expected TG: 3.5° P/1.014
- Expected ABV: 5.8%
- Expected bitterness: 35–40 IBU

Notes: Fuller's prefers Tipple and Concerto, varieties of spring barley with high nitrogen content. English base malts are hard for homebrewers to source, so use any variety your local store stocks. For dry hopping, use whole-leaf Goldings if available, and add only during conditioning.

NEXT STEPS

Two elements to consider tweaking are hops and yeast. Traditional English breweries still observe the bittering/aroma distinction between hop varieties. (You'll note that Fuller's still uses Target, an 11 percent alpha acid hop, to bitter.) You can experiment. Most of the hops will display different qualities depending on when they're added during (or after) the boil. This is no more evident than in the classic English hop, East Kent Goldings, which can seem comfortingly homey and fruity in one beer but bracingly spicy and floral (as lavender is) in another. Most of the hops that derive from English stock seem to have this mutability, so they're fun to play with.

KNOW YOUR ENGLISH HOPS

English hops are known for their fruity, earthy quality. Below are the flavor and aroma characteristics of the classic varieties.

Admiral (13–16% AA): An intense, resinous hop, with notes of orange and herbs.

Boadicea (8–10% AA): A mild, floral variety that offers apple blossom aromas.

Bramling Cross (6–8% AA): A somewhat rough, peppery hop that has notes of black currant and citrus.

Challenger (6–9% AA): Bittering is clean and rounded, with a cedary quality; when used in late additions, it will produce green tea and sweet floral notes.

East Kent Golding (4–6% AA): The most important English hop, and one of the most versatile. It can produce marmalade or honey fruitiness, floral notes of lavender or lemon blossom, or herbal notes of thyme and pepper.

First Gold (7–10% AA): A fruity hop that at times produces tangerine, orange marmalade, magnolia, and spice.

Fuggle (3–6% AA): Along with EKG, the most ancient, classic English hop. Produces a warm, delicate earthy bitterness and gentle forest-floor aromatics. Fuggle is a dying breed in England, but it is being replaced by Willamette, a hop of mostly Fuggle parentage.

Northdown (7–10% AA): Another hop with classic English flavors of cedar and forest, berry, and subtle floral notes.

Pilgrim (9–13% AA): A blend of fruity, berrylike flavors with a distinctive spicy note; can read as mildly lemony in some cases.

Progress (6–8% AA): An earthy, spicy hop that has notes of honey, mint, and grass.

Target (9–14% AA): One of the most intense English hops, Target provides a sharp spice-to-citrus bitterness along with hints of flower and sage.

AND A WORD ON YEASTS

Yeasts are no less important. Many traditional breweries such as Fuller's have strains dating back decades (at least). That makes them distinctive but often finicky. Steve Barrett, the longtime head brewer (now retired) at Samuel Smith's, described his extremely flocculent house yeast. "The rousing effectively means that we pump from the bottom of the tank up and . . . it keeps the whole thing in a dynamic state." During fermentation, beer sprays out of a fan into the famous Yorkshire squares, a process that sends the yeast back down into the beer. "It's quite unusual to do that during fermentation. You wouldn't expect to be throwing your yeast through the air." Yet this is what happens to yeast that has spent decades in the same brewery — it develops its own peculiarities.

Since the process of producing house character takes decades, it's not practicable for the homebrewer to wait for the process to happen naturally. One trick is to experiment with multiple strains. Indeed, English breweries do it themselves. Adnams, from Southwold, on England's east coast, pitches a mixed strain for their traditional ales (like Fuller's, they also experiment with stronger, hoppier, American-style ales). "One is flocculent, one not, and they don't work well alone but do harmonize," says owner Jonathan Adnams. "It's not 100 percent under control," he says, laughing, "but we manage." You're looking for interesting esters that will add character, so consider blending English strains or an English strain with one of the more sedate Belgian yeasts, such as an abbey strain.

Parti-Gyle Brewing

Fuller's conducts one of the more remarkable practices in the brewing world, parti-gyle brewing, and you can, too. The process is so obscure now that most people slightly misunderstand how it works. The idea is to pull multiple worts (or gyles) off a single mash, boil them as usual, and then blend them back together to get beers of different strengths. (Most people understand the first two steps but not the third.) Fuller's uses the parti-gyle system to produce the three workhorses in the brewery's line: ESB, London Pride, and Chiswick Bitter, as well as a slightly obscure stronger beer, Golden Pride.

Fuller's parti-gyle works like this. They begin with a grist of 97 percent pale English spring malt and 3 percent light crystal. For efficiency they use two mash tuns, staggered so one is draining while the other converts. They begin by taking the first runnings from one mash tun of strong wort and then follow it with the second mash tun, combining the strong worts from both mashes in the same kettle. Next, they run the weak worts from both mash tuns into a second kettle. To repeat: both strong worts go into the same kettle, and both weak worts go into a second, different kettle. The runnings at the end of the second mash are barely more than water — the wort has a gravity of just 1.005.

The boiling process for both worts is the same: 60 minutes, with two hop additions, just as in the recipe above. (The strong wort gets twice as many hops as the weak one for obvious reasons, but they are the same varieties in the same proportions.) Only once the worts are cooled and pitched with yeast do they begin to combine them to get the beers they want. ESB gets a larger proportion of the strong wort, a more balanced blend goes to London Pride, and the majority of the low-gravity wort is used for Chiswick.

I suspect there might be subtle benefits to blending different worts (differing levels of hop utilization or Maillard reactions, for example, but John Keeling, ever the flinty, pragmatic brewer, dismisses this entirely. "It is quite simple really. Parti-gyles are the most efficient way of using a mash tun, both in terms of speed and in terms of extract. It is not complicated and is rather simple and elegant."

How to Do It at Home

Conducting your own parti-gyle is entirely feasible, but it requires a fair amount of juggling and the use of random vessels during blending. As chilled wort was sloshing into side pots during the blending, I became a bit anxious about sanitation, but just make sure your yeast is ready to go and you shouldn't have any trouble.

The procedure is straightforward enough. You begin with a boatload of grain and make two mashes. The first mash will go into a kettle for boiling while you draw off the second mash. Because the first mash converts starches to sugars, the second mash is more of a grain rinse — and this is good, because it means you can have it in the kettle within a half hour so the first kettle doesn't have to sit as long once it's done boiling. You'll use the same hop varieties in both batches, adding them at the same time (though you'll add about twice as many in the first wort as the second).

Now the math. Here's a handy rule of thumb: if you divide your mash into two gyles, the first half will contain two-thirds of the sugars. I'm terrible at math, and knowing that has been extremely useful when I'm trying to figure out my initial recipe. If you make an initial mash that produces a wort of 1.080, you should be able to get close to 1.040 with the second wort. You'll probably lose some efficiency with a higher-gravity mash, so make your recipe based on 70 percent efficiency.

Once you've boiled your two worts, take gravity readings, and then prepare to blend. If you're doing two beers, the math is easy — take gravity points away from one wort, and they'll reappear in the other. If you're splitting the wort into three beers, the math becomes more challenging, but remember that your final three worts will have as many total gravity points as your initial two. (If you start with gyles of 1.080 and 1.040, your three beers will have 1.120 points of gravity among them.) When you distribute them to the three worts, they should still add up to 1.120.

In addition to gyles of bitter, the process would work with a number of different types of beer: American-style hoppy ales (an IPA, pale ale, and session IPA), dark ales (export stout, dry stout, and mild), wheat ales (wheat wine, American wheat, session wheat), and so on. And Keeling is right about one thing: it is a very efficient way to make multiple batches of beer.

CHAPTER 3

MILD ALES

Understanding British beer begins in the cozy warmth of the local pub. Mild ale is one of those rare styles of beers to fully display its delights only after two or three pints — preferably in the company of people you enjoy. For centuries the pub has been the focal point of British drinking, and the beer served there was made to be drunk in sessions lasting hours. Today those sessions are fueled by cask bitter or light lagers, but in the middle of the last century, seven of ten pints served were mild ale, a creamy, usually dark ale of very modest strength.

Originally, the word "mild" meant sweet young beer, not yet tinged by the drying effects of wild yeast. It wasn't a style but a category of beer, and milds might have been light or dark, weak or strong. In their modern form milds have evolved into something like a style, though they may still be light or dark (most are the latter). They are unfailingly light of alcohol now, typically at or below 3.5%. Most have little hop character to speak of, and some are sweetish and full bodied. Others might make up for the lack of hops with a layer of bitter, coffeelike roasted malts. Whatever the formulation, milds are built to be drunk in bulk, to taste as pleasant on the first sip as on the fourth pint, a trick that isn't as easy as it sounds.

EST **Mighty Oak** 1996
Brewing Company
ESSEX, ENGLAND

The trajectory of British brewing mirrored America's in many ways, with inexorable consolidation leading to a market dominated by giants, a situation that sparked a small-brewery revival. In Britain, however, many of these new breweries sought to restore tradition rather than upend it. When John Boyce founded Mighty Oak in Essex, he wanted to brew classic pub ales made from English malts and the kind of hops grown just across the Thames river to the south in Kent.

Boyce has been working in breweries since 1975 and brings a deep appreciation of traditional English beers to Mighty Oak, which he founded in 1996. The brewery has a broad range of regular and seasonal offerings, but it is best known for its mild, Oscar Wilde. An all-malt dark mild of comparatively strong heft (3.7%), it has won both Champion Mild of Britain (twice) and Champion Beer of Britain, making it one of the most celebrated beers on the island.

Understanding Mild Ales

Americans have a hard time appreciating mild ale, a style rarely brewed stateside. They are in many ways the polar opposite of the strong, intense ales that most American beer geeks love, and in order to properly appreciate them, you have to abandon the IPA mind-set. Mild ales are gentle to the point of innocuousness and in the wrong hands become insipid. Their essence is complexity through subtlety, and in the right hands — and with some attention — you'll be impressed by how layered and delicious they are. If you approach a mild looking for shafts of intensity, you'll always walk away disappointed. For those willing to listen carefully, however, milds offer flavors that whisper rather than shout, and good ones feature surprisingly complex layers of flavor.

One thing to look for in a mild is a full, silky body. This is a big part of what keeps them interesting over the course of a session. The sense of fullness in such a light beer doesn't require a lot of residual sugar, so while they may taste full and a bit sweet, good milds don't get gummy on the tongue and begin to cloy. Unlike bitter, which is a fairly narrow style, mild ale is much broader, and breweries add distinctiveness by the use of different hops, malt, or yeast.

Many English milds are made with a decent proportion of sugar in the grist — often dark sugar, which adds color without roastiness — which further smooths and softens the palate. Since Americans have developed a taste for all-malt beers, these milds may be a bridge too far. All-malt milds, balanced either with a perceptible hop note or roasty malts, are more likely to edge (barely!) into the American palate. That's what John Boyce brews, and it's the kind of recipe he offers.

Brewing a Mild Ale

There's nothing particularly difficult about brewing a mild ale — unless you want to use invert sugar for a traditional midcentury-style mild (see Making Invert Sugar, page 34). I would strongly recommend a British base malt to add depth to the malt profile. A warm mash and longer boil will help add body and flavor. Water adjustments are optional, but Boyce notes that "a relatively high alkalinity is used" to make milds, and "where required, salt (sodium chloride) is added, not traditional brewing salts."

MALT BILL

---

6 pounds Maris Otter pale malt (89%)

0.4 pound UK 60L crystal malt (6%)

0.3 pound UK black malt (5%)

SINGLE-INFUSION MASH

153°F (67°C) for 75 minutes

90-MINUTE BOIL

1 ounce East Kent Goldings, 90 minutes (5.0% AA, contribution of 19 IBU)

1 ounce East Kent Goldings, 5 minutes (5.0% AA, contribution of 4 IBU)

FERMENTATION AND CONDITIONING

Ferment with Wyeast 1469 (West Yorkshire Ale), White Labs WLP022 (Essex Ale), or your choice of British strain. Lower temperatures (65 to 68°F [18–20°C]) will suppress esters, while warmer ones (72 to 76°F [22–24°C]) will encourage them, so proceed as befits your preference.

PACKAGE

Cask- or bottle-condition. If kegging, limit to 2.0 volumes and serve at 55°F (13°C).

- Expected OG: 9.3° P/1.037
- Expected TG: 2.5° P/1.010
- Expected ABV: 3.5%
- Expected bitterness: 18–22 IBU

JOHN BOYCE
—
MIGHTY OAK

Notes: Yeast selection will dictate a lot of the character. To get a classic mild profile, do not choose especially dry strains. Ester production is fine, but those that accentuate malt are the best. For a fuller body consider mashing at an even higher temperature — around 155°F (68°C) should do.

NEXT STEPS

Although John Boyce prefers all-malt ales, in England a good many of them are made with sugar. Which kind of sugar? Well, funny you should ask. Back in 2011 I was touring the Greene King Brewery in Bury St Edmunds. We began the tour, as all tours of Victorian breweries do, at the top — in this case on the roof so we could look out over the verdant countryside. The head brewer at the time, John Bexon, pointed to a field of sugar beets. That seemed fortuitous, I thought, sugar that close by. But Bexon crinkled his nose as if offended by a foul odor when I asked if he used them in his beer. I pointed out that Belgian breweries used beet sugar, with no apparent harm done. "I know, but it's *beet*. It's the wrong sugar profile." (It turned out his view was hardly rare among his countrymen.)

In mild ales the "right sugar profile" is obtained by the use of a peculiarly English (and old-timey) form of sugar called invert. Invert sugar is made by cleaving sucrose (like you get in beets and cane) into glucose and fructose — two highly fermentable forms of the sugar molecule. In Britain invert sugar comes in a range of colors; it can, in beers such as stouts and milds, add color along with high fermentability. Invert sugar is readily available in the UK but isn't sold in the United States; I'm told Lyle's Golden Syrup is a reasonable alternative. If you want a no-hassle sugar-based mild, you can substitute regular sugar — either table sugar or dextrose (corn sugar) — for a portion of the pale malt grist and proceed as usual. Homebrew shops typically sell dark "candi" sugar for Belgian beers, and that can be used in place of some of the black malt for a less roasty mild. Of course, that wouldn't pass English muster, so instead try a darker cane sugar such as Demerara or turbinado. If you are really hellbent on making a traditional mild with dark invert sugar, have a look at Making Invert Sugar on page 34.

Other variations to consider: first, the pale mild. Although relatively rare, pale milds do still have a following. It's not always obvious what distinguishes pale milds from basic bitters, but you should be looking for a richer body and more complex malt flavor with the mild. I would not use sugar in this recipe. Instead, consider touching up the malt bill with specialty malts. A smidgen of Gambrinus honey malt can sweeten the palate, while biscuit malt will enhance the bready qualities. Other malts may add character to any mild, pale or dark. Briess now makes a mild malt, which is slightly darker and leaves more body than regular pale malt. You might also try a small amount of oats (no more than 5 percent) to add a further silkiness to your mild.

Milds are great beers for investigating yeast characteristics. Since they're so naked, the yeast has a chance to shine. Milds are also a great style for experiments in fermentation. Split a batch, and pitch the same yeast, but ferment one side cool and one side warmer.

In England hops are used in milds as accents, adding woody or fruity or marmalade notes to the finished product. Most American brewers (you know who you are) will probably transgressively pump up the IBUs to something north of 20 and possibly double or treble the finishing hops. (Don't give me that innocent look.) That's perfectly fine, and if an "American mild" ever emerges, it will probably be a hoppier variety. Keep in mind that roasty notes clash with hops, so look for malt-hop balance if you do decide to boost the lupulin.

Making Invert Sugar

You have decided that nothing but the most authentic treatment is good enough for your mild, and you will, by God, use invert sugar to make it. (At least once.) I admire you, because the process of making that invert sugar is laborious and slow. Don't let me dissuade you, though — mild made with invert *will* taste different from an all-malt mild, and you might prefer it.

In the UK invert sugar comes in four types (numbers 1–4), growing darker as the numbers increase. The invaluable Ron Pattinson, an English historian living in Amsterdam, gives the easiest and simplest instructions for making your own invert, and there's no reason to deviate from his method.

By tradition (and why else would you be making invert sugar?), you want to start with cane sugar. The British bias against beets is not confined to John Bexon, and Pattinson suggests a less refined form of cane sugar, such as muscovado or Demerara — often called "raw" sugar in the United States. That's fine, but note that the darker impurities are essentially molasses, and they can result in sugar tinged with that characteristic flavor.

The procedure is simple enough to understand — but remember to bring your patience along as well. For every pound of sugar you plan to invert, bring 1 pint of water to boil. Remove from the heat, and dissolve the sugar in the water. Add ¼ teaspoon of citric acid per pound of sugar, and then put back on the heat and raise to 230°F (110°C), stirring frequently. Once the concoction reaches 230°F, you raise the temperature as slowly as possible until it reaches 240°F (116°C), and then the fun begins. The next step is holding the sugar at between 240° and 250°F (121°C) while it slowly caramelizes. Pattinson suggests the following times to make sugars similar to commercial varieties:

No. 1 (golden): 20–30 minutes

No. 2 (amber): 90–120 minutes

No. 3 (brown): 2½–3½ hours

No. 4 (dark brown): 4–5 hours

Invert No. 3 is the classic preparation for a dark mild. If you're interested in a pale mild, you could get away with a shorter caramelization — a smaller investment that would nevertheless allow you to see its effect on body and flavor.

The Virtues of Invert

Homebrewer Bill Schneller regularly brews milds and English throwback styles of beers and has become accustomed to whipping up batches of invert. He speaks for traditionalists who, unlike Mighty Oak's John Boyce, believe it adds its own character. (Boyce: "Generally microbreweries in the UK produce all their fermentable sugars from malt and grain-based adjuncts, including malted, torrefied, or roasted wheat, oats, and rye.")

Schneller says, "The importance of invert is the flavor more than anything else, which is why I always make it with a less refined, more flavorful sugar. If you make No. 2 or No. 3, it has a rich flavor and adds a lot of dried fruit notes to the beer. I think it's far superior to dark crystal malt for those kinds of flavors in English or Belgian beers. It's why most homebrewed ales don't taste the same as commercial UK examples, but sugar still has a stigma among homebrewers. It's gained more respect as a quality ingredient, but there are still a ton of people who think sugar is cheating or is a cheap ingredient. You can't make mild or Burton ale without dark sugars. Well, you can, but they won't be very interesting." Again, Boyce would take issue with this point, but it's far from a heterodox one.

CHAPTER 4

IRISH STOUTS

irst things first: yes, I *do* recognize that Ireland is not a part of Great Britain and that, indeed, that has been a matter of some controversy for the past five hundred years. I mean to cause no offense. But the truth is that in beer terms, Irish stout is a tributary in the river that runs through the neighboring island. (And the influence goes both ways — Guinness was for a long time the only dark ale regularly available in pubs in Britain.)

Everyone knows this ale (for some people, it's the only ale they know), yet rarely do we stop to appreciate its quirks. The standard Irish stout is pub-strengthened at around 4% and meant to be drunk in sessions. And yet these beers can be flavor powerhouses, with tons of acrid malt bitterness often backed up by strong hop bitterness. Guinness gets credit for introducing a nitrogen dispensing system, and this presentation adds a creamy fullness to the equation. What you end up with is an assertively flavored session ale with a deliciously silky mouthfeel. For such a small beer, it's quite a trick.

EST **Porterhouse Brewing Company** 1996
DUBLIN, IRELAND

As closely associated with beer as Irish culture is (only the Czech Republic can rival it), it's surprising how few breweries were, until recently, located there. The reason, of course, was the unique dominance of what Porterhouse brewer Peter Mosley calls the "large brewer in Dublin." Nowhere in the world does one brand so dominate its home country. That's why, when Liam LaHart and Oliver Hughes opened their own brewery in Dublin 20 years ago, it bordered on radical.

To enter such a market, Porterhouse led with a stout as a luring mechanism. "Once we had them in the door," Mosley explains, "we could show them what other beers we could do and also how styles could be reinterpreted. They were in a position to look at our other stouts, which would be different, but still stouts nonetheless." Porterhouse added a more robust 5% stout to its standard version and later helped reintroduce the world to oyster stout.

Ireland is still trailing behind other European countries in terms of total breweries, but the number is growing rapidly. Porterhouse, which has earned itself a case full of trophies, showed that it was possible to open a brewery in Guinness's backyard and succeed. There are now Porterhouse pubs in three Irish cities, as well as in London and New York. Even in the city of Guinness, people can be persuaded to branch out and try different Irish stouts, so long as they're a recognizable expression of the tradition and made to the highest standards.

BREWMASTER PETER MOSLEY

Liam LaHart and Oliver Hughes started out as pub owners, and when they decided to expand into brewing, they needed someone with experience who could help them realize their vision. They turned to Peter Mosley, referred to them through a mutual friend. Mosley got his start at a small brewery in Bradford, Yorkshire, but decided to augment his biotechnology degree with a diploma from the famous brewing program at Heriot-Watt in Edinburgh. At Porterhouse he's authored a range of beers, including hoppy ales, strong ales, and even a few lagers. But it's the stouts for which Porterhouse — and Mosley — are known, local Dublin products that are very slowly changing the way people think about Irish stout.

Understanding Irish Stout

Stouts came from porters, and porters came from London; they were the world's first super-style. At the dawn of the industrial age, London's great breweries began making a strong, dark beer that was aged in wooden barrels, becoming dry and vinous with time. Sent out in the holds of British ships — which by that time were encircling the globe — it inspired breweries elsewhere to start copying it. One of the first countries where this happened was Ireland, in the 1760s.

The old London porters were made with acrid brown malt, which was both rough and not especially good for brewing. (It was harsh, and one of the reasons brewers aged their porters was so the beer would mellow.) Brown malt had a paucity of the enzymes needed during mashing and so made for inefficient brewing. Brewers realized this with the invention of the saccharometer in 1784. Pale malts were far better, they learned, and here is where Dublin's brewers made an important change. While London brewers carried on with brown malt, Dubliners instead switched to a blend of pale malts and black malts. For the first time there were two different types of porter. Those lines stayed separate, and eventually

Dublin's dark ales (later called stout) flourished, while Britain's drinkers turned to mild and bitter.

Modern Irish stouts are further distinguished by unmalted roasted barley, an ingredient Guinness started using after 1880. Roasted barley imparts a dry, astringent, coffeelike bitterness — the flavor we now identify as distinctive to the style. The "great gravity drop," which occurred when grain rationing forced brewers to make low-alcohol beer, crushed the British brewing world in the first half of the twentieth century. It didn't affect Ireland as viciously, but over the course of the century, standard Irish stouts nevertheless settled into strengths roughly equivalent to those across the Irish Sea.

 A true Irish stout should have a strong dark color, black at first glance, though a deep ruby would be more correct on closer examination.

– PETER MOSLEY, PORTERHOUSE BREWING COMPANY

What else? Well, let's turn to Mosley, who has a wonderful description at the ready. "A true Irish stout should have a strong dark color, black at first glance, though a deep ruby would be more correct on closer examination. It will typically have a roasted malt flavor, with some bitterness and even a slight sourness, one not always derived from the roasted malt and barley. The ABVs tend to be quite modest, in modern times typically between 4 and 5%. Stouts should also have a rich, full-bodied mouthfeel, traditionally from the roast barley. In an ideal world the head should also be creamy white and contribute to the sensation of a full-bodied beer. Domestically this is very important." I couldn't have said it better myself.

We shouldn't conclude without nodding to a variant of the style that retains some of the hallmarks of the porters of yore and that takes tangible form in Guinness's booming 7.5% Foreign Extra Stout (FES), which has been sold in different forms across the globe since 1817. It is clearly within the family, with roasted, ashy malt, but with this strength and density it is the opposite of a session beer. Other breweries have dabbled in export stouts, but they don't have large commercial appeal like their smaller cousins, so they're rare and not always as characterful as you'd like them to be. Irish brewers also seem to ply those waters only rarely; Porterhouse's strongest stout, for example, is just 5%. Even on the strength of Foreign Extra Stout alone, the strong Irish stout has long mesmerized drinkers across the globe.

THAT OTHER LARGE BREWER IN DUBLIN

It would be wonderful to tell you the ways in which Guinness deviates from Porterhouse, but Diageo's brewing jewel is kept hidden away from prying eyes. One is no longer allowed to tour the brewhouse, and when I spoke to master brewer Fergal Murray, he was careful not to divulge any of the more important secrets. I was particularly interested in the acidic tang that appears in the beer they sell as Extra Stout in the United States. It's an echo of descriptions from decades past, when the beer was still aged and slightly soured in wooden casks — Michael Jackson, in his *Beer Companion,* wrote that Foreign Extra Stout "featur[es] lactic, winy, and 'horse-blanket' (*Brettanomyces*) notes." Mosley hinted at it when he said Irish stouts might have "even a slight sourness."

But Murray seemed mystified at the suggestion. "We wouldn't describe it as a sour note. The roasted barley probably impacts that. The pH of the beer is probably lower than — as a stout there's a lower pH. There's no acidification process."

We talked further, and he came around to the points he thought most valuable to know, but which you and I will find wanting. "If you're writing a story on stout, you talk about roasted barley, you talk about Guinness in its unique mystery, you talk about stout yeast, and we talk about hop flavor and the impact of what nitrogen will have done to the world of beer. Five things stand out: roasted barley, hops, yeast, Guinness mystery, and then nitrogenation." Those are great points for the advertising department, but they're not so useful for those of us interested in the brewing process.

All was not lost; he *did* mention something I found most curious. All Guinness, even FES, is now high-gravity brewed. "It's a high-gravity brewing process. Starts as high gravity and then prepared for different packaging formats for around the world. You're talking about 22,000 kilograms of grain being converted and an original gravity in the region of 1.080. It's a 6.5-million-hectoliter brewery [5.4 million barrels] that with tweaks can go up and down." Guinness now has a state-of-the-art brewery, but one that has substantially shifted the way beer is made at St. James's Gate. "It's been an amazing journey in the last 10 years of doing things differently compared to what would have been done for the first 240 years."

So in terms of brewing a traditional Irish stout, I think Mosley's experience is more valuable to the homebrewer — even without the unique mysteries.

Brewing an Irish Stout

In terms of technique nothing here will look unfamiliar, especially if you've already brewed some of the English styles: a single-infusion mash, simple hopping regime, standard ale fermentation. The key points to note involve ingredients. Mosley advises: "The roast barley / roast malt balance is important. Roast malt lends a high degree of astringency to the beer so should be controlled, though a little is good for that point. Beware when you go above a ratio of 3:1 barley to malt, though."

You may have read something about the peculiarities of water and their effect on Dublin's stouts, and Mosley verifies this point, though perhaps not in the manner you expect: "Liquor quality is vital to stouts to emphasize the malt character; generally soft water should be used with low chloride and sulphate levels." (Water is a funny and misleading topic in beer. The idea that cities have uniform water profiles is not entirely accurate. Dig a 100-meter well there, and you're liable to get much harder water than a shallow well a mile or two over here. And in any case, modern breweries almost always treat their water.) So follow Mosley's advice here, not whatever you may have read elsewhere about hard, alkaline water being ideal for stout.

IRISH STOUT

PETER MOSLEY
—
PORTERHOUSE

MALT BILL

6.75 pounds pale malt (75%)

8 ounces roasted barley (6%)

1.5 ounces black malt (1%)

21 ounces flaked barley (14%)

5 ounces crystal malt (4%)

SINGLE-INFUSION MASH

151 to 153°F (66–67°C) for 90 minutes

60-MINUTE BOIL

0.75 ounce Galena, 60 minutes (13% AA, contribution of 35 IBU)

1 ounce East Kent Goldings at very end of boil (5% AA, contribution of 1 IBU)

FERMENTATION AND CONDITIONING

Ferment with a fairly neutral ale strain, such as Wyeast 1728 or White Labs WLP028. Mosley observes, "We use a flocculent ale yeast strain; we do not look for a tremendous ester profile, as it distracts from the malt character. Many English ale yeasts should suffice." Ferment cool, around 65 to 66°F (18–19°C), to inhibit ester production.

PACKAGE

Bottle or keg, or if you're feeling adventuresome, keg on nitrogen. It requires a separate draft system, and if you buy one over the Internet, you'll have to find a place to fill it where you live (federal law prohibits shipping full canisters). Like so many things in homebrewing, the initial investment isn't cheap. If you regularly brew beers that work well on nitro, though, it can be a worthwhile expense.

- Expected OG: 11° P/1.044

- Expected TG: 2.5° P/1.010

- Expected ABV: 4.5%

- Expected bitterness: 35 IBU

Notes: "High temperature reduces the fermentability and increases mouthfeel; also extracts beta-glucan from the barley, again increasing mouthfeel." Galena hops are not required to bitter. I noticed that a lot of Porterhouse beers use this variety (now quite rare in the United States), and I asked about it. Mosley replied that "our choice of Galena is purely random actually. It has a high bittering potential. No other reason!" So follow your bliss on hops, but shoot for a bittering charge that delivers around 35 IBU.

NEXT STEPS

Mosley's recipe is offered as a starting place, but he encourages tinkering. "The obvious area to vary is the roast barley to roast malt ratio." It's worth stopping for a moment to acknowledge the differences in these grains. Roast or black malt has a sharp, acrid flavor that comes across like char. Brewers use it sparingly (Mosley's recipe only calls for 1 percent black malt) to add a layer of burnt flavor and deepen a beer's color.

Roasted barley, by contrast, is more complex and will add more to your beer. Black malt will produce a mocha head, while roasted barley will keep it lighter — important for the visual presentation of an Irish stout. It also gives the stout that characteristic ruby color Mosley describes. In terms of flavor, roast barley gives a more roast-coffee flavor than pure char. Think French roast. Whereas black malt is very dry and astringent, roast barley is sweeter, with nutty, malty notes.

Mosley's recipe has a ratio of 5.6:1 roast barley to black malt, and he says the ratio should never go above 3:1 in terms of the amount of black malt you're using. He also notes that "crystal malt is not essential." If you like a drier stout, you can reduce or eliminate it.

The recipe Mosley provided will make a classic Irish stout — a 4.5% session ale. American homebrewers will no doubt begin to wonder how to scale up that recipe to make a stouter stout. Indeed, you may even be thinking of whipping up a sturdy 7.5% export stout. All well and good, but there are a few things to keep in mind. Mosley: "As strength increases, it is important to remember that the adjuncts should stay the same. Do not vary them all pro rata or you will end up with a beer that is very roasted!" That is to say, if you're using a fairly roasty recipe for a 4% stout, don't keep the percentages the same as you scale up.

I spoke with the founding brewer, Darron Welch, at Oregon's Pelican Brewery about how he does this to make Tsunami Stout — possibly the most-lauded strong Irish stout made in the United States. (It's won six Great American Beer Festival medals, including two golds.) He agrees that you need to keep the roast down when you're scaling up the recipe. Tsunami uses dark chocolate, black patent, and roasted barley in roughly equal parts. He doesn't use crystal malt in Tsunami Stout.

> [Mixing the barley] gives the beer both the dry
> roasty edge of a dry stout but balances it with
> coffee notes and dark chocolate character. Shoot
> for 10 to 11% of total extract coming from the three
> roasted grains.
>
> — DARRON WELCH, PELICAN BREWERY

Otherwise, the recipe can stay much the same as outlined by Mosley. "Standard clean-fermenting ale yeast at moderate temperatures works best, letting the malts and grains be the star. Bittering hops should be something like Magnum or Northern Brewer, varieties that give a clean, neutral bitterness without harshness or other distracting flavors. I would not recommend C-type hops for this style of beer. If you do use C-hops, you'll end up with more of an American-style stout — a lovely thing in its own right, but not really a classic export stout."

One important difference is mash temperature. Extra body is good for low-ABV stouts, but stronger ones should be dry. "These beers are so much more balanced

Oyster Stout

In London, porters evolved into stouts, and stouts evolved into a category in which just about everything was considered fair game — milk and cream, oatmeal, even meat — until at some point some brewer somewhere decided to brew with oysters. The idea strikes one as objectionable on its face, but breweries such as Porterhouse started reviving the tradition a decade or two ago. Oyster stouts are, against all expectations, fairly tasty. They aren't fishy (bivalvey?) but rather slightly briny; a stout with an ineffable mineral edge. (Mosley: "The flavor is subtle and tends to be described as 'marine' or 'iodine.'") Most people can't put their finger on the oyster's contribution but find these stouts richer and more interesting than a regular plain. Indeed, Porterhouse's Oyster Stout may soon become the brewery's best-selling stout.

They're pretty easy to make (if expensive). "We add the oysters, out of their shells, at the very end of the boiling process along with hops and copper finings." You want fresh, raw oysters, and a dozen ought to do. At Upright Brewing the oysters come packed in brine, which the brewery also throws in (like Porterhouse, they add the oysters at the end of boil). Some breweries have "dry-hopped" their oyster stouts with the shells, but this seems like an act of poetry, not science.

and drinkable if they are well attenuated," Welch says. "We start at 17 Plato and finish at 3.5 Plato. To achieve this, we mash at a fairly low conversion temperature, about 140°F [60°C]."

Finally, although some stronger Irish stouts are noted for their acidity, Welch discourages it. "I do not spend any time worrying about souring Tsunami Stout, despite what old homebrew books have to say. Here at Pelican we have produced some one-off stouts using acidulated malt and I was never very happy with the results. I would avoid all mash souring, wort souring, acidulated malts, etc. Keep it straight ahead — this is a straight-ahead style."

· CHAPTER 5 ·

OLD ALES

ave you noticed that British beer styles are very often just adjectives turned into proper nouns: bitter, mild, brown? Add "old" to the list. But what does "old" in this context mean — old as in historic, or old as in aged? Yes.

Old ales are a variety of strong ales, and they have been made for a very long time in Britain. Their lineage goes back to the arrival of hops on the island, which made it possible to make stronger beers and mature them without making a tun of vinegar. A generic category of beers (you'll find them referred to as "old," "stock," or "stale" in historic texts), they were stiffly hopped and put into casks to ripen. There, native wild yeasts turned them dry and gave them sherrylike flavors. Eventually, breweries began to understand the microbiology of beer and eliminated wild yeast from their facilities, and old ales became weaker and sweeter — like the modern standard-bearer, Theakston's Old Peculier. A few breweries, such as Benskins, Gales, and Greene King, kept making the aged wild versions, but their numbers have dwindled to just Greene King today (though Fuller's bought Gales and is purportedly going to resume making Gales Prize Old Ale in London).

For the homebrewer the most interesting versions of old ales are the ones that both hint at antiquity and are also aged with wild yeast. One of the few styles that are hard to find commercially, they deliver quite a bit of "wow" factor with their rich, malty body; robust strength; and layer of fruit and dryness that comes from the *Brettanomyces*. They are one of the few styles that continue to evolve and improve in the bottle, making them ideal cellar beers — another reason they're great for the homebrewer.

EST Upright Brewing 2009
PORTLAND, OREGON

When Alex Ganum founded Upright in 2009, he was inspired by the farmhouse beers of Belgium and France. The brewery's standard line was a series of saison-ish beers, each named for a strength in the Belgian degree system, Four through Seven. But it wasn't saisons to which he was devoted so much as the farmhouse approach; Ganum's process is instinctive and improvisational. Once when he was mashing in a batch of beer, I asked how wet he liked his mash to be. I assumed he'd give me a ratio of water to grain, but instead he said, "I go by feel." In the years since Upright launched, Ganum's brewery has developed a wonderful pilsner that has become a favorite of local restaurants, as well as a line of delicate barrel-aged beers, many made with fruit or spices.

Farmhouse ales are far from his only love, however. In fact, the first beer made at Upright — batch #1 — was their remarkable old ale, Billy the Mountain. Ganum has a love of English brewing, and early on he brewed an oyster stout and an English IPA as well. But among his English ales the real triumph is Billy the Mountain, the most interesting and accomplished old ale I've ever encountered. Upright ages a portion for three years on *Brettanomyces*, and then blends the aged stock back in with a portion of fresh beer. Bottled still, the wild yeast rouses itself and gobbles up fresh wort, carbonating the beer in the bottle.

BREWMASTER ALEX GANUM

Originally from Michigan, Ganum began his brewing career with a stint as an intern at Ommegang. Before that he attended culinary school, which gives a clue to his approach to brewing. He builds his beers from a sensory map in his head, using different ingredients and processes to add textures and subtleties to each recipe. He eventually went to work as an assistant to Dan Pedersen, an innovative brewer working extensively with Belgian styles at BJ's in Portland.

When Ganum opened Upright, he envisioned making beers "inspired by historical records and the dedicated few who have kept traditions alive." His approach remains the same, and his beers have a timeless quality, incorporating local ingredients, open fermentation, barrel aging, and his hands-on approach.

Understanding Old Ales

People come to old ale unexpectedly, if at all. Ganum first discovered old ales when he was at culinary school. He and a close friend went to Higgins, a legendary Portland institution that pioneered not only farm-to-table cuisine but also pairing beer and food. "It was a big deal, as experiences that nice were uncommon for us, so we planned to go on a sleepy Tuesday and relish the night over a few hours, asking the server to take her time because we wanted to enjoy a beer with each course and some in between as well. To cap the evening, I chose a vintage Gales Prize Old Ale, and that still, thick, bizarre beauty remains in my fondest memories today, 13 years later." He continued to buy them, finding some flat and dry, others richer and livelier; his interest grew, leading eventually to Billy the Mountain.

What makes old ales so interesting is how the density of the base beer interacts with the *Brettanomyces*; to my palate there has always been a sensory relationship with beers like those made by Liefmans and Verhaeghe (less so Rodenbach), with a rich sweetness of malt balanced by a steely blade of leather and acid. All of those beers are made in something of a similar fashion, with wood aging at the center. In the European cellars huge oaken vats not only serve as a resting place for ale, but their thick staves develop an ecosystem for microorganisms that successively inoculate each batch.

The last regularly brewed old ale is made by Greene King, which blends a very strong wood-aged beer with fresh, weaker stock to make Olde Suffolk (Strong Suffolk in the UK). That beer, at just 6% ABV, has been sanded down to suit modern tastes. Nevertheless, it's an impressive beer, with a touch of iron and balsamic from the vatted beer, brightened with soft, fruitier notes of the young beer blend.

Brewer John Bexon (now retired) described the aging beer as we stood next to the vats in the cellars underneath Greene King in Bury St Edmunds. "What we've got here are hundred-barrel vats that contain 12% ABV Five X, probably about 90 bitters, and they'll sit in there for two years. There's a microflora embedded in the grain of the oak that inoculates and perpetuates maturation. It's very low pH, and the resultant flavor is more or less like slightly sour sherry two years on."

There's not a lot of trickery to old ale. It does take time and attention and the curiosity to appreciate a "thick, bizarre" beer.

Brewing an Old Ale

If you're making one of the classic old ales with *Brettanomyces* (modern versions are just a type of strong ale), the trick is to restrain the yeast's effect so it doesn't overwhelm the rich malt body. Greene King and Upright do this by blending portions of aged beer with fresh beer. Greene King makes two different beers, but Upright uses all the same base beer for Billy the Mountain.

"We simply blend in one of the three-year-old casks and immediately refill it with the blend, so there is actually a bit of really old beer going back into the cask for a batch three more years out." He blends at a 3:1 ratio, young to aged stock, and bottles without priming, counting on the active *Brettanomyces* to carbonate the beer. "Bottle conditioning should be at least a month, if not longer." After that, he notes that "it changes drastically over the first year" as those yeasts get going. Like Orval, beers made like this are many beers in one.

Ganum recommends just adding *Brettanomyces* at bottling, but it's also a good opportunity to blend lots if you've got multiple carboys in process.

OLD ALE

ALEX GANUM

UPRIGHT
BREWING

7.25 pounds Briess Ashburne mild malt (40%)

7.25 pounds two-row pale malt (40%)

1.2 pounds light/medium crystal malt (45L) (7%)

1.2 pounds medium crystal malt (60L) (7%)

1.2 pounds dark crystal malt (120L) (7%)

2 ounces back malt (<1%)

¾ cup molasses (at end of boil)

SINGLE-INFUSION MASH

149°F (65°C) for 45 minutes

90-MINUTE BOIL

2 ounces Willamette, 90 minutes (5% AA, contribution of 31 IBU)

1 ounce Willamette, 20 minutes (5% AA, contribution of 9 IBU)

1.33 ounces Goldings or Willamette at whirlpool (5% AA, contribution of 5 IBU)

FERMENTATION AND CONDITIONING

Ferment with an English strain that produces a nice ester profile and soft finish — Ganum recommends Wyeast 1318/1928 or White Labs WLP026/WLP023. It's fine to ferment in the mid-60s, Ganum says, "as the gravity will encourage plenty of ester formation."

PACKAGE

Kegging is fine if you're not adding *Brettanomyces* (see Next Steps on page 52). Only bottle-condition, without priming, if you do use the *Brett*.

- Expected OG: 20° P/1.082

- Expected TG: 4° P/1.016

- Expected ABV: 8.5% at bottling

- Expected bitterness: 40–45 IBU

Notes: Ganum is not picky about the hops and suggests Mt. Hood and Fuggles as alternatives. "The hop character we shoot for is not intrusive or pungent, just a nice grassy or herbal flavor that blends in. Having something with a bit of floral character is nice as a contrasting note to the intense malts." He has used a variety of different crystal malts, leaning toward English varieties. The Briess Ashburne mild is a slightly darker base malt that will contribute a toastier, English character to the beer.

BILLY THE MOUNTAIN? THAT'S PECULIER.

There's something about old ales that provoke fanciful names. Curmudgeon, Old Tom, Peleg, Fisticuffs, and The Rev. James are just a few of the delightful names breweries have attached to their old ales. Theakston's Old Peculier, probably the world's most famous old ale, is another good example. Language nerds will note that the beer's name is spelled oddly — Peculier, not Peculiar. If you look closely, you'll see that the label has a funny little logo that reads, "the Seal of the Official of the Peculier of Masham." A peculier, it happens, is an obsolete ecclesiastical court — and also a great name for an old ale.

Upright's Billy the Mountain, another odd name, comes from a Frank Zappa song. (Ganum, much inspired by music, named his brewery after the upright bass.) The song, which takes anywhere from half an hour to an hour to play, involves the tale of a mountain that, flush with riches earned while posing for postcards, goes on a series of adventures involving the draft, red-baiting, and Las Vegas. Another excellent choice of name for an old ale.

NEXT STEPS

The most important element in an old ale — arguably the element that makes it an old ale — is the effect of wood-borne *Brettanomyces*. For the homebrewer, replicating this is more challenging. When commercial breweries age a beer in a liquor or wine barrel, three things happen. First, barrels arrive at breweries "wet"; that is, the staves are soaked with wine or liquor, and this leaches into the beer during aging, inflecting the beer with its flavors. Second, the beer may pick up some wood flavors — tannins, vanilla, and so on — though since the barrels are used, these notes are generally subtle.

Finally, and most important, wooden barrels are oxygen permeable, and they feed the action of aerobic microorganisms such as *Brettanomyces*. It's this last effect that makes English old ales so distinctive. Barrels are sensitive to environmental changes, humidity, and temperature, and each one will contribute its unique flavors to a beer as the environment and yeasts interact.

The easiest approach to get wild yeast is to just pitch it straight. Ganum recommends *Brettanomyces clausenii* (Wyeast 5151PC or White Labs WLP645), a gentler strain that has the added benefit of having come from English stock ales. "Don't add too much *Brett*," he advises, "especially if you intend to age the beer long, or it will simply end up out of balance." (A single pack/bottle of yeast is fine, but don't create a starter.) Ganum also suggests aging the beer on oak chips or oak spirals to add that characteristic wood-aged flavor. These come in both American and French oak and in a variety of "toasts" (the amount of heat applied to cure the wood).

There are three types of oak products on the market: chips, beans/cubes, and spirals, and all work well. The thing to know is that the amount of flavor they impart is proportional to their surface area. Oak chips have the greatest surface area and require the least amount of time. No matter which product you use, you'll want to taste the beer periodically to assess the wood-flavor level. Rack after primary fermentation, and add the oak — an ounce should be fine. (Many people worry about sanitizing the wood, but by the time you add them, you'll have plenty of alcohol to do the sanitizing for you.) Give it a week if you're using chips, and then monitor every few days until you've reached your desired level. It could take a few weeks depending on the type and amount of oak you've used.

Oh, one more thing. People go through a lot of effort soaking their wood chips in bourbon to get the effect the pros do with distillery barrels. Don't bother. If you want a dash of bourbon, just add the bourbon straight — it's a whole lot easier to adjust for flavor and doesn't take days or weeks of prep.

Different Oaks, Different Toasts

Not every barrel is the same. Some are made of American oak, others of European species. Some are "toasted" by fire, others burned to create a layer of char. When professional breweries reuse barrels, they're usually trying to infuse their beer with wine or liquor. But when distillers and vintners use barrels, they're interested in what the wood itself contributes — and if you buy oak chips, spirals, or a new barrel, that's what you'll be getting as well.

Wine barrels are toasted rather than burned, in a range running from light to heavy. The toasting process breaks down lignin, cellulose, and hemicellulose (wood sugar) into simpler substances. Lignin breaks down into vanillin — the source of oak's calling-card flavor. At higher temperatures it breaks down into volatile phenols such as guaiacol, which gives a smoky flavor. When heated, hemicellulose releases sugars and creates those toasty notes. Heat can also destroy compounds, which happens to tannins — another signature quality of wood — when too much is applied. Generally speaking, these are the qualities that emerge from different toasting levels:

Light. Earthy and mild; increased tannins

Medium. Rounder and sweet, with gentle spice, toast, and vanilla/butterscotch

Medium Plus. More intense vanilla, chocolate, brown sugar

Heavy. Smoky, roasted flavors such as coffee, black pepper, diminished tannin

Different species of oak also contain different levels of key compounds. American oak contains more potent flavor and aroma compounds and fewer tannins, while French oak has the reverse. (It's amusing to see Europeans gently disparage American oak when they say French oak is more "elegant" or "noble.") American oak is heavy on the vanilla, while French oak suggests sweet spice flavors such as cinnamon and allspice. You may also encounter Hungarian oak, which is the same species as French oak, and it falls midway between the intensity and balance of American and French oak.

Barrel Aging

For a long time, the only option you had for barrel-aging beer was doing it in a standard wine or bourbon barrel — a challenge (to say the least) for the average homebrewer. Companies have begun to make smaller barrels available for the homebrew market, however, in volumes as small as 5 gallons. They're even reasonably affordable (less than $200 at the time this book was written). There is a downside, though. The effect of a barrel on beer is directly proportionate to its size. The greater the surface area-to-volume ratio, the more wood character and oxygen the beer will be exposed to.

American breweries haven't had a chance to experiment with bigger vessels very much, but Belgians are well aware of this issue. When I toured Rodenbach, brewer Rudi Ghequire told a story about how the brewery kept building larger and larger wooden tuns (called foeders) until in the 1930s they built several 650-hectoliter giants — that's 554 barrels, or 17,000 gallons. "They discovered that the beer maturation was not going so fast as in vats of 180 hectoliters." He went on to describe this relationship. "The reason is very simple: the maturation speed depends on the average of the inner side surface and [volume]." Bigger vats also have thicker oaken staves, and this further retards the amount of oxygen that gets to the beer. Or put another way, the smaller the barrel, the thinner and more permeable the staves — and consequently, the more oxygen that seeps in.

For slow-maturing beer going through a *Brettanomyces* fermentation, speed is not a virtue. A lot of the character comes from ester production — it's what gives Rodenbach its characteristic flavors — and that takes time. Regarding his own (smaller) foeders, the lambic maker Frank Boon told me, "The finest tastes, [the finest] esters are built slowly. It takes time: time, time, time. It's a time-consuming way of making beer." Exposing wild ale to too much oxygen will send it running straight to the dry, leathery state, and this may give the beer a harsh edge.

If you want to commit a barrel to wild yeast (and remember: once you inoculate beer in wood with *Brettanomyces*, you have a *Brett* barrel forevermore), using it to make old ale is a great solution. Since you'll be blending only a portion of the barrel-aged beer into the final batch, the *Brett* will continue to evolve when added to the fresh beer. Begin tasting the barrel-aged beer at about six months and monitor it for flavor. It may be ready then or in a few months. It definitely won't need to go the full three years that Ganum's wild batch of Billy the Mountain does.

Once you feel the barrel-aged beer has a nice balance of flavors, blend it to a finished product of 25 percent barrel-aged and 75 percent fresh beer. Bottle without priming and wait at least a month before sampling. Once you have a *Brett* barrel in the house, you can use it to inoculate other wild ales in a variety of methods. (See Brewing Wild, page 257.)

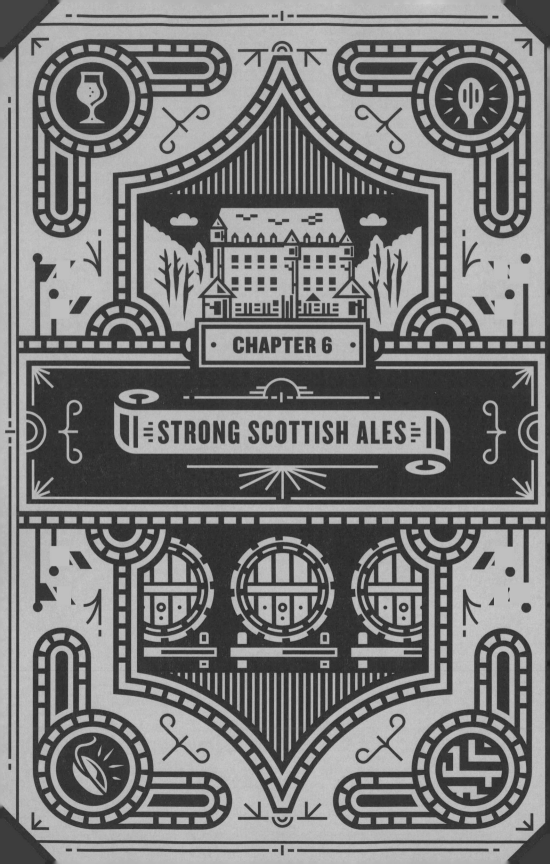

CHAPTER 6

STRONG SCOTTISH ALES

Scottish ales may be the most misunderstood — and misrepresented — styles among American drinkers and brewers. Several myths continue to cling to the Scottish tradition like lacing to a glass, and they prove even more difficult to wash off. This is unfortunate, because the reality of Scottish brewing is more interesting than the myth — and the beers are tastier than Americans often believe.

What are those myths? That Scottish ales are smoky and syrupy, to begin with. Americans also repeat reports that Scottish ales lack hops because of their rarity, not because of brewer choice. And many people repeat the notion that Scottish ales are or were boiled for extreme periods (this is actually a supporting belief for the central smoky-and-syrupy myth). In reality, most Scottish ales are satiny and extremely well balanced; malty, yes, but never syrupy.

Above all else, Scottish ales are meant to be drunk rather than fussed over, so whether they are very light or skull-splitting heavyweights, approachability and balance are placed at a premium. Finally, and importantly, no Scottish ale brewed in Scotland tastes of smoke — unless, perhaps, it was aged in a cask of Islay whisky. With their balance, malty sophistication, and smooth, moreish bodies, you could make an argument that, from a sensory perspective, anyway, their closest kin are the lagers of Bavaria, particularly bocks. Bocks? Yes, and isn't *that* interesting?

EST **Traquair House** 1694

INNERLEITHEN, SCOTLAND

The brewery at Traquair (*truh KWAIR*) House, an estate dating back 900 years in the Scottish Borders south of Edinburgh, is one of the most interesting in the beer kingdom. The commercial history of beer in the UK is comparatively recent; it was for centuries primarily a domestic activity, and even after the emergence of commercial brewing, an estate, not a corner brewery, is where you would find the very best ales. Traquair is one of the extremely rare examples of one of these old estate breweries, though fortunately the owners now sell some of their precious production to those outside the gates.

The current resident of the home, Catherine Maxwell Stuart, 21st Lady of Traquair, relayed to me the "modern" era of brewing history, which dates back to 1694. Stray records tell the story. By 1738 the brewery was situated in the former coach house. They know this, she writes, "as there is a receipt for the purchase of the copper." The brewery itself was shelved in the early 1800s and sat for another century and a half or so until the 20th Laird of Traquair, Peter Maxwell Stuart, discovered it and decided to start brewing again in 1964. Lady Maxwell Stuart recalls, "The brewery had simply become a family junk room and forgotten about entirely. What was unique about Traquair was that all of the equipment and vessels still remained in place, down to the stirring paddles and old oak fermentation tuns."

Remarkably, Laird Peter basically just hooked up the old equipment — which, though probably quite an impressive kit for its day, was by then four decades older than the United States — and started brewing again. There's a wonderful short film from 1975 archived at the National Library of Scotland that shows Maxwell Stuart mashing in. Hot liquor pours down a wooden trough into the mash tun, which Maxwell Stuart stirs with an original mashing fork. You can even see the laird and his daughter, the current lady, using large perforated spoons to speed cooling, which of course took place in a coolship.

In 1994 Traquair installed a modern brewery (the old one is still in place, called to duty for special beers), but brewers continue to ferment in open oak tuns. Peter Maxwell Stuart began with the original vessels he discovered, but over time, as the old staves wore out, they've been replaced by newer oak tuns. These fermentation vessels, along with local spring water, are what Catherine Maxwell Stuart credits with giving Traquair House ales their distinctiveness. No doubt that's true. But the story is no less important; in a country where nearly every working brewery had shut down by the 1990s (only six remained), Traquair House provides a unique connection to the country's amazing brewing history.

BREWMASTERS IAN CAMERON AND FRANK SMITH

Ian Cameron started working at Traquair 35 years ago, first as a groundsman. Not too much later, he began assisting Peter Maxwell Stuart in the brewery and was appointed head brewer in 1987. Frank Smith's story is similar, though more recent. He began working at Traquair 25 years ago. (Twenty-five years is "recent" in a place that counts in centuries, not years.) After Cameron's retirement in 2016, Smith took over as head brewer.

Understanding Scottish Ales

When you walk into a Scottish pub today, the beers you find on tap are not a huge departure from those found in pubs to the south, but the Scottish tradition offers many points of departure from the English. We think of Scotland as a remote, cloistered land, but in fact, it has long been every bit as worldly as England. Scotland is where the idea of capitalism was born (Adam Smith was born in Kirkcaldy, Fife), and the country has long been connected to the world through shipping lanes. In 1860 French scientist Louis Figuier called Scottish beer "the strongest and best beer made in Great Britain. It is distinguished from all other domestic beers in its alcohol content, beautiful amber tint, and balsamic taste."

Beer is one of the many products shipped out of its ports, and the flagship style in the nineteenth century was a beer called Edinburgh Ale; it bore some resemblance to England's Burton Ale, but as Figuier's quote suggests, it was considered more refined and sumptuous (although it clearly bore a nineteenth-century kiss of wild yeast). For the most part, this tradition of strong ales vanished after the world wars, but Traquair offers a glimpse back. Like the Edinburgh Ales that were being brewed when the brewery was mothballed two hundred years ago, modern Traquair House Ale is strong, amber-colored, and malt accented.

> **In 1860 French scientist Louis Figuier called Scottish beer "the strongest and best beer made in Great Britain. It is distinguished from all other domestic beers in its alcohol content, beautiful amber tint, and balsamic taste."**

In that wonderful archival footage from 1975, the laird is asked to describe his ale. "It's a very strong, highly flavored beer about two and a half times the strength of ordinary beer," he begins. "It's slightly sweet. It's got a malty flavor, which is absolutely unique in the brewery world." With a recipe adapted from one of Traquair's historical formulations, Traquair House Ale is probably a decent evocation of those nineteenth-century ales.

In general, the keys to understanding Scottish ales — and their differences from English ales — lie in malt and yeast. These beers are defined by malt. Even very light session ales will have a pronounced malt flavor. All beers, from the weakest to the strongest, have a kind of silkiness that comes from the malt; in lighter beers it adds mouthfeel, but in alcoholic beers it undermines the cloying heaviness that strong low-hop beers sometimes have. The malts will contribute flavor and aroma as well — and they are the central focus of the palate.

Hops don't interfere much with the presentation of malt, but neither does the yeast — another point of departure from English ales. Esters are not prized, and Scottish ales are clean and neutral, almost like lagers. Yeast character is so de-emphasized that when I visited Belhaven, Head Brewer George Howell told me, "Nobody knows precisely where [the] yeast came from." In fact, it was common for the Edinburgh breweries to share strains, and Belhaven regularly sourced theirs from Tennent's or Scottish & Newcastle.

THERE'S NO SMOKE IN THIS SCOTCH

For reasons lost to memory, the first American craft brewers thought Scottish ales should be smoky. One might hazard a guess that they were conflating beer and whisky, but whatever the thinking, early brewers tended to fold a bit of smoky distiller's malt into their grist. It was so common that the American Scotch ale has become its own style, codified in such places as the BJCP guidelines ("perceived as earthy or smoky") and Brewers Association style guidelines ("Though there is little evidence suggesting that traditionally made Scottish Ale exhibited peat smoke character, the current marketplace offers many examples with peat or smoke character present at low to medium levels").

It's true that the horse has left the barn — American Scotch ale *has* become its own style, and the smokiness perpetuates itself. But for our purposes, it's important to recognize that this is a purely American invention.

Brewing a Strong Scottish Ale

In my correspondence with Catherine Maxwell Stuart — who acted as the go-between with brewers Ian Cameron and Frank Smith — she introduced the recipe and formulation with this comment: "I should firstly say that we consider it impossible to replicate our ales on a homebrew scale because of two important factors: the pure spring water, which is unusually soft here, and, of course, the fermentation in oak vessels, which give the ales their unique complexity of flavor and characteristics."

It's a bit difficult to assess the attributes of soft water in a finished beer, but the oak? Yes, it plays a central role in Traquair's ales. House Ale has one of the most unusual palates I've encountered in a British beer. The writer Roger Protz describes it as an "amontillado sherry character," and I think he's right. Fermenting a beer on wood, especially just for four or five days as Traquair does, should not have a profound effect. Yet somehow it does. I have searched my palate for evidence that there are wild yeasts involved, but aside from a lighter body than I would expect in such a big beer, it's not there.

Perhaps oxygen has something to do with it? The sherrylike note does suggest the play of oxygen, but it would seem to be in the wood far too briefly to actually pull much through the staves. The wood in Traquair offers a perfect case of unexplainable "house character." How to replicate this? Well, you could try open fermentation (described in chapter 8), and, if you were feeling experimental, add some wood chips during primary.

MALT IS KEY

Whatever that house character is, the beer — like all Scottish ales — gets the rest of its flavor punch from the malts. Scottish ales build the entire operation on their tawny malts, and much of what seems to come from other influences is heavily filtered through this malty lens. This is especially true in Traquair, which builds melanoidins through its long boil, building up the rich, malty flavors that support those sherry notes. It's critical to use UK malts here, though they need not be Scottish. Floor malts will add a nice flavor of authenticity if you can find them.

The historian Ron Pattinson has challenged the conventional wisdom that Scottish brewers subjected their beers to long boils; looking through nineteenth-century Scottish brew logs, he found that they were actually shorter than contemporary English ales — often just an hour. Traquair *does* use a long boil — two hours. What's more, they add hops at the beginning of the boil, which stiffens the bitterness. This effect is not dramatic in Traquair because the low-alpha East Kent Goldings are very mild, but it is possible to detect a tiny bit of spikiness. If you substitute higher-alpha hops in your beer, you might consider adding them at 90 minutes.

Finally, it's important to use a fairly neutral yeast. This is one of the hallmarks of Scottish brewing. Unlike their brewing neighbors to the south, the Scots don't favor fruity strains. What's more, they ferment cool to inhibit ester production. The differences between lighter Scottish and English ales are hard to perceive, but this is an important element.

MALT BILL

12.25 pounds British pale malt (98%)

0.25 pound roasted barley (2%)

SINGLE-INFUSION MASH

148°F (64°C) for 1 hour

120-MINUTE BOIL

1.5 ounces East Kent Goldings, 120 minutes (contribution of 26 IBU)

0.5 ounce East Kent Goldings, 10 minutes (contribution of 3 IBU)

Ferment cool with a fairly neutral yeast strain such as Wyeast 1728 or White Labs WLP028. The Wyeast strain tolerates cooler temperatures, so try 58°F (14°C); bump that up to 64°F (18°C) if you're using White Labs.

PACKAGE

Bottle-condition or keg.

- Expected OG: 17° P/1.070
- Expected TG: 3.7° P/1.015
- Expected ABV: 7.2%
- Expected bitterness: 29 IBU

IAN CAMERON

—

TRAQUAIR HOUSE

Notes: Traquair water is very soft, but most Scottish water is hard. You'll obviously get a different profile depending on your water preference. Note that if you conduct a 2-hour boil, you'll lose greater volume than you would in a 60- or 90-minute boil. Primary fermentation for Traquair takes 4 to 5 days, but if you ferment cool, yours may take longer. In addition to fermenting on wood, Traquair basically uses open fermentation (covering the wooden tuns with a loosely fitting wooden lid), which would be appropriate here; Caledonian and others ferment in open containers.

NEXT STEPS

There should be no smoke in your traditional Scottish ale, but spice — that's another matter. Based on archaeological digs at Fife and on the Orkney Islands, it's likely people were brewing beer in Scotland 4,000 to 6,000 years ago. Since these Neolithic brewers were very far from the nearest hop bine, they spiced their beer with other herbs, particularly heather. This tradition continued on with the Picts, whose heather beer was so famous it entered folklore. Heather ale continued on well after hops arrived and only died out in the mid-nineteenth century.

Heather is the most famous Scottish brewing spice, but it is far from the only one — bog myrtle and meadowsweet are other classic examples. Traquair recalls this history by using coriander in their Jacobite Ale. That beer is made much the same way as House Ale, described above, but with just a tiny bit more roasted barley (2.5 percent) and a gravity of 1.078 / 19° P. To re-create Jacobite Ale, add an ounce of coriander with the second hop infusion. If you want to recall the long history of Scottish brewing, substitute heather. It's a subtle herb and hard to overdo, so add up to 5 ounces with the second hop infusion.

Part 2

German

TRADITION

hen we think of Germany, we think of lagers. It's where lagers were invented, and modern brewing (at least precraft) is essentially German brewing. But that tradition is actually *Bavarian*; Germany as we know it today was for much of its history fragmented and ruled by different kings. Everything north of Franconia was ale country until the nineteenth century. The beers made there bore far closer resemblance to the ales made in neighboring Belgium than they did the lagers in Bavaria.

A writer in the late 1500s cataloging German beer mentioned examples made with henbane (which can cause insanity), laurel, ivy, and even chimney soot. Sour beers were ubiquitous, as were bizarre, super-high-gravity beers that were barely alcoholic. This was decades after Bavarians had adopted *Reinheitsgebot*, the famous purity law, and Northerners would continue making these strange ales for hundreds of years before Reinheitsgebot finally went national at unification and lagers slowly began to creep northward — ultimately taming the ale brewers.

So there were two very different traditions in German brewing, and the remaining beers, at least, still stand testament to that history: altbier and kölsch, Berliner weisse and gose. If we think of Germany as having a single national brewing tradition, an approach that applies as well in Cologne or Leipzig as Munich, though, we're not really wrong. As the various states and principalities that now constitute Germany came under the same flag at unification, so too did the disparate approaches to brewing.

Coming into the twentieth century, then, were these twin impulses in German brewing — the highly controlled, pragmatic Bavarian approach and a flamboyant, daring, and just plain weird ale-brewing approach. Even today, at places like Uerige, where they still use a coolship and drip chiller, there are funky practices going on. Yet while some of those old ales have managed to hang on, in the end, the Bavarian way did ultimately win out.

The Impact of Reinheitsgebot

You could think of the Bavarian approach as one symbolized by Reinheitsgebot, a rule that originally eliminated a lot of the funny business among lager breweries in the 1500s. It stipulated that only products made with barley malt, hops, and water could be called "beer" (Bavarians were well aware of yeast but considered it an agent, not an ingredient, so omitted it). It in many ways codified a way of thinking about beer as much as it did the techniques and ingredients one could use. After reunification, leaders put the new country's breweries under this same law. All the nonconforming northern oddball beers were treated with asterisks (and in truth, as early as 1551, even Bavarians were making exceptions for beer brewed with coriander and laurel), and their place was carved out in the modern all-German Reinheitsgebot to bring all German beer under the same umbrella.

> **Reinheitsgebot stipulated that only products made with barley malt, hops, and water could be called "beer."**

Over the course of the twentieth century, that Bavarian pragmatism took hold even in the north, so that now even most ales are brewed with the same level of precision lagers are. Where wild bacteria and open fermentation are still used, they don't happen in the rustic, uncontrolled settings they do in Belgium. Uerige uses a coolship, but it doesn't allow a single stray cell of wild yeast into the cooling chamber. Students now go off to learn brewing at one of the universities (two of the most famous are in Bavaria), and they are taught a standard style of brewing. The notion is that if you can brew a light lager, you can brew anything — even gose.

Matthias Trum, who studied at Weihenstephan but oversees the smoky kiln at Schlenkerla, the rauchbier brewery in Bamberg, made this point when I visited. "The thing is, when you brew a beer and when you make a malt, there are a couple thousand variables which you can tweak. And *that* they can teach you extremely well at Weihenstephan." The weird stuff you are left to figure out on your own (or learn, as Trum did, from your father). And there *are* little pockets of weird stuff, but it is very much diminished from its nineteenth-century standing.

What it means is that while there are many styles in Germany, the method of brewing them now forms a single tradition, so whether a brewer is making weizen, helles, or Berliner weisse, she will use a similar approach. Here are a few of the key points.

DIFFERENCES IN BASE MALT. I didn't really understand malt, particularly base malts, until I traveled through Germany. When Americans build their malt-forward beers, they do so by layering in specialty malts to produce these flavors — caramel, biscuit, roast, and nuts. Except in a few rare cases, German beer depends on base malts to drive flavor. Many brewers study malting in brewing school and have specific demands about the way their malts are prepared.

Americans know Weyermann Malts, which is essentially synonymous with "German malt"; what they may not realize is that there are dozens of malt houses in Germany, and breweries choose their products based on the ways they want their base malts to perform and taste. Although it's a subtle element, when you're drinking 10 kölsches in Cologne or sampling helles and weissbier from different breweries across Bavaria, your palate becomes attuned to these subtle experiences, and you begin to see how much a base malt can define a beer.

DELICATE HOPS. German beer just isn't hoppy. This may be the reason American craft breweries have been slow to go in the direction of German beer. But the hops Germans use *are* particular. The undisputed king is Hallertau Mittelfrüh, a landrace variety that comes from the Hallertau region just north of Munich. It has a delicate, herbal/peppery quality that accentuates many beer styles perfectly and is said to have a "harmonic bitterness" — which in this case isn't entirely spin. Other classics are Spalt, Hersbrucker, and Tettnanger, and they all bear some of the same qualities — delicate spicing, fresh herbal notes, and sometimes lightly floral aromas.

Over the years breeders have made some high-alpha varieties, but these mimic the "harmonic" bittering, and classic aroma hops are used later in the boil. In the past decade hop growers have introduced some newer varieties that have something of the New World in them, but even these are comparatively restrained in their quality. German beers favor balance over boldness, and German hops must be sedate enough to allow those famous base malts to shine through.

BALANCE AND RESTRAINT. Since the word "balance" keeps popping up, it may seem unnecessary to call it out, but in terms of brewing approach, it's a critical element. German brewers seem allergic to flamboyance. Even when they're making a gose or Bavarian weissbier — quite odd beers when you think about them — they rein in the flavors so that they come into gentle balance. The only extant German beer that violates this convention is Berliner weisse — but tellingly, it is essentially extinct in the country of its birth. All of this may change, but whether you're brewing a kölsch, gose, weissbier, or helles, if you want it to taste German, you must resist the urge to amp up the flavor volume. That's just not the German way.

Germany doesn't get nearly the credit it should for the diversity of beers its brewers make. Depending on what you consider a style, Germany is home to something like 15 native extant styles. Many are extremely similar: the differences between a helles, märzen, pilsner, schwarzbier, and maibock mainly come down to malt bill. But this is a country with the world's only salted beer (gose); a wild ale (Berliner weisse); a rustic, yeast-driven ale (weizen); a tradition of farmhouse brewing (especially vivid in the Zoigl region); lagered ales (kölsch and altbier);

brewery-kilned smoked beer (rauchbiers); and all of this in addition to those lagers that made the country famous.

Of all the breweries I've visited, those in Germany surprised me the most. I expected to find a country where the brewers were dogmatic and incurious. Instead, I found the most knowledgeable brewers in the world, and the ones who were the most attentive to world brewing trends. It's true that Germany is not home to a lot of experimentation (yet), but this has more to do with the drinkers than the brewers.

Returning again to Schlenkerla's Trum, he described what he was up against. He continued on. "If you now start doing a totally new beer because you think, 'I want to diversify, and I want new customers,' you will get *some* new customers. The Reinheitsgebot is the holy cow. If someone found out that someone was not brewing to Reinheitsgebot, they would not survive."

There are no beer geeks in Germany. I mean, there are people here who love beer and drink it every day, but being so [avid] about it — it's just not what Germans do.

— MATTHIAS TRUM, SCHLENKERLA

So Trum and other inventive brewers such as Schneider & Sohn's Hans-Peter Drexler mine their wonderfully rich history and find wildness in tradition. When he wants to introduce a new beer, Trum looks into the past to finding interesting beers and resurrects them. Drexler has gone so far as to barrel-age his weizenbock, picking up a distinct *Brettanomyces* note. He's on the leading edge of hops experimentation, pointing out that using juicy, flavorful new varieties in his weissbier in no way changes the method of production. "If you take different varieties of hops or malt, you can do so many different things," he told me. "I think it's more interesting to work with the raw materials to create new things."

My sense is that things are going to start changing soon. Clever brewers will first begin to push the envelope in terms of flavor without harming any sacred cows. The excitement that has punctuated craft brewing's rise in other countries will spread to German drinkers, and over time we'll begin to see a "new" German tradition emerge. For now, it's enough to step back and appreciate how diverse the old tradition still is.

· CHAPTER 7 ·

BAVARIAN LAGERS

*L*agers were born in Bavaria sometime around the end of the 1300s and soon became a fixture there. Yet despite the ultimate dominance of lagers worldwide, it took another 350 years before anyone started paying much attention to this odd style of beer made in cool caverns dug into the hillsides in a remote, rural part of the German-speaking world. All that time spent languishing in obscurity gave Bavarians time to perfect their technique and even become a bit hidebound about it. (Reinheitsgebot came out of this tradition, and it is nothing if not hidebound about the proper ways to make lager.)

The early lagers were made of darker malts and were by definition *dunkel* (dark) lagers. At first that was out of necessity: aside from the "wind malts" made by drying in the sun, it was not possible to kiln malt to a pale hue. It wasn't until the 1830s that history began to change. That was when two scions of famous brewers, Spaten's Gabriel Sedlmayr II and Klein-Schwechat's Anton Dreher, traveled to Britain to discover how the English were making pale ales. Upon their return both created lighter malts named for their homes — Vienna and Munich.

In Munich Spaten debuted a dark amber lager in 1841, nudging Munichers toward lighter beers. Munich malt also changed the character of dunkel lagers from rough, roasty affairs to rich, smooth ones. But still, Munich was a dark-beer town, the undisputed king of lager making, and people weren't about to give up their chestnut beers, no matter how much excitement pale lagers were creating in Vienna and Pilsen.

Decades rolled by before anyone dared attempt a pale lager in Munich, and it was — again — Spaten that broke the ice. The brewery released the first true *helles* (bright) beer in 1894, and it nearly caused a schism among Munich's breweries, many of whom felt that pale lagers were an offense to the city's rich dunkel lager heritage. Of course, the traditionalists lost the battle, and helles eventually found favor. You'll still find both helles and dunkel in nearly every watering hole from Würzburg to Wallgau, though now helles has overtaken dunkel in popularity. Over the centuries Bavarians also added various types of bocks and märzen/festbiers, as well as heavily influencing the lagers, such as schwarzbier and pilsner, popularized farther north.

For anyone who has spent time in the dappled shade of a Bavarian biergarten, the name of Florian Kuplent's brewery will be obvious: those trees soaring overhead are usually chestnuts. Bavarians and fans of Bavarian beer see that name and they think: weissbier, pretzels and weisswurst, biergarten. Kuplent, an immigrant who spent the early part of his career working and studying in Bavaria, delivers all these goods.

In reality, Urban Chestnut channels the mood of Bavarian conviviality more than it tries to re-create a perfectly German experience. There's no *Schweinshaxe* or *Aischgründer Karpfenfilet*, and the taplist features some very un-Bavarian specialties, such as a double IPA, an English porter, and a French saison. But even in these deviations there's often a knowing wink — German malt and Hallertau hops that find their way into recipes, a softness in the palate, a sense of balance even in bouncy American beers.

The taste of Bavaria really pops in the classic preparations of the beer invented there, particularly Kuplent's rendition of kellerbier, an unfiltered helles. Zwickel is a great way to bring American audiences to the beer of his homeland; it is brewed in the traditional fashion, with decoction mashing and German ingredients, but has a hazy, yeasty appearance that makes it more familiar. Urban Chestnut makes all the classics, at least periodically — dunkel, weissbier, doppelbock, and märzen. And to emphasize its connection to Bavaria, in 2015 Urban Chestnut announced the purchase of Bürgerbräu Wolnzach, a small brewery in the Hallertau region, just north of Munich.

OWNER/BREWMASTER FLORIAN KUPLENT

A voracious brewer, Florian Kuplent started out at Brauerei Erharting, near the Austrian border, having convinced the local brewmaster to take him on as an apprentice. He went on to study brewing at the Bavarian College of Food and Beverage Science, later earning a master's at Weihenstephan in malting and brewing science. From there Kuplent brewed all over the world, from Connecticut (New England Brewing) to Meantime (London), Beck's (Bremen),

Duvel Moortgat (Belgium), and elsewhere. He finally landed in St. Louis to work at Anheuser-Busch; he left there in 2010 and opened Urban Chestnut in 2011.

Understanding Bavarian Lagers

I was sitting in front of my third or fourth half-liter of Bavarian helles when I had one of the most important beer insights of my life: *I finally understood malt.* Helles beers bore American beer geeks because they seem so unyieldingly mild. You can search the whole of Bavaria and never find a sharp edge. But strip everything down to its bare essence, and you begin to make unexpected discoveries.

Each helles had a similarity to the last — it's one of the least varied beer styles on the planet — and yet each helles was also different. I later learned that one of the main reasons for this is there are tons of malt houses throughout the country. I was surprised to never encounter a brewery that used Weyermann, the only German malt house I knew. (This was even true in Bamberg, Weyermann's home.) Each malt was slightly different, resulting in flavors that varied in surprising ways helles to helles.

> **As a brewer you have maybe 25 percent chance to influence the profile of your beer in the brewhouse; 75 percent of the character is set at the malthouse. And of that, more than half is from the field.**
>
> **— JÜRGEN KNÖLLER, BAYERN BREWING**

And actually, what I really understood were base malts. Americans basically ignore base malt as a flavor element. If we want to add nuts or biscuit or graininess, we do it with specialty malt. By contrast, base malts are critical to the flavor and aroma of German beers. Helles is the perfect beer style to encourage you to develop an appreciation for the diversity of these base malts on a beer. That difference that I kept finding always related at least in part to the difference in these base malts — some are sweeter, some grainier, some warm and biscuity, some like honey. Other factors such as yeast and technique play a role, but I quickly became a connoisseur of this very elemental part of the beer. It was a revolutionary lesson, and one Americans are often slow to appreciate.

Florian Kuplent echoes my discovery. "I would go even a step further," he says. "I am a big believer that the European-grown barley varieties are a big driver of flavor in helles-style beers. At Urban Chestnut we actually import all of our malt (made from barley grown mostly in Bavaria) to ensure the highest quality ingredients. At a previous employer we ran tests with domestically grown barleys and were never able to reproduce the flavor that we got with imported European barleys."

Dunkel lagers are not terribly different from one to the next in mood and temperament. They are simple little beers made for quaffing by the liter. Helles lagers are often made with just a single malt and a single hop, and dunkel lagers can be made that way as well, using Munich rather than pilsner malt (though typically Munich is only a portion of the grist). Again, any beer with such stripped-down recipes — particularly lagers, which start out pre–stripped down — must depend mightily on the quality and interest of those few ingredients. With dunkel lagers the malt in question is Bavaria's most famous, Munich — that same malt that ushered in the very slow move to lighter beers. As with the different pilsner malts used to make helleses, Munich can produce different kinds of dunkel lagers.

I wish everyone could spend a week or two sitting in Bavarian biergartens, slowly attuning their palates to these subtle malts. The next best thing is to experiment with these styles in your own brewing and see for yourself. (But don't rule out a trip to Germany, either.)

Brewing a Bavarian Lager

Brewing a good helles is an art form par excellence. Indeed, when Germans go off to learn how to brew beer, they're first taught how to make pale lagers, the theory being that if you can master the technique to make a good helles — or German pils — you know how to brew all styles. Alan Taylor, who went to brewing school in Berlin, explained it this way (though he acknowledged that it's true for helles beer as well): "The German philosophy is if you can make this beer — in which you can't hide anything — if you can make that beer with all the technological tools we give you in your tool kit, you can make anything. You can make a hefeweizen; it's slightly different, but it's the same principles. You use different ingredients, you use a different mill setting for the wheat, you use different mash schedules, you use different yeasts, you use an open fermenter, but you know all about that because you learned how to make a pilsner beer."

In a beer with such slim margins for error, consistency is very hard to manage. Shifting any variable — mash temperature, hop variety (even hop *year*, since the variation in crops year to year is evident in such delicate beers), pH — will have a noticeable effect on your beer. For the homebrewer, though, that's mostly good news. It means you likely won't be able to achieve the kind of consistency professionals manage, true, but it also means you can easily observe the effect of changes in, say, malt type. The sensitivity of this style is brutal for consistency, but it's great for transparency.

There are no real tricks to brewing a great lager. Many small breweries still decoct their lagers, but many larger breweries don't. Even highly sophisticated breweries like Weihenstephan (uses decoction) and Ayinger (doesn't decoct) come down on different sides of the question. The recipe that follows is for a helles beer and does not call for decoction. If you wish to do a single or double decoction, it's certainly an option (see chapter 12 for instructions). Florian Kuplent sent along both methods as possibilities.

The more important point is that whatever ingredients and methods you choose, pay particular attention to what happens when you brew and take detailed notes. When you brew a helles again, do the same thing. Since these beers are so sensitive to change, you'll have the chance to see the effect subtle differences make on the way the beer tastes.

MALT BILL

8.5 pounds German pilsner malt (97%)

0.25 pound CaraHell malt (3%)

STEP MASH

122°F (50°C) mash in

144°F (62°C) for 30 minutes

162°F (72°C) for 30 minutes

172°F (78°C) mash out

90-MINUTE BOIL

0.5 ounce Hallertau Mittelfrüh, 90 minutes (4.0% AA, contribution of 8 IBU)

0.4 ounce Hallertau Mittelfrüh, 45 minutes (4.0% AA, contribution of 5 IBU)

0.75 ounce Hallertau Mittelfrüh, 10 minutes (4.0% AA, contribution of 5 IBU)

FERMENTATION AND CONDITIONING

Ferment with Wyeast 2206/2308 or White Labs WLP830/WLP833 at 46°F (8°C) (fine to let it rise to 50°F [10°C]) for 7 to 10 days. Condition as cold as possible (down to 30°F [–1°C]) for 3 weeks.

PACKAGE

Keg is ideal to preserve the beer's clarity — particularly for homebrewers who can't filter. The yeast in bottle conditioning may add haze at opening. If you do bottle-condition, try chilling the beer in the bottle after re-fermentation is complete to clear the yeast.

FLORIAN
KUPLENT

URBAN
CHESTNUT

- Expected OG: 12.1° P/1.049
- Expected TG: 2.8° P/1.011
- Expected ABV: 5.0%
- Expected bitterness: 18 IBU

Notes: The boil length is not critical, but it will impact hop utilization and evap-oration, so adjust your recipe if you choose a 60-minute boil. It depends on your system — Kuplent says that "we boil between 60 and 90 minutes in our breweries." Since this recipe calls for a 90-minute boil, you'll want to adjust the hopping rates to achieve the target bitterness. Kuplent also notes: "I believe strongly in yeast strain selection and condition, as well as the amount of pitching yeast. I think this is being neglected by many brewers."

Ester production is directly affected by pitch rates, so if you underpitch your yeast, even if it's healthy, it will kick off esters. Consider creating a starter for your yeast to ensure clean fermentation. You may wish to conduct a diacetyl rest, raising the temperature to around 65°F (18°C) for 2 days following fermentation. Crash the temperature as cold as possible (down to 30°F [–1°C]) for maturation/lagering.

NEXT STEPS

Aside from the question of decoction (see page 132), Bavarian lagers do not invite a great number of embellishments or options. These are beers you improve incremen-tally, through modest changes in ingredients or process. It's sort of like playing darts: you understand the theory, but it all comes down to practice.

As mentioned, these beers are also great at revealing subtle differences, such as how different base malts or hops affect the flavor. Americans don't have access to many of those myriad German brands of malts, but we do have a number of pilsner malts to choose from. Compare Weyermann with domestic, French, Canadian, and even Belgian pilsner malts. Similarly, German hops aren't as flamboyant as American varieties (it's the rare drinker who can distinguish between Hersbrucker and Spalt). A helles is essentially a SMASH recipe (single malt and single hop), so swapping out Hallertau Mittelfrüh and trying one of the other classic German varieties will help you become familiar with them.

Beyond that, it's practice, practice, practice.

GERMAN HOPS

German hops are famous for their delicate spicy to herbal quality. They are not all interchangeable, though. Below is a list of a few of the key varieties to know. German hops are grown in the Tettnang, Elbe-Saale, Baden-Bitburg, Spalt, and Hallertau regions — and some of these locations give their names to the hops. This is why you sometimes see things like "Tettnang Tettnanger" — it indicates both the region and the hop variety. There are elements of terroir in hops, but this list discusses general qualities without getting into regional variations (though buy German hops when using these varieties — American-grown German varieties are quite a bit different).

Hallertau Mittelfrüh. The most famous German landrace hop; spicy and herbal, it is famous for its "harmonious" bitterness (a German description, but apt).

Hersbrucker. Another landrace variety, it has mild, balanced characteristics of spice and fruit along with a lightly floral aroma.

Perle. Developed at the German hop research center in Hüll in 1978, Perle is balanced and delicate, with spicy notes and a touch of fruit.

Saphir. Developed at Hüll in 2002, it has characteristically German spicy notes but also some citrus (often described as tangerine).

Spalt. Another German landrace variety, it is mild, lightly herbal, and fruity.

Tettnang. The last of the famous landrace varieties, descended from Saaz, Tettnangs have a distinctively tangy, almost citrusy quality (but not in the American mode).

Researchers have been busy developing new varieties that work well in more hop-forward beers (and especially weissbier) but that may be a little too assertive for Bavarian lagers: Hallertau Blanc, Hüll Melon, and Mandarina Bavaria. They are, however, worth checking out for your other beers.

Dunkel Lager

A simple variation on Florian Kuplent's recipe above is for a dunkel lager. These are soft, malt-accented dark beers found all over Bavaria. Even more than helles lagers, dunkel lagers are characterized by malt flavors — and unlike schwarzbiers, they don't have any roasty flavors. Kuplent suggests a recipe of 92 to 95 percent Munich malt, 3 to 6 percent caramel malt (CaraMunich, for example), and 1 to 2 percent black malt for color. For the rest of the process and ingredients, follow the included recipe.

Other Lagers

Lager brewing is a Bavarian tradition. Beyond helles and dunkel lager, bocks (mai-bocks, doppelbocks, eisbocks), Oktoberfest/märzens, German pilsners, export lagers, and schwarzbier all grew out of this tradition. Using the template from this chapter, you can create these styles by tinkering with the recipes. In each case shoot for a hop profile using one of Germany's classic varieties. German brewers often use high-alpha varieties such as Magnum to bitter, but always use noble-type hops later in the boil.

GERMAN PILSNER (4.5–5.5% ABV, 25–40 IBU). German pilsners are very similar to helles beers, differing only in hop intensity. Use a grist of 100 percent pilsner malt or pilsner with 1 to 3 percent acidulated malt and hop to preference.

MÄRZEN (5–6.5% ABV, 18–30 IBU). Märzens have become lighter in recent years, looking more like pilsners than the autumnal-hued beauties they once were. For a rich, traditional märzen, consider a base of pilsner malt with up to 50 percent Munich or a blend of Munich, Vienna, and pilsner.

MAIBOCK (6–8% ABV, 15–30 IBU). Maibocks may be pilsner pale, golden, or almost amber. Depending on the color you wish, use 0 to 10 percent Munich, 0 to 25 percent Vienna, and the remainder pilsner malt.

DOPPELBOCK (6.5–10% ABV, 20–40 IBU). Doppelbocks are typically darker, so start with a base of 50 to 70 percent Munich malt with a touch of debittered roast malt (1 percent), and a balance of pilsner malt.

SCHWARZBIER (4.5–5.2% ABV, 20–40 IBU). Schwarzbiers can be made with very diverse grists, including Munich-heavy examples with modest roast malt or versions that use less Munich but more roast. Use a grist of 20 to 67 percent Munich, 2 to 10 percent roast malt, and the remainder pilsner malt.

Lagering

Commercial breweries have precise control over their fermentation and conditioning temperatures. Homebrewers rarely have the equipment to chill their beer, or if they do — in the case of a fridge, say — they lack the ability to shift from relatively warm fermentation temperatures (46°F [8°C]) to freezing temps used at conditioning (30 to 33°F [−1−0.6°C]).

There are ways around this. Some homebrewers plug in external thermostats that allow them to raise their fridge/freezer temperatures to the mid-40s F (7–8°C). Others have rigged up insulated boxes cooled by minifridges or jury-rigged other systems. There are even devices that will cool beer in a carboy. These are all fine solutions — for many brewers, tricking out a system is half the fun. But there is also a time-honored low-tech solution to lagering: winter.

In chilly parts of the country, brewers can use an assist from Mother Nature. Depending on the month and where you live, you can stow carboys in the cellar, outside, in sheds, or in garages to achieve typical fermentation and lagering temps. Huge fluctuations can be a problem, so it's better to have an intermediate area — such as a garage — when outside temps are bouncing around.

For lagering you want temperatures below 40°F (4°C); if it's warmer than that where you plan to lager, you can help keep the carboy cold by packing it in a cooler with a block of ice. So long as it's not terribly warm, the ice will melt slowly and keep the carboy at excellent lagering temperatures. Professionals are pretty fussy about their lagering temps, but you won't ruin a beer if for some reason your carboy drifts above 40°F (4°C) or even 50°F (10°C). The final product may just be a bit rougher, but it will not ruin the beer.

CHAPTER 8

WEISSBIERS/WEIZENS

Summer is the time most beer is consumed, and a good many of the world's styles taste best in the heat of July. But give me a choice, and I will always select that cloudy, bubbly potion that comes served in a "vase" — the Bavarian weizen. It's the perfect summer beer (which is why so many Bavarians choose it when they're sitting in biergartens), with a soft, banana fruitiness balanced by a clovey phenolic snap. Add the clouds of wheat and yeast, further clouds of head billowing out, and a crisp, bready finish, and it quenches like no other beer.

Brewers know that weizens are a product of yeast, but they may not realize that there are complex chemical reactions that affect the degree to which the yeast will produce those wonderful esters and phenols. It begins with the mash schedule and, in the most traditional Bavarian breweries, continues on in open fermentation. Learning these techniques will give you more control over your weizen, allowing you to adjust the phenols and esters to your taste.

EST **Schneider & Sohn** 1855

KELHEIM, GERMANY

Very few breweries can claim to have saved a style — especially one as important to modern brewing as weissbier — but Schneider is one. The style, which has roots going back six hundred years, was wildly popular in the eighteenth century. But by 1812 tastes had turned away from wheat beers, and there were just two breweries left making it. When Georg Schneider decided to take out a lease on a weissbier brewery in Munich in 1855, it seemed like a quixotic venture. Brewing weissbier had for centuries been a right granted by the state, but he fought and won the right for any brewer to make them. His advocacy for weissbier was pivotal, and most of the credit for saving the style goes to him. He later moved the brewery to tiny Kelheim, where it still keeps the spirit of weissbier alive.

Schneider still adheres to the most traditional methods of making wheat beer. The brewery is configured especially for this purpose. In fact, until an expansion in the mid-2000s allowed the brewery to make alcohol-free beer, the only beer the brewery *could* make was wheat beer. (Now they have conditioning tanks, though the wheat beer never touches them.) Like all traditional breweries, Schneider ferments its beers in open vessels, and Schneider Weisse is never filtered nor does it go to a conditioning tank. Instead, it is dosed with a bit of wort called *speise* (food) in the bottle and finishes developing its character there.

Despite this traditional bent, Schneider is also on the leading edge of innovation. Master Brewer Hans-Peter Drexler, impressed by American hopping, began working with local hop growers in the Hallertau region to develop new and interesting varieties; they turn out to harmonize wonderfully with the flavors in the yeast. Drexler has also initiated a barrel-aging program for his legendary weizenbock Aventinus. Weizens are one of the few success stories in a country that drinks less beer each year, and Schneider has been at the forefront of their popularity.

BREWMASTER HANS-PETER DREXLER

Although he looks too young for this to be possible, Drexler arrived at Schneider in 1982 and has been the master brewer since 1990. Despite his long tenure, Drexler has helped guide Schneider to the vanguard of German brewing, forming one of the first transatlantic partnerships with an American brewery to produce collaboration beers. He has experimented with new hops and even, shockingly, Cascade and Nelson Sauvin hops in his ever-growing portfolio. Nevertheless, Drexler doesn't see anything transgressive about the beers he's making. "[Reinheitsgebot] means we have three raw materials to work with: hops, malt, and water. If you take different varieties of hops or malt you can do so many different things."

Understanding Weissbiers

There are three important elements driving the character of a weissbier: the use of wheat for flavor and appearance, strident effervescence, and those important esters and phenols that dominate the palate. Let's take them separately. Wheat generally composes the majority of the grist and gives a weissbier both its dry, clean flavor and the famous billowing cloudiness. Wheat isn't the only important player, though. Barley contains compounds that interact with yeast to produce those all-important spicy phenols. Fortunately, the wheat flavor takes care of itself; the turbidity and phenols, however, require the brewer's attention.

Barley contains an organic compound called ferulic acid that can be converted during fermentation into 4-vinyl guaiacol — the phenol that tastes like clove. "We are very interested in having the raw materials bring a lot of the ferulic acid to the wort and get a lot of vinyl guaiacol in the beer," Drexler says. "The wheat malt brings other characteristic aromas, but the clove aroma mostly comes from the barley malt." Ferulic acid is freed during mashing but only within a band of temperature between 104 and 113°F (40 and 45°C), known as a ferulic acid rest. The longer you hold the mash at that rest, the more phenolic the beer — that makes sense — but there's a trade-off: ester creation falls during this period, too. If you want a balance, 10 minutes seems to be the sweet spot.

Now what about those esters? Fermentation temperature affects them (yeast produces more esters at higher temperatures), but an even more important consideration is the fermenter itself. In commercial brewing, traditionalists believe only open fermentation produces the rich ester profile the best weizens exhibit. At Ayinger, where they spent millions of dollars building a new brewery and abandoning old techniques such as decoction mashing, they nevertheless preserved an open fermentation room for their weissbiers. The science seems to support it. In his excellent book *Brewing with Wheat,* Stan Hieronymus reproduces German research illustrating that an open fermenter produces more than twice as much isoamyl acetate (the classic banana ester in weissbier) than a cylindro-conical tank and a third more than other closed tanks.

Carbonation levels are often overlooked in weissbiers, but if you can't stack a 2-inch head on the top of your weisse vase, you're missing half the fun.

The final element is effervescence — though here homebrewers may find the effect easier to achieve than do commercial brewers. In traditional weissbier, breweries add a dose of speise (literally "food," or in this case wort) to bottle-condition their beer. They aim for carbonation levels as much as twice as high as standard beer. (Most ales contain 1.5 to 2.5 volumes of carbonation; weissbiers have from 3 to 4 volumes.) Carbonation levels are often overlooked in weissbiers, but if you can't stack a 2-inch head on the top of your weisse vase, you're missing half the fun. Besides, the creamy body and refreshing crispness come in part from that lively carbonation.

WHEAT, WEIZEN, WEISSE

The terms "wheat," "weizen," and "weisse" are interchangeable when we're talking about Bavarian wheat beers, but they're not synonyms. "Weizen" literally means "wheat," but "weisse" (weiße) actually means "white." Centuries ago wheat malt was dried at a low heat and took on a whitish cast — particularly in comparison to the barley beers made with fire-roasted malts. So "white beers" did generally refer to beers made of wheat — and still does. But it's nice to know the subtle differences.

Brewing a Weissbier

When you look at the formulation on page 86, you'll see what odd ducks weissbiers are. At Schneider Hans-Peter Drexler uses a one-mash decoction but, "when we do a microbrew in our pilot plant (100 liters), we use an infusion process." He then detailed the *seven* rests I repeat. The point of these rests is to do all those things that make wheat beers so distinctive — esters and phenols; billowing, cloudy bodies; rich, wheaty flavor. Most homebrewers won't have the system to complete them all accurately, but it's worth monkeying with different rests and seeing how the beers change when you collapse some of them versus doing more. (Some of the outcomes that a commercial brewery seeks when using all these rests, such as stability and shelf life, aren't that important to homebrewers.)

Another very important consideration is the flavor balance you're seeking. Bavarian weissbiers span a range that includes ones that lean heavily on the banana to spicier ones that are only accented with banana. The natural action of the yeast will work to create isoamyl acetate without much tinkering by the brewer, but getting the phenols dialed in is more work. In my experience, commercial breweries often favor banana to clove, which by itself can create the impression of imbalanced sweetness in a low-IBU ale. If you like spicier weissbiers, consider using open fermentation (see Open Fermentation, page 88), but at least be sure to do a rest to release ferulic acids.

WEISSBIER

HANS-PETER DREXLER

—

SCHNEIDER & SOHN

MALT BILL

5.33 pounds German or French wheat malt (60%)

3.5 pounds German pilsner malt (40%)

STEP MASH

Mash in at 95°F (35°C) for 10 minutes to release ferulic acid.

122°F (50°C) for 10 minutes (protein rest)

131°F (55°C) for 15 minutes (protein rest)

144°F (62°C) for 10 minutes (amylase rest)

155°F (68°C) for 20 minutes (amylase rest)

161°F (72°C) for 20 minutes

172°F (78°C) mash out

60-MINUTE BOIL

0.25 ounce Herkules, 50 minutes (14.5% AA, contribution of 13 IBU)

0.25 ounce Hallertau Tradition, 45 minutes (4.5% AA, contribution of 3 IBU)

FERMENTATION AND CONDITIONING

Ferment with a Bavarian weissbier yeast (Wyeast 3638 or White Labs WLP351). The brewery pitches at 63°F (17°C) and lets the temperature rise to 73°F (23°C). If you lack temperature control, pitch at around 68°F (20°C) and try to keep it from rising too much. (Ayinger pitches and holds their weissbier at 68°F.) Schneider only needs 5 days for complete primary fermentation before bottling. Give the beer 21 days to bottle-condition — a week for maturation and 2 to settle the yeast and finish maturation.

- Expected OG: 13° P/1.052

- Expected TG: 12° P/1.011

- Expected ABV: 5.4%
- Expected bitterness: 16 IBU

Notes: The mash schedule is very complex for breweries that don't have sophisticated systems. If you collapse the first two steps, it's important to have one rest somewhere between 104 and 122°F (40 and 50°C) so that the malt releases the ferulic acid that will be converted into 4-vinyl guaiacol. Drexler notes that a stop at 113°F (45°C) will produce "a distinct phenolic note" (that's the classic ferulic acid rest temperature).

During fermentation Schneider actually drops the beer down to 54°F (12°C) at the end of fermentation, but "it is important for our process, but not for a home-brewer." About the malt Schneider uses, Drexler writes: "We use special varieties that work for the farmer (yield, less disease, no fusarium) and for the brewer (influence of the beer's flavor and aroma by ferulic acid/4-vinyl guaiacol). Those varieties are Anthus, Maltop, or Hermann." If you brew year to year and find the phenol levels change, it may not be your process, but the barley. Drexler says, "We try to get a lot of this vinyl guaiacol to get a typical aroma in the beer. But it depends on the year; not every year is the same." Of course, American homebrewers don't have many German malt varieties to choose from, so work with what you can find.

NEXT STEPS

There is a small revolution going on in Germany, and Hans-Peter Drexler is among the leading revolutionaries. He was first inspired by, of all things, American pale ale 15 years ago. "I remember I was very impressed with the beers of Sierra Nevada. Very, very nice beers. I thought it should be easy to match the American citrusy Cascade hops with Bavarian-style weissbier, so we started to brew Edel-Weisse with them." That led him to think deeply about the limits of what "German" beer really was.

> For me it's interesting to play with old tradition.
> In Germany Reinheitsgebot means we have three
> raw materials: hops, malt, and water. If you take
> different varieties of hops or malt, you can do so
> many different things.
>
> — HANS-PETER DREXLER, SCHNEIDER & SOHN

The next step was integrating the American mode of hopping in with indigenous varieties. Just down the road from Kelheim are the famous Hallertauer hop fields. In the past decade farmers, working with the German government, have been producing new hops such as Polaris, Hallertau Blanc, Huell Melon, and Mandarina Bavaria. Drexler has combined newer-variety hops with his weissbier to create the kind of potions that Americans love — using the same techniques. "We do both, late addition and dry hopping, depending on the beer style and recipe." As Drexler suspected, the peppery phenols and bright esters harmonize wonderfully with citrusy, fruity qualities imparted by American hops.

If you want to try your hand at these hybrid ales, make the beer exactly as you normally would through the first part of the boil, but add aroma hops the way you

DIVING DEEPER

Open Fermentation

A few years ago I encountered some research discussing the effects that fermenter shape and design had on ester production. At first glance that struck me as totally bizarre — why would the shape of a fermenter affect flavor? When you think about it a bit, though, it starts to make sense. The agents of flavor are tiny beings, so it stands to reason that the physical environment will affect their behavior. In weissbier, the best way to pop the esters and phenols is with open fermentation. Part of this has to do with CO_2 levels, which inhibit ester production — and which are lowest in open fermenters. It's not clear why phenols develop more fully in open fermentation, but breweries have consistently found it to be so.

Open fermentation is risky in the home brewery. Even in a commercial brewery, it can be a challenge. When we walked into the fermentation room at Schneider, Drexler literally flinched. "The challenge of this system is the hygienic problem of the open fermenters. Everything has to be very, very clean, and these open fermenters are hard to control." This is all true, and open fermentation in the home brewery is would for a juicy pale ale or IPA. Citrusy hops are ideal, and herbal hops can add some nice textures, but avoid especially dank, sticky varieties. Experiment with all the techniques Americans use, from hop bursting to using hop backs to dry hopping.

In working specifically with weissbiers, Drexler adds the following tidbits of advice: "Open fermenters bring more aromatic beers, and this masks aggressive hoppy notes. To remove the kräusen from the top of fermenters makes the beer smooth and balanced, and bottle conditioning brings more balance into the beer if you use real speise (wort) instead of sugar." The results can be impressive — and are still Reinheitsgebot compliant!

not without risk. But it's also true that professionals are not only worried about losing one batch to spoilage but inadvertently introducing a pernicious wild yeast or bacterium into their brewery. Homebrewers don't have to worry about that.

The easiest method is to use your brew kettle as the fermenter. They are typically wider than plastic vessels — another advantage in ester production. Make sure you begin with a yeast starter and that it is in the very active stage of fermentation when you pitch. Place your open fermenter in a clean, still part of your house where small beings (children, pets) are forbidden, and pitch the yeast.

Keep the lid on the fermenter until you start to see froth building, and then move the lid to the side so that there's a gap for air to enter. You want the gap to be large enough so that air does enter — the whole point of open fermentation is to put the fermenting wort in contact with the air. (I suppose courageous brewers could fly totally commando, but that sends a chill up my spine.) So far, my experimentation with open fermentation hasn't led to any infection.

WEISSBIER VARIATIONS

Once you know how to brew a classic weissbier, it's easy to produce the common variations you find throughout Bavaria. Use roughly the same proportion of wheat in these beers (50–60 percent) and follow the same mashing schedule.

Dunkelweizen. The term dunkel ("dark") is relative, and dunkelweizens are usually amber to light brown. You have a couple of choices in how to add color. You can add small amounts of dark malt, which will preserve the classic flavor profile but stain the beer darker. You can also use a darker wheat caramel malt such as Weyermann's Carawheat, which will give the beer a nutty, fuller flavor.

Weizenbock. A typical weissbier style brewed to doppelbock strength (7% and higher), these beers still have the same fruity esters and spicy phenols but have stronger malt flavors and a noticeable, warming alcohol sensation. As a point of departure, you can use the identical recipe as listed above, but shoot for a gravity of 1.076/18.5°P.

Rauchweizen. A quite rare style of weissbier made with smoked malt, rauchweizens still have the fruity and spicy yeast character, in addition to the smokiness of a rauchbier such as Schlenkerla or Spezial. As a beginning point, use the basic weizen recipe and substitute 10 to 15 percent of the pilsner malt with smoked malt.

· CHAPTER 9 ·

ALES OF THE RHINE

Say the words "German beer" and the mind turns to "lager." But that association is off — it's really Bavaria that equals lager. The northern half of modern Germany was until the twentieth century entirely devoted to ales, so much so that in 1603 the Cologne town council actually *banned* lagers. Altbier, kölsch, gose, Berliner weisse — when you start thinking about it, you realize that all the early indigenous styles were ales. Two cities are still devoted to ales, though slightly different varieties — kölsch in Cologne (Köln) and altbier in Düsseldorf.

Visiting these cities is a strange experience. We live in a time where everything is globalized and local stores have products from around the world. But visit Cologne and Düsseldorf and you find that the rules of globalization don't apply. In these cities you find only the local beer in the pubs (and everywhere else; even at Chinese restaurants) — but leave them, and those styles vanish. These sister cities form little bubbles of beer culture, and within them the styles flourish (though makers of altbier are falling fast).

Although expectations of these beers force them to conform to narrow criteria, each brewery manages to carve out different flavors and aromas within the style, and locals are devoted to their favorites. Spend some time in these cities, and you see why — after a few days, distinguishing between Schlüssel and Füchschen and Früh and Päffgen is as easy as telling the difference between your mother and your father.

EST **Hausbrauerei Uerige** 1862

DÜSSELDORF, GERMANY

Germany is loaded with interesting old breweries, but my vote for most interesting is Hausbrauerei Uerige. By German standards it's not especially old, dating just to 1862, when brewmaster Wilhelm Cürten bought the property and converted it from a wine tavern into a brewery. In the local dialect the word for "grumpy" was *uerige* (pronounced something like *OOR eh guh*), an adjective locals used to describe Wilhelm — and, eventually, the brewery.

Both the pub and the brewery still feel like something out of 1862. After leaving the kettle, hot wort goes to a coolship (*kühlschiff*) — a wide, flat pan used to cool beer before the invention of wort chillers — a vessel almost obsolete even in Belgium, where it is used in lambic breweries. From there it goes over an old drip chiller (pipes running with cold water), another nearly obsolete piece of equipment, before heading to the fermenters. And the fermenters are, of course, open.

The brewery is entwined in the pub, which wraps itself around vessels and tanks, filling in nooks and corners but often overlooking part of the brewery. Hop wreaths hang from the walls, stained glass adorns the windows, and heavy wooden casks full of altbier sit on the counter, waiting to fill cylindrical glasses to 0.25 L (a quarter liter).

Several brands of altbier still exist, but Uerige's remains the world standard. The regular alt is Düsseldorf's most bitter, though it is a soft, noble-hop bitterness further softened by rounded, almost burnished malts. The brewery also makes a special, stronger version of the beer called Sticke, which is served only twice a year (on the third Tuesdays of October and January). Another, even stronger version, Doppelsticke, is made for the US market. Both of these beers are dry-hopped and have reached the status of legend.

BREWMASTER CHRISTOPH TENGE

In Germany being a brewmaster is a technical qualification that requires an advanced degree, so it's common to see that a German brewer has attended Weihenstephan — a brewery with the Harvard of brewing schools. Rarely, though, has a brewer *taught* there, as Dr. Christoph Tenge did for six years. Tenge also served stints as quality compliance manager and brewing manager at the Spaten-Franziskaner Brewery in Munich.

It must have been something of a transition to go from using state-of-the-art brewing equipment at an AB InBev plant (Spaten's) to juggling coolships and drip chillers at Uerige. But it says a great deal about Uerige's commitment to quality that they were able to lure Dr. Tenge to Düsseldorf, where by all appearances he is flourishing.

Understanding Altbiers and Kölsches

It is reasonable enough to call altbier and kölsch "ales," but that term doesn't go far enough. In German they are known as *obergärige*: "top-fermenting." (Uerige is sometimes called Uerige Obergärige Hausbrauerei.) But they're also called *lagerbier*. This points to the twin qualities that define these beers. They are brewed with ale yeasts and fermented at ale temperatures — and consequently contain ale-made esters. But then they're racked to the cellar (or lately, glycol-clad conditioning tanks) to lager for weeks or in some cases months. What do you get for all that lagering? A clarion beer that has a lagerlike crispness and smooth, clean lines. It shares the best of both worlds.

Of the two beers, altbier appears to be considerably more difficult to duplicate outside its home city. Kölsch is a delicate, light beer made with a simple malt and hop bill. Breweries put their stamp on a kölsch by using more or fewer hops and tilting them toward either the zesty or the floral side and by coaxing lightly fruity flavors from the yeast — honeydew melon, pear, apple blossom. Their crisp finish is accentuated by a mineral twist from the water.

Altbier appears just as simple and elegant. It is said to be a hoppy style, but the dominant characteristic is a downy softness that comes from the malt. Hops are added at the beginning of the boil and often never again — and yet, because brewers use classic German hop varieties, they coax woody, peppery flavors from them. It is very common to find a caramel note that calls to mind slightly blackened sugar. Finally, there's something of a mineral note that comes through noticeably on the palate. When Americans have made this beer, the hops are generally too bitter, the malts not soft enough, and the mineral note absent.

Brewing an Altbier or Kölsch

There is an elegant simplicity to brewing ales in Cologne and Düsseldorf. In Düsseldorf they're often served at the brewery from wooden casks perched on the bar. Though neither are they naturally carbonated within the casks nor do they pick up any character from the wood (they have plastic linings), this presentation does remind one of English cask ales, and there is a similarity. Some of the breweries making these beers are brand-new and highly technical; others are antiques. If you know the key flavor elements, altbiers and kölsches can be made on simple equipment, just like cask ales. And as with cask ales, the execution is the important part.

There are a couple of things to keep your eye on when brewing an altbier. Despite what you may have heard, this is a malty style. Altbiers taste a bit fuller and richer than kölsches, and smooth, flavorful, aromatic malts are a must in the style — IBUs are not. The malt bill and mashing regime will help create the character you want, so don't deviate overmuch. The second thing is the hops — which while singing backup are nevertheless important. If you want to try to capture the flavor of Düsseldorf, I recommend sticking with these low-alpha German varieties as the recipe instructs. Despite the sole addition of hops near the start of the boil, some of the flavor and aroma will carry over, even after 70 minutes.

With a kölsch, the more important factor is the right yeast strain, which will add a soupçon of esters but leave the malt and hop flavors unmolested. It's one of the styles that makes homebrewers look good because the yeast does all the heavy lifting, and the brewer gets the credit for striking what looks like a difficult balance. Just don't let the temperatures rise too much during fermentation.

Finally, there's the matter of water. In most of the Cologne kölsches and all the Düsseldorf altbiers, there is a noticeable structure in these beers that comes from hard water. It's unmistakable and quite important in their drinkability. This is especially true with altbiers. I've sampled many American versions that seem washed out and flabby without it. I asked Dr. Tenge whether it was added intentionally, and he said the flavor is native to the city. "It is still the traditional way we brew our beer here, developed in this area according to the available water quality. All the altbier brewers around here use the Düsseldorf [water] without much treatment, from their own well or the local supplier, but the quality looks quite the same. That typical hard water seems to be responsible for what you call a mineral taste."

> **There is a noticeable structure in these beers that comes from hard water. It's unmistakable and quite important in their drinkability.**

It's not critical to adjust your water for a kölsch; it is for altbier. Use a water adjustment tool (Brewer's Friend has a good one) to amend your water so that it's similar to Düsseldorf's: calcium (90 mg/L), magnesium (12 mg/L), sodium (45 mg/L), sulfate (65 mg/L), bicarbonate (220 mg/L).

ALTBIER

CHRISTOPH
TENGE
—
HAUSBRAUEREI
UERIGE

MALT BILL

8 pounds pilsner malt (96%)

4 ounces cara malt — CaraRed or CaraMunich I (3%)

1.5 ounces German roast malt (1%)

STEP MASH

135°F (57°C) for 10 minutes

145°F (63°C) for 30 minutes

162°F (72°C) for 20 minutes

172°F (78°C) at sparging

80-MINUTE BOIL

0.2 ounce Magnum, 70 minutes (15.0% AA, contribution of 11 IBU)

2.5 ounces Tettnanger or Spalter or a 50/50 blend, 70 minutes (4.0% AA, contribution of 38 IBU)

Ferment with Wyeast 1007 or White Labs WLP036 at 68°F (20°C), with an option to do so in open fermenters. After initial fermentation settles, drop to 50°F (10°C) and let it continue to terminal gravity. Rack and condition for 4 weeks as cold as possible (down to 32°F [0°C]).

PACKAGE

Keg or bottle.

- Expected OG: 12° P/1.048

- Expected TG: 2.5° P/1.010

- Expected ABV: 5.0%

- Expected bitterness: 45–50 IBU

Notes: The brewery uses "very hard water." Uerige's initial fermentation takes just 2 to 3 days before it's transferred for cool maturation. Tenge said wryly that while Uerige's own yeast is the most suitable strain, "unfortunately (or indeed not), it is not freely available."

NEXT STEPS

This is one style that doesn't benefit from a lot of tinkering. From a sensory perspective, altbiers occupy a little world that is quite distinctive, but they are close enough to other styles that it's easy to nudge them too far, making them taste American or English. Christoph Tenge illustrates just how narrow that flavor band is when he dissuades brewers from using the wrong hops. And in this case, he's talking about *German* hops. "I would not exclude hop varieties like Perle or Hallertauer — we have also good experience with Hallertauer." Other varieties are going to change the essential character of this beer immediately; the room for improvisation is slight.

One thing you can do is make stronger versions. Uerige Sticke is 6.5%, and Doppelsticke is 8.5%. If you scale up the recipe, consider reducing the cara from 3 percent to 2 percent, especially for very strong beers. Uerige's Doppelsticke is rich and creamy, but it shouldn't be overly heavy. The most important change is dry hopping; both Sticke and Dopplesticke are dry-hopped with Spalter during maturation. The effect is not dramatic and just adds an aromatic component to the nose, so just use an ounce or two depending on the beer's strength. Uerige's Sticke is lagered 8 to 10 weeks, and Doppelsticke 12 to 20 weeks.

MAKING A KÖLSCH

A long-standing and mostly playful rivalry exists between Düsseldorf and Cologne (at Reissdorf, a kölsch brewery, a smiling Frank Hasenkrug told me "we don't say the name of that town [Düsseldorf] here"). For all that, the beers and beer culture of the two cities are quite similar. In both cities the beer is served in small, cylindrical glasses, and the waiter will keep dropping fresh ones in front of you until you wave him off. In both cities the waiter will leave a tick mark on the beer mat for each fresh glass he's dropped off. In both cities the beers are fermented with ale yeasts and lagered. But in one city the glasses are slightly larger, and in one city the beer is pilsner pale instead of deep copper. Much is made of small differences.

In the home brewery you will find them remarkably similar. I've seen some reference to Cologne water as soft, but that's inaccurate. It's hard (so hard that Reissdorf softens it), and a mineral note is common in the city's beers. The following instructions work well without water amendments, but you'll want somewhat hard water for the authentic flavor of Cologne.

The malt bill, of course, lacks a darkening agent. Kölsches are not quite as light as pilsner, so add a bit of Munich to the grist (start with 5 percent and adjust to preference) to add a deeper golden hue. A kölsch malt has recently come onto the American market, and it gives a richer maltiness to a beer. It's a bit dark, so you could add 25 percent pilsner to lighten it. A portion of wheat is acceptable but uncommon.

You can use the same mash schedule as altbier. Although Reissdorf does not want their mashing schedule publicly disclosed, it's quite similar to the one Dr. Tenge outlined. Bitter with a Halletauer-type hop such as Herkules, Merkur, or Tradition, and add an aroma charge with 15 minutes left in the boil with Hallertauer, Perle, or Saphir. Unlike altbier, kölsch is a broader style that can have malt-forward expressions like Reissdorf's or fairly hop-forward versions like Gaffel. Shoot for anything up to 30 IBUs with abandon, and go higher if you're feeling bold (or American).

Ferment with one of the standard kölsch strains (Wyeast 2565, White Labs WLP003/WLP029) at cool temperatures between 65 and 70°F (18 and 21°C). Lager cold for 3 to 4 weeks. Some kölsch strains produce a lot of sulfur, and the lagering time with those is not optional (lager until the sulfur is gone). You may also ferment kölsch in an open container as Sünner still does.

· CHAPTER 10 ·

GOSES

Even a decade ago a chapter on gose (*goes-uh*) would have been preposterous. A style that survived in the former East Germany for two decades until going extinct in 1966, it enjoyed the most tenuous of revivals in its homeland, being produced by just two breweries. Gose has all the hallmarks of a niche style, a tart wheat beer made with coriander and salt, of a type that is usually more popular with brewers than drinkers. It *is* odd. The first time I tried it, it reminded me of *lassi*, a salted yogurt drink from India, not beer. Northern Germany has been the home to a host of really weird ales — all of which have died or are on life support — and gose was a charter member.

But this is the little style that could. Amazingly, Americans in particular have taken to it and, in contrast to the witbier revival, have made every kind of conceivable variation, adding blood oranges (Anderson Valley), hibiscus (Widmer, Boulevard), cherry (Victory), cucumber (Seventh Sun), yuzu (Westbrook), lemon-basil (Schlafly), and on and on. The addition of salt makes goses thirst-quenching and also gives them a culinary dimension. Breweries have keyed off both of these elements to make their revival goses, and now it's hard to imagine any variation that wouldn't be considered a reasonable departure.

When I was on my book tour promoting *The Beer Bible*, I stopped in to breweries and alehouses across the country; everywhere I went, I kept seeing gose. Of all the places I stopped, only a few *didn't* have one on tap. They are clearly popular for their interesting palate and mutability, and that, of course, also makes them perfect for homebrewing.

EST **Bayerischer Bahnhof** 2000
LEIPZIG, GERMANY

Gose dates back as far as five hundred years, having gotten its start in Goslar, about smack dab in the center of northern Germany (though long before there was a Germany). It took two hundred years to migrate to Leipzig, the city that would make gose famous. Leipzig is where the style would find its revival, thanks to a gose fan named Lothar Goldhahn. The owner of Ohne Bedenken, an old gose house in Leipzig, Goldhahn wanted to be able to serve one of the city's famous beers to customers. He contracted out the production of gose to various breweries, but none made it full-time until Bayerischer Bahnhof opened its doors in 2000.

Owner Thomas Schneider was committed to bringing gose back to Leipzig permanently and set about creating a version of the old beer that could be reliably produced with consistent results on modern equipment. Brewer Matthias Richter told me, "In the past gose was fermented spontaneously. Thus, there was a good chance that the beer had a weird taste. We only changed the recipe of the Original Leipziger Gose to the extent that it is compatible with modern brewing technology. With the brewing being nowadays monitored and controlled, we have a distinctive, consistent gose taste."

The brewery is located in Leipzig's old, still-functioning train station (the "bahnhof" in the brewery's name) and makes a range of beers, including a pils, a Berliner weisse, experimental beers, and even a Baltic porter. It may not be their best seller, but the most influential beer — at least on this side of the Atlantic — remains the gently tart, saline gose. As German drinkers grow ever more adventuresome in their beer preferences, there's some reason to think gose may once again flourish in Leipzig.

BREWMASTER MATTHIAS RICHTER

Richter got his start working for a large brewery now in the Radeberger group called Ur-Krostitzer, where he learned brewing and malting. He continued his studies at Berlin's VLB brewing school, where he earned his brewmaster diploma. While at VLB, he started working with Bahnhof, and when the founding brewer decided to leave in 2002, Richter was offered the position. In addition to his work with Bayerischer Bahnhof, he consults with clients across Europe and in the United States.

Understanding Goses

The gose made at Bahnhof is the latest incarnation of what has been an evolving style. Gose was originally spontaneously fermented — a common practice hundreds of years ago. Those goses would have had a blend of yeast and bacteria and would probably have tasted like young lambic or the Hoegaarden beers of the time. Goses evolved, though, and in the nineteenth century they were made without boiling, a method that would have been useful in sparking a lactic fermentation. In this iteration the palate changed so that lactic tartness was central to the palate, much like Berliner weisse. In the early twentieth century it was described as *more* sour than Berliner weisse — quite a trick — but elsewhere was described as "strong." It was said to be good for the blood but also reputed to be a potent laxative. (Make of *that* what you will.)

The gose made by Bahnhof has a tangy, orangey aroma, a distant evocation of a wit. The coriander is more an essence, though. It's wheaty and lightly lactic, nothing like the sharp sour of a traditional Berliner weisse. What really makes Bahnhof's gose stand out is the salt. Salt infuses this gose, from the first sip through the final swallow. In fact, I licked my lips a few minutes after I finished the beer and they were still salty. American versions I've tried have tended to downplay this note, to their detriment; there's something incredibly interesting and moreish about a salty-sour beer.

There's something incredibly interesting and moreish about a salty-sour beer.

What Americans have learned, however, is that the salt is perfect for goses containing fruits or vegetables. It could be that the basic version of the beer is too odd for palates in the United States, but by adding another flavor the whole experience becomes more familiar. Ales made in what is now northern Germany were once very weird and experimental — easily as strange as anything made across the Belgian border. It would make perfect sense to the eighteenth-century Leipzig brewery to take the basic gose template — lactic sour, salt, wheat — and layer in other ingredients and flavors as suited the brewer's fancy. They would be as "traditional" as those made by American breweries today.

Brewing a Gose

Goses are essentially wild ales — they get their most important quality from *Lactobacillus* — so the decision about how to sour the mash is the first and most important consideration. To make Bahnhof's gose, Richter begins by cultivating lactic acid in his cellar from the naturally occurring bacteria found on the wheat. (According to Reinheitsgebot, brewers may not add chemical lactic acid. They must create it naturally.) He then blends an acidified wort with a standard wort to achieve a consistent pH level. There are other methods, and we'll address those in Next Steps.

Oddly enough, Richter ferments his gose with a weizen yeast, but ferments in a cylindro-conical tank to restrain ester and phenol production. He also skips the ferulic acid rest, further limiting the phenolic potential. Richter advises, "If you like to have a noticeable wheat taste, you should use wheat yeast you would normally use for a wheat beer. Otherwise, you can use any neutral top-fermenting yeast; for example, a yeast for a kölsch."

Seasoning the gose is, far more than spicing a wit, a matter of brewer preference. Richter says with salt, "you'll have to try for yourself through trial and error" what amount works best. In *Brewing with Wheat*, Stan Hieronymus quotes Richter as saying he adds 500 grams of table salt to a 15-hectoliter batch — or about 1.25 teaspoons per gallon. Trust Richter on this one, though; salt is such an assertive ingredient that overdoing it could easily ruin a batch of beer.

GOSE

MATTHIAS RICHTER

BAYERISCHER BAHNHOF

MALT BILL

4.25 pounds German pilsner malt (50%)

4.25 pounds wheat malt (50%)

SOURING TECHNIQUE

See Fermentation and Conditioning below. For an alternate method, see Next Steps.

STEP MASH

144 to 147°F (64–67°C) for 15 minutes

162°F (72°C) for 30 minutes

60-MINUTE BOIL

0.5 ounce German Northern Brewer, 60 minutes (8.0% AA, contribution of 14 IBU)

0.5 ounce cracked coriander seed, 15 minutes

1–1.5 teaspoons table salt at knockout

FERMENTATION AND CONDITIONING

Ferment at 68°F (20°C) with a 1:1 ratio of *Lactobacillus* to regular ale yeast. Wyeast 5335/White Labs WLP677 (lacto) with 3056/WLP300 (wheat) or 2565/WLP029 (kölsch).

PACKAGE

Bottle-condition or keg.

- Expected OG: 10.5° P/1.042
- Expected TG: 2° P/1.008

- Expected ABV: 4.5%

- Expected bitterness: 10–15 IBU

Notes: Matthias Richter has the spirit of a homebrewer, and he encourages everyone to experiment as they go along. Nearly everything can be adjusted to your preferences, from the boil time (up to 90 minutes), hop variety and amount (though hops should be at most a subtle note), and the salt and coriander amounts. One of the biggest decisions is how sour you want your gose to be. To begin with, choose lacto-to-yeast ratios of between 1:3 and 2:1. When pitching yeasts with bacteria, you lose flexibility in adjusting sourness, but it is by far the easiest method.

NEXT STEPS

Gose is a great style of beer to practice souring techniques. You're working mainly with *Lactobacillus*, so the different approaches can be compared in a relatively scientific setting (that is, you don't have to figure out what wild *Brettanomyces* or other wild microorganisms are contributing). Richter suggests two more methods of souring a gose in addition to pitching mixed cultures: sour mashing and kettle souring. These accomplish the same thing but in slightly different ways. In kettle souring you're pitching a pure *Lactobacillus* culture in wort, while in a sour mash you're encouraging native *Lactobacillus* on the grain to produce lactic acid.

Sour mashing is an old practice — and in the United States, a backwoods technique used to make whiskey — but it is very risky. As the name suggests, you make a regular mash and then let it sour over the course of hours or days. Wild *Lactobacillus* on the grain will stir themselves and go through a lactic fermentation, but there are a lot of other wild microorganisms on the grain as well, many of them in the food-spoilage class. Once those fellows get going, your mash may smell any manner of putrid (garbage, rotting vegetables, stinky feet, and so on).

Kettle Souring

In Portland, Oregon, Breakside Brewing's Ben Edmunds has used a number of techniques to make his tart beers — including gose — and he discourages sour mashes. "Sour mashing is a dubious technique all around. As someone who has done it a number of times, I can't say that I recommend it. The pickup of enterobacter and other bugs that live on malt is almost always a certainty. If the goal is to reduce mash pH, just use food-grade acid, acidulated malt, or a pure lacto culture."

Edmunds prefers kettle souring. Using this technique, he conducts a lactic fermentation on wort rather than in the mash, holding the wort for up to 72 hours in his brew kettle. A portion of the acidified wort is then blended with fresh wort and pitched with regular yeast, where both acidified and fresh worts go through a standard alcohol fermentation. The resulting beer will have a predictable pH level and won't contain any of the off-flavors that sour mashing might produce.

Edmunds recommends souring about 15 percent of the wort but prefers his goses to be only lightly acidic. "By the time the kettle is full, we have achieved our target pH of 3.7 to 3.8, which is where the beer stays the rest of the way through fermentation." If you want a sharper gose, you could increase the sour wort to 20 percent. With 20 quarts in a standard batch, the math here is easy — you'll be souring either 3 or 4 quarts of wort per batch. (Of course, if goses made with these percentages are still not tart enough for your liking, you can continue to increase the amount of kettle-soured wort.)

At least three days before brewing your gose, prepare 3 or 4 quarts of wort, using the same mashing regime as for a standard gose. (You could even use a blend of wheat and extra-pale dry malt extract if you want to skip the mash — but make sure you prepare a wort of around 1.042.) Cool the wort to 115°F (46°C), pitch a *Lactobacillus* culture (Wyeast 5335/White Labs WLP677), and hold it for three days. *Lactobacillus* is an anaerobic bacterium, so you want to seal it off from ambient oxygen. "As far as sealing the vessel goes, I'd suggest something as simple as Saran wrap for an overnight souring," Edmunds advises. The first 12 to 18 hours are the most critical, because that's when the pH is high enough for contamination to set in. "Once below a pH of 4.5," Edmunds says, "you're mainly safe from any aerobic contamination."

Setting Up a System

You'll have to rig up a system for holding the wort between 105 and 120°F (41 and 49°C). If you have a small cooler, a simple way to do this is to put the wort inside a container sealed with plastic wrap, and put this inside a bath of warm water in the cooler. Start the bath at 120°F (49°C) and check every 12 hours. When it falls to 105°F (41°C), replace some of the water and bring the temperature back up to 120°F (49°C).

One caveat to this system comes from Solera Brewery's Jason Kahler, who also regularly uses kettle souring in his brewery. He believes a lower temperature results in happier bacteria. "I believe that 110 to 115°F [43–46°C] is the highest you can go with *Lactobacillus* before you damage it. Beyond that, I think you might kill it." He conducts his lactic fermentation between 85 and 90°F (29 and 32°C). "I think that with bacteria, like with yeast, the lower range of its comfort zone is generally cleaner. It might take a little longer, but I think it's cleaner. That's my theory." I've had fine results from Edmunds's process, but if you want to work with cooler temperatures, follow the same procedure, but keep the bath between 85 and 100°F (29 and 38°C).

If you use this technique, you'll then brew the gose according to Richter's recipe but reduce the ingredients to make 4 or 4.25 gallons of 1.042, 10 to 15 IBU wort. Add the soured portion of the wort to the boil to kill the *Lactobacillus* and continue as with a regular batch, chilling to 65°F (18°C) and pitching with either a weizen or a neutral German ale yeast.

· CHAPTER 11 ·

BERLINER WEISSES

 decade ago you would have been hard pressed to find more than a handful of commercial Berliner weisses in the United States. (Note: Although most Americans pronounce it "vice," in German it's "vice-uh.") One of the venerable old styles from the wild and wacky ale country of northern Germany, it was basically extinct, even in its hometown, a decade into the twenty-first century. The style dates back to at least the 1600s and was an emblem of the city for centuries (Napoleon's troops called it the "Champagne of the North"). It is an odd beer, though, rarely stronger than 4 percent but powerfully flavorful, with a bright tartness the intensity of lemon juice. That was not the flavor twentieth-century palates wanted — even as distantly ago as 1938, it had only 3 percent of the market in Berlin — so brewers began taking shortcuts in the brewing process and adding sweet syrups to lure customers. This did not revive the style, which continued its steep descent toward a historical footnote.

Fortunately, this odd beer *does* have a palate that folks in the twenty-first century admire — at least some of us. Americans took it up tentatively, but successes such as Dogfish Head's Festina Peche encouraged more experimentation. Made properly, it has depths unusual for beers three times its strength. There's an initial blast of eye-opening lactic tartness, but soon after the mouth adjusts to the shock, drinkers will discover a whole buffet of flavors underneath the acidity. It is light and has a refreshing wheatiness and, like lemonade, is a perfect quencher on a hot summer afternoon. Fortunately, Berliner weisse is now a fairly regular guest on brewery lineups, and even in Berlin there are signs of a revival. The twin trends of intense flavors and sessionable strengths have given Berlin's famous old ale new life.

EST ## Zoiglhaus Brewing 2015
PORTLAND, OREGON

A decade and a half ago, Alan Taylor was studying in Germany. While he had done some homebrewing in college, he wasn't studying beer but Middle High German, an abstruse academic field in which he hoped to receive his PhD. But as time went on, his passion for linguistic studies waned. Fortunately for the beer world, he took the opportunity to enroll at the VLB brewing school in Berlin. That course correction put him on a path that would eventually lead him to become one of the most knowledgeable brewers of Berliner weisse in the world.

There are two famous brewing schools in Bavaria, but VLB's location puts it in German ale country, giving Taylor a chance to look closely at the city's house style. He interned at breweries while in school, and after earning his degree he brewed broadly in the United States and Germany. "I interned in Berlin," he begins, detailing his long ramble, "studied in Berlin, worked in Bavaria, then was at Full Sail, Spanish Peaks, Gordon Biersch [in the United States], then returned to Berlin and ran Brauhaus in Spandau." When he finally returned to Oregon (where it all started), he worked for Widmer Brothers until deciding to open his own brewery.

Even then events didn't unfold in a linear fashion. He had a name and a logo, but he couldn't find a building to house Zoiglhaus. Eventually, he agreed to work for a tiny brewpub in downtown Portland called PINTS, which until that time had focused on English-style ales. Taylor quickly switched focus, adding a series of wonderful German-style beers, including a celebrated schwarzbier, a helles, and a kölsch. His pièce de résistance, though, is a Berliner weisse released in summertime that has layers and layers of complexity.

While waiting for Zoiglhaus to become a reality, he became a part owner with Chad Rennaker of PINTS, and together they opened another brewery in Albuquerque. In September 2015 Zoiglhaus finally became a reality in Portland's outer east side.

Understanding Berliner Weisses

One tart sip of Berliner weisse suggests a very old lineage, and indeed that is the case. The style dates back to at least the 1600s and may go even further back. For centuries it was an exalted local product celebrated far from home. In 1879, Englishman Henry Vizetelly wrote, "The beer is drunk in preference when it is of a certain age, and in perfection it should be largely impregnated with carbonic acid gas and have a peculiar sharp, dry, and by no means disagreeable flavor." That description could act as a blueprint for the style even 13-plus decades later.

The predominant flavor is a lactic zing, and the beers are so dry they finish out around $1° \text{P}/1.004$. Roiling effervescence isn't a target everyone hits, but the "Champagne" reference illustrates how long it has been a feature of the beer. Vizetelly may have been especially prescient when he described its "peculiar sharp" quality, for although the tartness comes chiefly from a lactic fermentation, wild yeasts are an important part of the flavor profile. They help develop critical esters that round out the profile of this little titan of flavor. (And little they should be. Although some modern Berliners are 5%, it has long been considered a *schankbier*, a German strength designation that tops out at about 8° P.)

Finally, there's the matter of the acid. How tart should a Berliner weisse be? Some American examples are just a bit puckery. I think there is no right answer here, at least by historical standards. Brewing methods varied over the decades, and one could mount a defense for just about any level of acid. But if we're looking at the pre-debased twentieth-century examples, I think the answer is pretty damn tart. Many of those had a pH of around 3 — roughly the level of orange juice. Because there is very little sugar in a Berliner weisse (unlike orange juice), that tracks as pretty tart to the mouth. (Water, as a reminder, has a pH of 7.) After all, this is why Berliners started adding sugar syrups in the first place — it was a really tart style.

GREEN OR RED?

If you order a Berliner weisse in a pub, particularly in Berlin, you might be asked if you'd like it green or red. These are the colors of the syrups typically used to temper the tartness of a classic Berliner weisse — red for raspberry, green for *waldmeister* or woodruff, which tastes a bit like marshmallow. You can buy these syrups online if you're properly motivated — but *should* you?

I personally love the unadulterated flavor of a Berliner weisse and would never think of using them. But no less a traditionalist than Alan Taylor does — and if you buy a glass at one of his breweries, you'll be offered the choice. He believes it is an authentic expression of the style and doesn't seem offended that the syrups cover up the subtler elements of his brewing craft. So choose your color without shame (but include naked yellow among your options).

Brewing a Berliner Weisse

Like so many styles, Berliner weisse evolved. Depending on the era, it might have been made without hops and sans boil. In some cases, brewers hopped the mash before moving straight to fermentation. In other cases, it was boiled just briefly, for five minutes. Some brewers used smoked wheat malt (making something similar to a Lichtenhainer), and some used no wheat at all. ("Weisse," which we think of as shorthand for "wheat," actually means "white." Long ago most wheat malt was air-dried, so the beer it produced was milky pale, and an association developed. But it wasn't always ironclad, and records exist of all-barley Berliner weisses.)

In some eras the ales were sent to taverns to finish fermenting, while others were bottle-conditioned. It was pretty common for brewers to high-gravity brew Berliner weisses, watering them down after the brewing process. The indispensable Ron Pattinson has spent a lot of time studying old texts, and you can read more about Berliner weisse at his blog, *Shut Up about Barclay Perkins*, if you're interested in these myriad permutations.

So what is necessary, and what's just interesting? A baseline for these beers should include both the use of *Lactobacillus* and *Brettanomyces*. Although Berliner weisses are not known for their overtly *"Brett-y"* flavor — the lactic acidity is the dominant note — both of these organisms are necessary to create a "typical" profile. What's going on? A lot. Taylor showed me a study Berlin's VLB brewing school did of Berliner weisse and pointed out why *Brett* is so important. "One of the reasons to have *Brett* in there early is that it helps to amplify the amount of acids and esters produced," he explained. After it goes through a lactic fermentation, wild yeast can work with the acids and convert them into certain esters like ethyl acetate (pear or apple) and ethyl lactate (wine or coconut) during fermentation.

Taylor continued: "The ethyl acetate and ethyl lactate levels are significantly higher in the traditional product. Those esters are being created by the interplay of acid production from the bacteria and the *Brett* converting those to esters. As you see, *Brett* alone can't create the levels that the mixed culture examples have. *Lactobacillus* and *Brettanomyces* synergistically create a much more complex beer."

In beers where *Brettanomyces* is used in a mixed culture, rather than *Lactobacillus* alone, the beers will have 5 times the amount of ethyl acetate and 20 times the amount of ethyl lactate. They will also have the presence of some acetic acid, which is another marker of that "typical" flavor. The levels are not super high, but they are evident in the palate. "The acetic acid brings something along the lines of a Rodenbach note to the beer," Taylor says, "which I find appealing."

There's also the question of *Lactobacillus*. Like *Brettanomyces*, there are several cultures available, and they behave somewhat differently in beer. Some are tolerant of hop compounds, others intolerant (which may be why some breweries used hops and others didn't). Some prefer cooler temperatures typical of *Saccharomyces*, while others like blood temperatures. Most important, all create somewhat different compounds during fermentation, which will give beer different flavors. White Labs offers *L. brevis* and *L. delbrueckii*, and Wyeast adds *L. buchneri* to the mix — though other strains, like *L. lactis* and *L. acidophilus*, have been identified in beer. Oh, and a bit of trivia. Wyeast's strain of *Lactobacillus* (5335) came from a sample Taylor brought back to Oregon from Berlin.

MALT BILL

2.67 pounds German pilsner malt (50%)

2.67 pounds German or French wheat malt (50%)

SINGLE-INFUSION MASH

151°F (66°C) for 75 minutes

15-minute boil

No hops

FERMENTATION AND CONDITIONING

Cool the wort to 120°F (49°C), and, if possible, flush the fermentation vessel with CO_2. *Lactobacillus* prefers an anaerobic environment. Pitch the *Lactobacillus*, and keep it between 110 and 120°F (43 and 49°C) for a week. Then taste it daily until it reaches desired level of acidity. A typical pH should be 3.2 or 3.3.

It's best not to expose it to air when you're taking samples, so if you can rig up a system that pulls out wort without exposing it to air, that's ideal. An excellent solution is fermenting directly in a 5-gallon keg, purging with CO_2, and drawing wort off for tasting directly from the keg.

Once the lactic fermentation is complete, chill to 68°F (20°C), and pitch both an altbier strain (Wyeast 1007 or White Labs WLP036) and a strain of *Brettanomyces*. Taylor suggests *B. lambicus* or *B. bruxellensis* (Wyeast 5526 or 5112 or White Labs WLP653 or WLP644).

PACKAGE

Bottle once the gravity drops to 1.004. Bottle conditioning is fine, or add speise to finish (see instructions on page 115). Shoot for very high levels of carbonation — four volumes at a minimum. This requires thick-walled bottles to prevent explosion. Let condition at least a month, though 3 to 6 is preferable. If kegging, let stand 1 month and carbonate heavily before serving.

ALAN TAYLOR

—

ZOIGLHAUS

- Expected OG: 7.5° P/1.030

- Expected TG: 1° P/1.004

- Expected ABV: 3.4%

- Expected bitterness: 0 IBU

Notes: Taylor notes that Berlin's water is hard, and he adjusts his liquor by adding calcium sulfate, calcium chloride, and magnesium sulfate. Because Taylor uses Wyeast's hop-intolerant strain of *Lactobacillus*, he doesn't use hops in the boil at all. "You can add one pellet of hops to the mash if you want, but make it a German variety," he jokes (I think).

The short boil sterilizes the wort, but take note: you will boil off very little of the water, so don't start with 6 or 7 gallons as you normally do when shooting for 5 gallons. In finishing the beer, Taylor emphasizes the effervescence. "Carbonate the hell out of it — Berliner weisse is even higher than Bavarian weissbier."

NEXT STEPS

Most of the styles in this book are brewed according to fairly narrow orthodoxies. Berliner weisse is not one of those styles. In Berlin the last two breweries making weisses into the modern era used very different approaches. Looking further back, you see even more variation. What seems more important is the final product: a usually low-alcohol, tart beer with roiling effervescence. If there is an orthodoxy, it might include the use of wild yeast (which would have been unintentional for most of Berliner weisse's history) to build complexity.

It's reasonable to deviate widely from Taylor's formulation so long as you keep these elements as your North Star. Many commercial breweries in the United States now use kettle souring to make Berliner weisse (see chapter 10), which is a perfectly reasonable approach. Using a small amount of hops (less than 10 IBU in any case, and probably closer to 5–8) and boiling the wort is acceptable, as is skipping them altogether, along with the boil.

It was common for some breweries to use a single decoction, but infusion seems just as traditional. Finally, you can use everything from 60 percent wheat in the grist all the way to none — and again, find plenty of support for your decision in the historical record. In commercial American brewing, Berliner weisses are regularly dosed with fruit, and although the Germans didn't do that, it seems firmly in keeping with the spirit of the beer, particularly given the later use of sugar syrups. In short, experiment, and have fun and find what works for you.

Using Speise

Although more associated with the weissbier from Bavaria, the use of speise is appropriate for Berliner weisses, too — and Taylor suggested it for this recipe. In German *speise* means "food," and it refers to wort added after fermentation to bottle-condition beer. Brewers do this with the same type of wort used to ferment the beer to carbonate a beer without altering its basic structure. In weissbier breweries finding wort of the same gravity and grist is easy; homebrewers generally have to plan ahead.

Since you want to use the same wort for the speise that you used in your beer, the easiest approach is just to use the same wort for both. The amount of speise you add to condition your beer depends on the gravity of the wort, the volume of beer you're carbonating, and the level of carbonation you want to achieve. There are ways to calculate this, and Stan Hieronymus describes one formula in *Brewing with Wheat*.

A far easier approach is plugging in the variables on one of the online calculators; I recommend the one at Brewer's Friend. An interesting wrinkle in this process is that the lower the gravity of your beer, the more wort you'll need to use to create a certain amount of carbonation. In a standard weissbier, you would need 3.5 quarts of 1.052 wort to reach 4 volumes. In our 1.030 Berliner weisse, you need 6 quarts.

If you want to try using speise, calculate how many quarts you'll need to use, and then pull off that amount right before you chill your wort. Flush the container you plan to use with CO_2, and refrigerate. When you're ready to add the speise back into the beer, bring it to a boil for 10 minutes to sterilize, chill, and add to the beer. If you're working with a large volume of speise, you could pitch the altbier yeast at bottling to ensure speedy bottle conditioning.

Part 3

Czech
TRADITION

he beer world is alive with odd paradoxes, but none comes close to this one: for the better part of a century, the word "beer" was synonymous with "pilsner," and yet Americans still have almost no sense of the Czech Republic's brewing tradition. Pilsners may have come from the Czech lands, but the American lager tradition is German. It was planted here by the thousands of German brewers who started immigrating in the nineteenth century, founding breweries that still bear some of their names. Even today, it's common for German brewers to immigrate to the United States and ply their trade here — but when was the last time you encountered a Czech brewer?

The Czech tradition is related to the German, but not as closely as you might imagine. Lager brewing was a Bavarian practice, and when Bohemian brewers started switching over to lager making, they turned to Bavarian brewers. Indeed, when the citizens of Plzeň (Pilsen) became fed up with the poor quality of beer in their town, they decided to make proper Bavarian-style lager. They sent their architect off to Munich to learn how to design the brewery and then turned to the Bavarian Josef Groll to brew the beer. The first four brewers making the first pilsner were, in fact, Bavarians. But this was all back in the nineteenth century, and a lot of beer has passed under the bridge since then.

The twentieth century was a time of massive change in brewing. It's hard to imagine, but *Brettanomyces* wasn't even isolated until 1904, illustrating how much brewers would learn in the coming decades. But that century wasn't kind to the Czech Republic. Following the collapse of the Hapsburg Empire, an independent Czechoslovakia was born in 1918, but it was not long for the world. True independence lasted only about 20 years, until Hitler's armies seized the Czech lands during World War II. That occupation was followed by Soviet domination, which lasted until 1989. In other words, Czechoslovakia was under occupation for about 50 years — five decades during which the rest of the world's breweries modernized and evolved.

In Bohemia during the twentieth century, brewing did not evolve; to the contrary, traditions solidified. When modernity finally visited the Czech Republic after the collapse of the Soviet Union, it found a country where old methods of brewing had become codified and therefore preserved. The metaphor I often use to describe the Czech affection for tradition is the grant you invariably find at every brewery. You may have seen one of these pieces of equipment in pictures of old breweries; it resides underneath the lauter tun in a recessed pocket with an array of many swan-neck faucets. The attached valves were used to regulate the flow out of the lauter tun on the way to the kettle. Because wort aeration is a concern, breweries elsewhere have long since abandoned them, but you'll find them everywhere in the Czech Republic — even in newer breweries such as those at Pilsner Urquell and Budvar — because they are traditional. (In the big breweries computers control them or skip them altogether, but their symbolic value is still strong enough that they are installed in the first place.)

Czech brewers have had to spend many years defending their old ways to brewers in countries where shining modern breweries delivered consistency and precision. But Czech brewers may have had the last laugh as the revival of small-scale brewing has led to a rediscovery of more hands-on methods. Now when we review the quirks of Czech brewing, it looks almost forward thinking. You could make a convincing argument that Czechs were the original craft brewers.

Here are a few of the hallmarks that define Czech brewing:

FLOOR MALTS. One of the biggest differences between the practices of Czechs and their neighbors to the west concerns malting. Czech brewers favor malts that are more like English than German malts. In many places they continue to practice floor malting, which creates malts that are rich and aromatic. Maltsters — sometimes still connected to breweries — wet raw grain and spread it out in warehouse-size cellars to germinate. They kiln the malt on-site (where it's known as "pale" malt, not pilsner malt) to a brewery's specifications. The tradition of malting was considered so important that the *sladmistr*, or malt master, was afforded more respect at a brewery than the brewmaster, which stands to reason when you recall what made that luscious beer from Pilsen so unusual back in 1842.

CZECH HOPS. This is one element of Czech brewing — the only one, really — that people are aware of, all thanks to the famous tangy Saaz hop (Žatec in Czech). And it is incredibly important to the tradition and the beer. The Saaz cultivar dates back to the Middle Ages, and its genome is splattered all over the world (Tettnang, Spalt, Sterling, Lublin, Sorachi Ace, and Motueka, to name a few). It is not just the most-used hop in Czech beers, it's also central to their flavor. Breweries infuse their beer with its unmistakable zesty flavor, adding more bitterness and flavor than you find in most lager beers. Eighty percent of the Czech crop is Saaz, and new varieties such as Premiant, Sladek, and Bohemie are close kin. Breweries do a lot to distinguish their lagers from others on the market, but using exotic hops is not among them.

DECOCTION. Decoction is the practice of removing a portion of the mash, boiling it, and returning it to the main mash to raise the temperature. It's an old method developed as a reliable way of converting the mash in an age before thermometers and advanced malting and farming techniques. Most of the world has abandoned the practice (including in the larger breweries in Germany), but it is universal in the Czech Republic. In fact, decoction brewing is so central to the Czech brewing tradition that the Ministry of Agriculture allows only beer made that way to be called *České pivo* (Czech beer). Czech brewers are adamant that decoction adds both the color and fullness that give their pale lagers their inimitable character.

FIRST-WORT HOPPING. This may not be ubiquitous, but it's common (both Budvar and Pilsner Urquell utilize it, for example). Czech breweries add their bitter hop charge when the wort is entering the kettle. It is said to produce a softer, milder bitterness — counterintuitive because the hops are exposed to heat longer in this method. The practice is so rare outside the Czech Republic that an American brewer once scoffingly told me that it was a technique only a homebrewer would use (as if that's a bad thing!).

A Word on Nomenclature

The Czech Republic has its own vocabulary for beer, one mostly unknown to Americans. We know "pilsner," and that's where the knowledge ends. (And even there, we don't have it right. In the Czech Republic, pilsner is not a style, it's a beer — Pilsner Urquell. If you order a pilsner in a pub, that's what they'll serve you — or they'll shoot you a weird look if you're in a Budvar pub. This is out of deference to the beer of the founding brewery. All other pale lagers, what we would call pilsners, are *světlé pivo* to Czechs.)

The Czech system for grouping beer runs along two axes: strength and color. If you imagine a chart in your mind, on the one side you would have beers of different strength categories based on the Plato scale and on the other a continuum of color running from pale to black. So you might have a 10° pale beer or a 12° amber or a 14° dark. But you might also have a 10° dark or a 15° pale. Here's a quick rundown of the terminology. If you want to impress your homebrew partner, suggest brewing a *světlý ležák* instead of a "Bohemian pilsner."

Stolní pivo, table beer up to 6° P. (They're so rare I've never seen one of these in the wild.) The pronunciation is roughly *stole nyee PEE voh*.

Výčepní pivo, from 7° to 10°. Strangely, výčepní comes from the word for taproom, and the term literally means draft beer. It is applied to all beer in this range, irrespective of package. Pronounced *vee chep nyee PEE voh*.

OTHER OLD TECHNIQUES. You don't have to tour scores of Czech breweries to uncover unusual practices. In one instance, I found a brewery doing a two-hour boil, adding hops at the start of boil and at two more 45-minute intervals and omitting a late addition — none of which I encountered elsewhere. Open fermentation is still fairly common, as is what I still think is maybe the weirdest practice of all: extralong lagering. I saw breweries lagering their regular pale lagers for three months and their special dark beers up to *nine* months. In some cases, breweries transfer the beer to lagering tanks before it is fully fermented, allowing it to finish at very cold temperatures over many weeks.

All of these practices were handed down from brewer to brewer and date back decades. I have no doubt that there are still other odd habits to be found in the mysterious Czech Republic, and I hope I have a chance to return many times to find them.

Ležák, from 11° to 12°. Again, to add to the confusion, ležák literally means lager — and again, it applies to all beer in this range whether lager or ale. Pronounced *leh zhak*.

Speciál, strong beers above 13°. Pronounced *spet zee-al*.

The colors are more straightforward — pale, amber, and dark, though for etymological reasons, I'm going to list them out of order; the reasons will soon be evident:

Světlé, or pale-colored. Pronounced *svet leh*.

Tmavé, or dark. Pronounced *t'ma veh*.

Polotmavé, which literally means semidark or half-dark, referring to a color in the amber band. Pronounced *polo t'ma veh*.

Černé, or black. Pronounced *cher neh*.

When you're ordering these, you can mix and match. That 12° amber would be a *polotmavý ležák*. A 10° pale would be *světlé výčepní*, and so on.

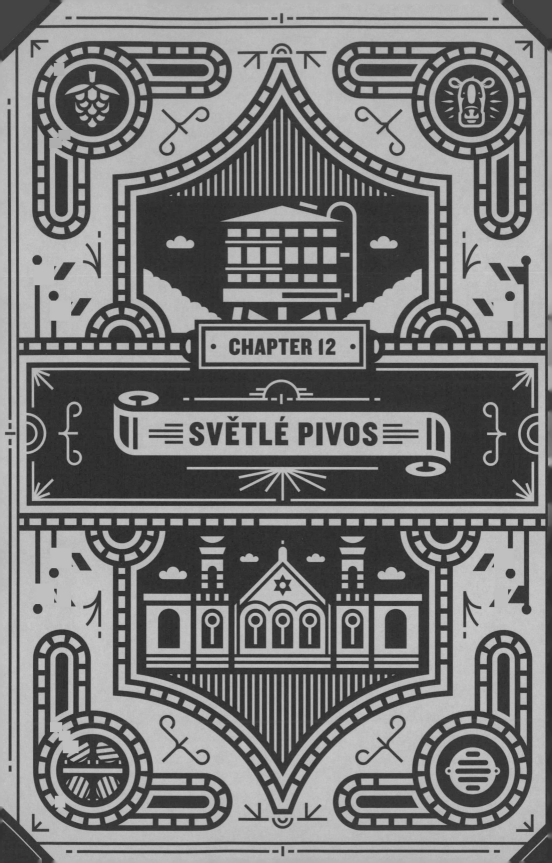

CHAPTER 12

SVĚTLÉ PIVOS

lmost all serious beer fans know that pilsners came from Plzeň (Pilsen) in Bohemia. It is the world's most famous style and is imitated in greater or lesser ways in every country that makes beer. What they are less familiar with are the světlý ležáks and světlé výčepnís — pale lagers — as they are made and consumed in their homeland. From a great distance all Czech pilsners look alike. If pressed, drinkers might admit that hoppy Pilsner Urquell, with its very round body and dollop of diacetyl, isn't actually that much like the drier Budvar, with its subtle kiss of bitterness. But eh, really, they're yellow and fizzy and mostly all the same, right?

If you spend time in more than a couple of Czech pubs, however, it quickly dawns on you that this is completely wrong. Let me offer an analogy by way of thought experiment. Put your mind on hoppy American IPAs, which from a great distance also appear a lot alike. Now imagine the perspective of a foreign beer drinker — a Czech, say — who believes he understands the style well enough because he has ready access to Dogfish Head 60 Minute IPA and New Belgium Ranger. Would you say he has an adequate understanding of American IPAs based on his sample of two beers? This is why knowing Pilsner Urquell and Budweiser Budvar does not give you a complete sense of světlý ležák.

The truth is that within the confines of just a few ingredients, breweries have managed to create beers with a range nearly as broad as American IPAs. I have had the good fortune of visiting a number of both pubs and breweries in the Czech Republic and have come to marvel at the differences in some of my favorite pivos: Únětické 12°, with its rustic haze and electric hops; creamy Pilsner Urquell, the unfiltered version of which is a revelation; thick, very stiff Kout na Šumavě, a beer some say is the best in the world; Na Rychtě Mazel, which slyly hides its luxurious honeylike malts behind a wall of Saaz; and the mysteriously deep golden U Tří růží Světlý Ležák, which seems to have a touch of stone fruit on the palate.

Because the ingredients, beer to beer, are so similar, these differences come largely from technique. Whether breweries are using double or triple decoctions, long boils, open fermentation, extralong maturations (or shortened ones), filtering or not filtering — all these choices shape the flavors each brewery wants. If you don't have the opportunity to visit Prague and taste these beers yourself, you can at least experiment with brewing methods and see how many variations you can make at home.

EST Pilsner Urquell 1838
PILSEN, CZECH REPUBLIC

When you sift through the history of beer and brewing, it becomes clear that single-origin histories usually turn out to be myth. Finding the one guy who did X is like finding the pot of gold at the end of the rainbow. Beer styles almost always evolve incrementally, with many fathers of invention. One very notable exception is the origin of pilsner, which we can trace back to Josef Groll (Brewer X?), a brilliant, dyspeptic Bavarian who briefly took a job in Bohemia and brewed the world's most important batch of beer there.

We start the story in 1838, when the beer situation in the small town of Pilsen had gotten so bad that the town fathers rounded up 36 barrels of inferior ale and dumped it in the town square. To rectify the woeful state of affairs, they decided to build their own brewery, and they wanted it to be the good stuff, the "Bavarian" beer (lager) that was starting to become popular in Bohemia at the time. The town fathers hired an architect, built a malt house and brewery, and set off to Bavaria to find the man to brew it. They brought back Groll, who etched his name in the history books by brewing a startlingly pale, coruscating lager on October 5, 1842. Thus was born pilsner beer. (Groll, described by his own father as "the rudest man in Bavaria," lasted only three years before he was sent packing — but by then he'd changed the world.)

That brewery came to be called Plzeňský Prazdroj — Pilsner Urquell — the fountainhead of pilsner — and as noted the only "pilsner" you'll find in Bohemia. When I visited one of the brewery's chief rivals, Budvar, the master brewer, Adam Brož, said, "It's really difficult to compete with Pilsner because it [defines] the style. It became the style of the pilsner type." His beer, he said, was not a pilsner. In old Bohemia Prazdroj's beer became immediately popular and began to influence other breweries.

Within decades the style was hopping international borders and inspiring imitators as far away as St. Louis and Milwaukee. Pilsner's most famous brewery led the international charge, shipping their beer across Europe and across oceans. As Urquell's current master brewer, Vaclav Berka, says, "Before the outbreak of World War I, the Burghers' Brewery had distributors in 34 countries worldwide."

Today visiting the brewery is a bit like making a pilgrimage. Pilsen is still a small town, and from the town square you can see the water tower across the Radbuza River from downtown — it's as dominant a feature on the skyline as the spire of St. Bartholomew. The campus sprawls over 89 acres, with beautiful nineteenth-century buildings gathered around a central cobblestone boulevard. Equally as impressive are the 9 kilometers of cellars beneath the brewery, carved out in a preelectricity age to house slowly maturing pilsner. The pièce de résistance of any tour is a cup of fresh beer straight from a wooden tank — consecrated water from the cathedral of beer.

BREWMASTER VACLAV BERKA

Pilsner runs through Vaclav Berka's blood — or bloodline. His father oversaw the fermentation department, and as a boy Berka would wander those long cellars where beer sat ripening. He stayed in the family business, studying fermentation in college. He interned at the brewery in the summer and brewed his first batch of pilsner at the tender age of 16. In 1980 Urquell gave him a job, and he briskly climbed up the ladder, becoming the chief of maturation within just two years.

More important, Berka was there after the 1988 Velvet Revolution that would ultimately bring privatization to Urquell. He was involved in the process of modernizing the brewery and converting his beloved old wooden vats to stainless and over the course of years worked to perfect a system that produced beer with the character of the original. He has worked in different capacities as brewmaster and currently holds the title senior trade brewmaster.

Understanding Světlé Pivos

Every beer-drinking country has a particular relationship to the beer it brews. In the Czech Republic, unlike many places, beer is treated as both a less exalted beverage and one more necessary; it's elemental, like water. You don't find Czechs rhapsodizing about their světlý ležáks the way American beer geeks do. Those displays are for luxuries. For Czechs pivo is a staple, mundane as the air they breathe but just as central to life. (It hardly bears repeating the well-worn statistic that the Czechs, at 143 liters of beer per person per year, far outdrink their closest rivals, the Germans, who put back a mere 110.) The vast majority of the beer Czechs drink is světlé pivos — pale lagers between 10° and 12° P (1.040 and 1.048).

In the United States we describe a style known as "pilsner" that is divided into two categories — German and Czech. According to this view, the difference is basically hops — there are more of them in the Czech pilsner, and they consist of that gloriously intense hop type, Saaz. German pilsners are less bitter and employ more sedate, lightly herbal German-grown hop varieties. Other than that, they're basically the same beer.

This view is flatly wrong. There are several distinctions, but the big difference lies in the base malt and the way that malt is used in the mash. All světlé pivos are made with decoction mashing, while fewer and fewer German breweries hang on to this old practice. The decoction process was originally used to make sure undermodified malt was fully converted during mashing. But it has an effect on the flavor and feel of a beer, too; the process of pulling out a portion of the mash and boiling it creates melanoidins, compounds that occur during Maillard reactions that both flavor the beer with bready or toffee notes and give it a rounder, richer maltiness.

At Budvar brewers ran an experiment in which they made their beer with a step mash and compared it to decoction mashing. Master brewer Adam Brož describes the results. "We compared decoction versus infusion in our small-scale brewery; always the beer brewed by the infusion process was emptier in its taste — the body was not correct for the lagers. Also the color changed. If you boil during the decoction, you prepare the compounds that cause golden color. So the infusion lagers were yellowish, not so full in their taste."

Because decoction is ubiquitous in the Czech Republic, many breweries use floor malts or malt their own barley, and they shoot for a quality that is rich and aromatic. This has been the case at Pilsner Urquell since it was founded, and it is still critical, since the brewery goes through a full triple-decoction mash. "While most brewers purchase malt from external suppliers," Vaclav Berka says, "the Plzeň brewery makes its own malt to be sure the product meets all criteria." The result is pale lagers with far more malt character than those across the German border. They are hoppier, for sure, but the malts are also more obvious — the equal of that stiff dose of Saaz in světlé pivos. Even among the German breweries that still use decoction mashing, the profile is a lighter, less malty beer. A helles is far closer to a German pils than the latter is to a Czech pils.

> **The Czechs, at 143 liters of beer per person per year, far outdrink their closest rivals, the Germans, who put back a mere 110.**

Brewing a Světlé Pivo

Světlé pivos are deceptively simple beers: pilsner malt (which is called "pale malt" in the Czech Republic), Saaz hops, and soft water. This is the most basic formulation, and the one most often used. The Czech Republic is starting to develop a craft brewing scene, and many local breweries are experimenting broadly — but not with their světlé pivos. A brewery may use a tiny bit of specialty malt or bitter the beer with Sládek or Premiant, but they would not deviate very far from the expected palate for this style of beer.

But that doesn't mean a brewery doesn't have room to put a stamp of originality on their světlé. Mashing regimes vary (double decoction is most common, but Urquell and others still do triple), with rest lengths and decoction practices differing brewery to brewery. Barley types and malt sources vary and, as in England and Germany, create different flavors. Boil lengths are typically 90 minutes but are sometimes as long as two hours. Some breweries use relatively few hops, while others load in bales. Conditioning times run the gamut from three weeks to three months.

In some ways the Czech světlé pivo is a more homebrew-friendly beer than a Bavarian lager. German brewing is now so refined and precise that replicating it on the home system is a challenge. Czech lagers are a bit more variable, and rusticity isn't necessarily a bad thing. A popular presentation in pubs is *nefiltrované pivo*, or unfiltered beer, and *kvasnicové pivo*, which literally means yeast beer and is also cloudy — something like German kellerbier.

In some regions of the United States, a haziness is considered a mark of artisanal authenticity, and that expectation is starting to happen in the Czech Republic, too. When Únětický Pivovar, a Prague-area brewpub, first released their two světlé pivos, they had shortened the lagering period to get them out on the market. They were hazy and not fully smooth — and people loved them. When they did start lagering for a month and introduced a bright version of their beer, people demanded the more rustic version. Or take Urquell, which in the Czech Republic is considered unusual. It is a světlý ležák — a pale lager of 12° — but at 4.4% ABV it has a fair amount of residual sweetness. It also contains a detectable level of diacetyl, which adds to the fullness of the beer. Half-liters arrive with mousselike heads and go down like special, rich treats.

All of this makes světlé pivos great beers for homebrewers to tackle. You're working with more flavors to begin with, so a little extra character or haziness from the brew system may well give it a delicious je ne sais quoi.

SVĚTLÉ PIVO

ADAPTED BY
THE AUTHOR

Note: This is a typical recipe for a světlý ležák, but not the one Urquell uses. Theirs uses triple decoction and a few other proprietary procedures and ingredients. This recipe is a composite of the information I learned after touring Pilsner Urquell, Budweiser Budvar, Kout na Šumavě, Únětický Pivovar, and others.

MALT BILL
---

9 pounds Czech pilsner malt (100%)

DECOCTION MASH

See Decoction Mashing at Home, page 130

90-MINUTE BOIL

2.25 ounces Saaz while bringing wort to boil (3.5% AA, contribution of 30 IBU)

1 ounce Saaz, 15 minutes (3.5% AA, contribution of 10 IBU)

FERMENTATION AND CONDITIONING

Ferment with Wyeast 2001/White Labs WLP800 at 48°F (9°C) for 12 days. Lager for 4 weeks at as near freezing as your equipment allows.

PACKAGE

Keg is much preferred over bottle conditioning to preserve clarity. If bottle conditioning, let beer warm to 50°F (10°C) to carbonate for at least 2 weeks and then crash to near freezing to clarify beer.

- Expected OG: 12° P/1.048
- Expected TG: 2.5° P/1.010
- Expected ABV: 5.0%
- Expected bitterness: 35–40 IBU

Notes: Berka emphasizes that this recipe is not the one Urquell uses ("The detailed recipe remains secret and is closely guarded," he told me, "passing from one brewmaster to the next."), but it is typical for Czech brewing. For the full description of decoction, see Decoction Mashing, page 132. Note that decoction processes vary widely, even within the constraints of a two-decoction mash. When you mash in, how long you boil, how thick the mash is — all these things will affect the wort.

Hopping rates and schedules vary dramatically, from the low 20s to over 40 IBUs. First-wort hopping (adding hops to the kettle during lauter and while the wort heats to a boil) is very common. Světlé pivo is not noted for rich aromatic hop additions, but modest late additions are fine. It's traditional to conduct primary fermentation for one day for every point of gravity on the Plato scale, but you can transfer to maturation whenever the beer reaches terminal gravity.

Yeast variety is not critical, though Berka notes, "Pilsner Urquell is fermented with the 'Pilsner H' yeast strain, which has a pedigree dating back to the yeast that Josef Groll used." A version of that strain is available from the commercial yeast banks. You might need to conduct a diacetyl rest. Diacetyl is a slick, heavy compound that gives beer the flavor of butter or butterscotch; it's actually a key ingredient in the artificial butter used on popcorn. Yeast will reabsorb the diacetyl naturally. Raise the temperature of the beer to 57°F (14°C) and hold for two days at the end of primary fermentation and you shouldn't have any trouble with diacetyl.

NEXT STEPS

We've talked about the fullness of body and flavor that distinguishes a světlé pivo from other beer. There's even a term in Czech to describe this quality. It's called říz and translates roughly as "cut." Evan Rail, an American who has been the most important English-language writer on the subject of Czech beer, describes it as the way a good beer strikes you; it can mean "character" or the sharp or full flavor of beer. When you make a světlé pivo at home, shoot for říz.

In the Czech Republic, breweries attain the quality of říz through different means. For a real outlier take the example of Kout na Šumavě, a remote brewery in a town that shares its name with a town two hours southwest of Prague, near the German border. The eighteenth-century building it occupies once housed a much larger brewery, but it had been long abandoned by the time Jan Skala decided to reoccupy it and open Kout na Šumavě in 2006. He brought in Bohuslav Hlavsa, an experienced brewer, to make the beer.

Everything Kout does seems odd. They conduct a two-hour boil and add hops in three additions — at the start of boil, again after 45 minutes, and finally after

90 minutes. That accounts for the strangely stiff-seeming bitterness, which is sharp and muscular, but only registers at just above 30 IBUs.

The fact that Hlavsa consulted two-hundred-year-old recipes discovered at the old brewery site may account for the long boil as well as the open fermentation and long maturation (three months for the 12° beer). But the very strange thing is that he also uses a dab of caramel malt in the grist. This is of course a shortcut Americans might take to approximate the flavors and roundness of decoction, but I'd never encountered it in a Czech brewery. (Hlavsa also uses triple decoction on his 12° beer.) It turns out that other breweries use color malts as well — though typically Munich rather than caramel. So while decoction is a given, it seems everything else is up for grabs.

In making Czech-style světlés myself, I have used more late-addition hops than is typical but found that most of the effort on late-addition hopping is lost on the beer during lagering. Still, there seems to be no strict rule on when or how many hops may be added — just that they should be in the Saaz family. Hopping is one of the main ways breweries distinguish themselves, and I could envision a future when breweries seek more saturated flavors and aromas from late-addition and dry hopping. I'd consider most hopping experiments largely acceptable as traditional variations.

DECOCTION MASHING AT HOME

Start with Bohemian pilsner malt, which was malted with decoction in mind. You're going to start with a somewhat wet mash of 2 quarts of water per pound of malt. Mash in at 122°F (50°C), and hold it for 10 minutes.

Next, pull a thick decoction of about a third of the mash. "Thick" here means a third of the barley, leaving behind most of the liquid wort. Enzymes are converting the starch in the liquid part of the mash, so you want to leave as much behind as possible for later steps. Stir the mash, and then remove with a colander. This will allow some of the liquid to run off. You can eyeball the third, too — this system allows for ranges rather than precise measurements. Move this decoction to a kettle (a smaller one if you have it), and begin heating. This decoction mash should resemble a slightly watery porridge.

You're going to raise the temperature slowly, making sure to keep stirring so that none of the grain gets stuck to the bottom of the kettle and scorches — you don't want scorched flavors in your světlé. Bring the temperature up very slowly, about 2°F (1°C) per minute if you can manage it. You're going to raise it all the way to 156°F (69°C), but the slow rise means conversion will be happening along the way.

Hold it for 10 minutes, then raise it to a boil, and keep boiling for another 15 minutes. If you're having trouble with sticking grain, it's okay to add a bit of water to make sure it's thin enough. Be careful while boiling, because the bubbling mash burps like the mudpots in Yellowstone, and you don't want to get splashed.

Return the decoction to the main mash. Ladle it over in portions, and watch the temperature of the main mash. You want to hit something in the 144 to 149°F (62–65°C) range for conversion, and since you'll be building body by boiling during decoction, a lower number in that range is better. If you hit your main mash temperature before you've returned the rest of the decoction, stop and let it cool, returning the remainder when the main mash cools down to 150°F (66°C) or lower.

After you've done the main starch conversion, it's time for the second decoction. Again, pull another thick third of the mash, and heat it in your small kettle. This time there's no need to stop at a saccharification rest since you've already done it in the main mash, and you can slowly bring it to a boil. Even though you're not looking for conversion during the heat rise, you want to go slowly to prevent scorching.

Return the decoction to the main mash, bringing it to 162°F (72°C). At this point you're ready to complete the mash as you would normally. After you boil, ferment, and lager — just another six weeks away! — you can sit down to a pint of your decocted světlý ležák and see for yourself if that extra effort was worth it.

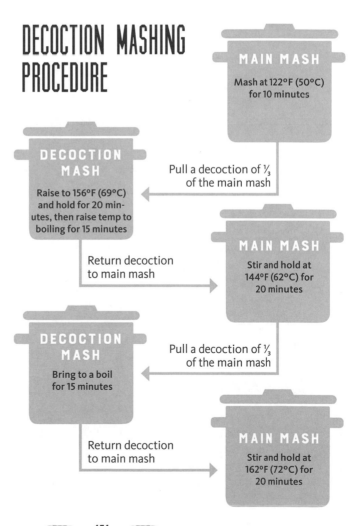

DECOCTION MASHING PROCEDURE

MAIN MASH
Mash at 122°F (50°C) for 10 minutes

Pull a decoction of ⅓ of the main mash

DECOCTION MASH
Raise to 156°F (69°C) and hold for 20 minutes, then raise temp to boiling for 15 minutes

Return decoction to main mash

MAIN MASH
Stir and hold at 144°F (62°C) for 20 minutes

Pull a decoction of ⅓ of the main mash

DECOCTION MASH
Bring to a boil for 15 minutes

Return decoction to main mash

MAIN MASH
Stir and hold at 162°F (72°C) for 20 minutes

Decoction Mashing

Decoction mashing was invented to solve some old barriers to a reliably fermentable wort. Using direct-fire heat and lacking thermometers, it was very difficult for breweries to proceed through precise steps during mashing. It was a clever system: so long as you could begin mashing at a reasonably consistent temperature, the process took care of itself. In a decoction mash you remove a portion of the main mash — malt and wort — and begin heating it.

In the old days they would have heated the decoction mash very slowly, knowing that as it went up in temperature, conversion of the grain would happen naturally. They ultimately heated it all the way to boiling, which helped create body-building melanoidins in the wort, and then returned the decoction to the main mash. Because it was boiling, the decoction raised the temperature of the whole mash to the next step. The process proceeded like this through two or three decoctions.

The earliest forms of this process utilized triple decoctions. That allowed breweries to do an acid rest (around 100°F [38°C]), a protein rest (122°F [50°C]), a saccharification rest (somewhere around 145°F [63°C]), and a final stage at mash out (167°F [75°C]). The reason had to do with primitive malting methods. Bayern Brewing's Jürgen Knöller describes the history. "In Germany it could be rainy and cold for like 10 years. Then you have barley with protein levels that are atrocious, with glucan levels you can barely live with. So that's why the Germans invented those complicated mashing methods, because [that way] you can achieve consistency of beer by technology."

A few breweries — notably Urquell — still use the technique, but they begin with specially malted barley. Most Czech breweries now do a double decoction, skipping the acid rest and mashing in around 122°F (50°C). With more modified modern malts, it makes sense to do a double decoction; a triple risks breaking down proteins too much and leaving the beer watery.

CHAPTER 13

TMAVÉS/ČERNÉS

Everyone knows pilsners (světlé pivos), of course, and I will confess that when I'm in the Czech Republic, they get most of my attention. But they are far from the only beers available, and depending on your proclivity, you might find the dark lagers — *tmavé* (dark) and *černé* (black) — more alluring. They have myriad charms. Some are as bitter and roasty as a cup of coffee (or an Irish stout, which some resemble), while others are as frothy, rounded, and sweet as a mug of hot chocolate.

In much the way that Czech light lagers can be quite varied in strength, profile, and even brewing technique, so too can the dark ones. When you see comparisons to German dunkel or schwarzbier, pay no attention. German styles have quite narrow prescriptions, and while you might find the odd tmavé that bears a resemblance to a dunkel (though I rarely have), you'll find five that don't. The American-born writer Evan Rail, who now lives in Prague, once pointed out that "if a brewery brews two pale beers and two dark beers, the dark ones will usually be stronger." It's about the only general guideline to dark lagers I found to be true. Everything else is up for interpretation.

EST Pivovar U Fleků 1499
PRAGUE

It is almost a necessary rite when you visit Prague: stopping in at Pivovar U Fleků for a mug of dark lager and a plate of something meaty with a side of dumplings. It's such an emblem of the city — along with the river, the castle, and, of course, defenestrations — that it's mainly a tourist stop now. Locals, who have lately enjoyed the renaissance of local brewing, mostly steer clear. This is unfortunate because the brewery is one of the world's great brewing treasures, and the beer made there one of the finest in a country lousy with excellent lagers.

U Fleků's sole beer is a rounded 13° *tmavý ležák* that weighs in at a surprisingly low 5% ABV. It is the only beer they make, and many Czech beer fans would argue that it sets the standard for the tmavé style. (I agree, though like Pilsner Urquell, which also sets the standard for světlý ležáks, it is unlike most other examples.) The brewery was founded in 1499, an astounding half a millennium ago, and unlike so many other breweries with claims of eye-popping antiquity, it's an accurate indication of how long they've been brewing there. For three and a half centuries, U Fleků brewed ales; it was in 1843 the Pštross family, then owners of the brewery, made the momentous shift to lagers. It's not surprising that first beer was dark; it was made just a year after Josef Groll brewed his famous lager in Pilsen. The Czechs were learning lager brewing from the Bavarians who (Groll's experiment excepted) brewed dark lagers.

Interestingly, there is no single recipe. U Fleků's Martin Plesný explains. "Every master brewer has his own way to brew the beer, and there is no exact written recipe. The method is basically inherited generation by generation, and the outcome should be always the same: a 13° dark beer of a smooth taste and a bitterness which is agreeable, not excessive." U Fleků recently made a transition from the longtime master brewer, Ivan Chramosil, to his young replacement, Michael Adamik. We will soon see if the old-timers note a shift in the flavor.

BREWMASTER MICHAEL ADAMIK

In 1921 longtime maltster and brewer Václav Brtník purchased U Fleků, and it was in the family until 1949, when the Communist government seized it from its private family owners. It was given back to the family in 1992, a year after Michael Adamik, a descendant of Brtník's, was born. He started studying brewing in high school, trained at U Fleků during school, and went to work there after graduating in 2010. In addition to being a master brewer, he's a successful motocross racer. Yet despite winning the South Bohemian Motocross Cup in 2014, he agreed in January 2015 to take over the mash paddle and become the latest brewmaster in U Fleků's long history.

Understanding Tmavés

Let's start with the name. What is the difference between a tmavé (dark) and a černé (black)? I put that to Martin Plesný, who offered this very Czech take on the matter. "As we understand it here in U Fleků, 'black' is simply darker than 'dark.' We call our U Fleků lager 'tmavé' — it is very dark brown but not completely black. I think the crucial question is: Could it be any darker? If the answer is no, then it's black. When yes, then it's still just dark. But in fact, the two terms are mutually interchangeable." To emphasize his point, he appended photos of three beers, variously called černés or tmavés, all of which were the same color.

> Traditionally, the term 'black beer' (schwarzbier) refers only to the darkest German types of beer. No such completely black beer is brewed in the Czech Republic (although it might have changed over the past few years with hundreds of microbreweries newly established).
>
> — **MARTIN PLESNÝ, U FLEKŮ**

In terms of the palate, it seems that older tmavés are often quite sweet or at least brewed with very high finishing gravities. The effect of sweetness is mitigated by a few factors in dark lagers: 1) lager yeasts don't add esters, which enhance the perception of sweetness, 2) roast malt offsets sweetness, and 3) lagering leaves the beers seeming drier than they really are. This is all true with U Fleků, which is an unusual beer, even by Czech standards. It is a 13° lager, placing it in at the *speciál* (special) category of robust-gravity beers. Despite this, it is only around 5%. That means it has a finishing gravity of around 3.5° P/1.015 ("around" because the recipes aren't fixed).

If you've had that beer, this probably surprises you. It definitely has a luxurious mouthfeel — it's on the mug-of-hot-chocolate side of the spectrum — but it is balanced, hugely drinkable, and, although sweetish, nothing like cloying. It is so moreish because the flavors balance between cocoa and a roastiness suggestive of medium-roast coffee.

Other tmavés are different. Budvar's *tmavý ležák* instantly recalls Dublin. Master brewer Adam Brož developed the beer in 2004 as a contrast to other dark lagers on the market. "It is quite dry, no sweetness," he said as we sampled the beer together, "which was unique in the Czech Republic when we developed this beer. Other dark beers in the Czech Republic were heavy and sweet, and we wanted something for regular drinking." Kout na Šumavě, by contrast, makes two heavy dark lagers, a 14° and a booming 18°, and brewer Bohuslav Hlavsa offsets their voluptuousness with stiff hopping.

German dunkel lagers usually lack a roasty note and instead showcase Munich malt. German schwarzbiers are roasty but lean bodied. Czech dark lagers have elements of both but are another category altogether. They have the roast of a schwarzbier but only hint at Munich malt, and they are generally full bodied in a way no German beer — even doppelbock — ever is. In other words, don't look to Bavaria and Thuringia; these are Czech through and through.

Brewing a Tmavé

Although we corresponded for weeks and brewery officials facilitated contact with brewer Michael Adamik, in the end U Fleků got skittish and declined to provide their exact formulation and process. Fortunately, Martin Plesný sent me a fascinating document that described the mashing process at U Fleků. It was taken from a history of the brewery, not a brewing manual, so it lacked detail. Still, what is present is remarkable: it describes a mash that begins at 100°F (38°C), goes to a protein rest at 122°F (50°C), and then goes all the way past the amylase rest to mash out at 167°F (75°C). This is unlike anything I've ever seen, and I had to track down a couple of local brewers to see if they thought it would even produce a fermentable wort.

The first stage is what some brewers call "doughing in," when the malt and warm water are blended to moisten the grain, a process thought to produce greater yield. The protein rest is another fixture of brewing with Czech malts, useful in breaking proteins down into amino acids and smaller proteins. With modern malting this is already accomplished, and using a protein rest needlessly thins out the body of a beer, something U Fleků was definitely not trying to do.

What comes next is the most interesting — a rest all the way up at 167°F (75°C), well past the safe window for starch conversion of 142 to 162°F (61–72°C). Holding the wort at this temperature denatures the enzymes and freezes conversion — important in beers like tmavés with richer bodies. But what about starch conversion? Two enzymes are used to convert starches to sugars: alpha amylase, which works best between 149 and 162°F (65–72°C), and beta amylase, which likes cooler temperatures between 136 and 150°F (58–66°C). The U Fleků process appears to skip them both, but in this case appearances may be deceiving. In fact, what is probably going on is a slow rise from the protein rest to mash out at 167°F (75°C), giving the mash something on the order of half an hour within the conversion window. It wouldn't produce a hugely fermentable wort, but that's fine; U Fleků uses this oddball process to build in all those rich, rounded malt notes.

A final comment: Did you see what else isn't mentioned in this description? Decoction. While that process will be used overwhelmingly to make these beer styles, U Fleků appears to have come to decoction late. This description suggests how varied Czech brewing may once have been, and it's a fun throwback method to experiment with. To conduct a typical decoction mash, follow the procedure from the previous chapter (page 130), using the grain bill given here.

Note: This recipe was based on notes from U Fleků, before the brewery decided it didn't want to divulge proprietary information. I've filled in some of the gaps with information collected at Budweiser Budvar and Kout na Šumavě.

Malt Bill

7 pounds Czech pilsner malt (74%)

1 pound dark Munich malt (11%)

1 pound dark CaraMunich malt (11%)

0.5 pound Carafa III malt (5%)

Step Mash

Dough in at 100°F (38°C)

122°F (50°C) for 5 minutes

Raise the temperature slowly to 167°F (75°C) (about 1°F [0.5°C] per minute)

Hold at 167°F for 10 minutes

120-Minute Boil

1 ounce Saaz while bringing wort to boil (3.5% AA, contribution of 15 IBU)

1 ounce Saaz, 60 minutes (3.5% AA, contribution of 13 IBU)

Fermentation and Conditioning

Ferment at 50°F (10°C) for 9 to 13 days with Wyeast 2308 or White Labs WPL820. Do a diacetyl rest, raising the temperature of the beer to 57°F (14°C) at the end of primary fermentation and holding for 2 days, then drop the temperature to as close to 32°F (0°C) as your system allows. Lager for 30 to 40 days.

PACKAGE

Bottle or keg.

- Expected OG: 13° P/1.053
- Expected TG: 4° P/1.015
- Expected ABV: 5.0%
- Expected bitterness: 28 IBU

Notes: Use soft, low-mineral water as is typical for Czech styles. Weyermann continues to expand its Bohemian malt line, and if you can source their dark malt, use 6.5 pounds pilsner and 1.5 pounds dark Bohemian malt. Weyermann Carabohemian, even more rare, can replace CaraMunich. The more you can find and use Czech malts, particularly floor malts, the more the flavor will turn toward the typical Bohemian profile (read: not German). Weyermann sources these malts from inside the Czech Republic.

A longer boil will help create melanoidins that enhance mouthfeel. U Fleků's beer is unfiltered.

NEXT STEPS

The main goal with a tmavé should be roundness of body, and finding a way to get a 13 Plato beer to finish out at nearly 4 Plato is the real challenge. Modern malting in particular makes this a challenge, and you might find that the U Fleků mash regime produces much drier beers than you wish. Conducting a double decoction (see chapter 12) will help by building melanoidins. You might also consider tucking in 1 to 5 percent caramel malts to build body if your tmavés are finishing too dry.

One other technique Czechs sometimes employ is a very slow fermentation at low temperatures. When they make their 14° tmavé, Kout na Šumavě transfers the beer to conditioning tanks when they are only about 60 percent fermented. The final phase of fermentation happens at 36°F (2°C) and may take up to 3 months to finish. Budvar is another fan of what brewmaster Adam Brož calls "deep fermentation" over very long conditioning times.

Part 4

Belgian
TRADITION

—

Belgium is a curious country. Its northern half is peopled by Flemish speakers (Dutch, basically) and the south by French speakers. A fissure of attitude separates these halves — known locally as Flanders and Wallonia — as decisively as language, and things got so contentious that for nearly two years in 2010 and 2011, Belgium limped along with a caretaker government as each member of the couple fumed about the other. The rivalries date back to the nineteenth century, and there's little hope things will get better any time soon. For a country without much national identity and few cultural touchstones, it may be that the only thing that really unites the country is beer. But unite it beer does and has done since the time of the Romans.

We know this because Julius Caesar wrote about his encounters with the pastoral Belgae tribes, whom he admired, calling them the "bravest of the three peoples" of Gaul. (He admitted that bravery may not have been the sole province of wine-drinking people.) But even before Caesar they were known for their beer — decades earlier the Greek historian Diodorus Siculus wrote that they "make a drink out of barley which they call *zythos* or beer."

Over the centuries Belgians brewed a rich tapestry of beer styles. In Flanders to the northeast, they drank dark beers. The region around Brussels and extending east constituted a wheat beer belt. In the south they drank rustic saisons. One of the best portraits of this diversity comes from the mid-nineteenth century, when a brewer from Leuven decided to tour Europe and document the brewing practices he found. Georges Lacambre's (sometimes rendered La Cambre) *Traité Complet de la Fabrication des Bières* is an amazing survey of traditional brewing of the time. His 1851 work, which expanded on writing done earlier in the century by two men, J. B. Vrancken and Auguste Dubrunfaut, details a fascinating world of brewing — great variation on the one hand and inconceivably baroque brewing methods on the other. Most of the beers he wrote about don't exist any longer, but we can see in these distant ancestors the DNA that would lead to most of the styles currently brewed in Belgium.

Modern Belgian beers have a reputation for quirkiness, and reading through Lacambre, you can see it has always been thus. He described around 20 different beers (he actually found more but took time to document only the "major" ones), and only one was what we'd consider "normal." To begin with, those old brewers used lots of different grains. Only three used all-barley formulations; oats were used in more than half the beers, and wheat in even more. Some brewed with spelt. The mashing regimes were very exotic. The reason had to do with taxes — fees were levied based on the size of their mash tuns, not their production volume.

As a result, they all used tiny tuns, which they packed with as much grain as possible. ("Turbid mashing," the method still used to make lambics, is a legacy of these laws.)

Breweries typically did a series of mashes to get all the sugars from those overstuffed tuns. Some had auxiliary vessels for mashing (apparently those weren't taxed); and one, bière blanche de Louvain, required five vessels as well as baskets and pans to strain and spoon out wort, not to mention "eight to ten strong brewers" to manage the ordeal.

Boil lengths were shocking. The *average* boil was 9 hours. Only four of the beers Lacambre found used boils of 3 hours or less, while five ran over 12 hours, and the longest took *20* hours. Drinkers regarded deep color as a sign of wholesomeness, so in most cases the long boils were used to darken wort. Brewers sometimes cheated by adding the mineral lime (not, strangely enough, dark malt), a practice Lacambre not unreasonably said was "very detrimental to the interests and even the health of consumers."

Writing a century later, the famous brewing professor Jean de Clerck did another survey of Belgium's extant styles and found many of the same ones Lacambre described, including blanche de Louvain, Peeterman, Diest, uytzet (uitzet), Antwerp barley beer, Hoegaarden, and Liege saison. Many of these were, alas, in their final days. Lager was already eating away at the traditional styles, which suffered from poor quality. Rustic wasn't always a positive adjective; the bottled lagers were more consistent and stayed fresh longer than local brews. The lambic maker Frank Boon witnessed the transition as it was happening in the 1960s. "I remember my uncles said that in the summer they could keep their beer for two weeks. Midsize breweries had beer that could keep one month or six weeks. In the 1960s, Stella Artois was the first to make beer that could keep for six months."

Modern Belgian brewing is a direct part of this long lineage, and we see in it many of the echoes of the past (18-hour boils excepted). Rustic grains, spices, dark beers, sour and wild-fermented beers, beers of impressive strength. But twenty-first-century Belgian beer is also a product of modernity, so methods have changed considerably. Moreover, despite brewing the largest range of indigenous beers, Belgium also has developed features that are consistent, or at least common, across the country. To wit:

YEAST CHARACTER. The word "Belgian," as used to describe certain kinds of beers, refers to yeast. Belgians practice "high fermentation" (warm fermentation), and it is often *very* warm when compared to other countries. Mid-70s F (24°C) for pitching is not unusual, and terminal temps in the 80s or 90s (27–37°C) is not unheard of. The result is beer with tons of fruity esters and spicy phenols. The fact that American brewers rarely have the temerity to let their temps run as high as Belgians when making these styles is evident in the subdued flavors that result.

SECONDARY FERMENTATION/BOTTLE CONDITIONING. Nearly every ale brewery in Belgium has a "warm room." It's a temperature-controlled room where bottles ripen while bottle-conditioning. For Belgians the carbonation is only a secondary effect — the real goal is secondary fermentation in the bottle. That's when the yeast flavors mature and evolve. It's why you mostly don't find Belgium's famous ales on tap; to properly develop, those beers must go through this secondary fermentation.

SUGAR AND STRENGTH. It's common for Belgian beers to be strong; 7% and higher is completely typical. To keep the beers light on the palate and attenuative, breweries regularly use sugar, often in high proportion. (Occasionally they use adjunct grains, often deploying a cereal cooker, to achieve the same thing.) Belgium has not had a strong history of hoppy beers, and one of the reasons is that these thin beers do not receive bitterness well. As the influence of American brewing arrived in Belgium, it took the breweries there a decade to figure out how to use hops without making the beers unpleasantly bitter. Also note: Nearly all breweries just use dextrose, not whatever it is Americans think "candi" sugar is. Plain old corn sugar is the ticket.

SPICES. Only a minority of beers contains spices — but perhaps more than the average drinker realizes. The judicious use of spice accentuates yeast characteristics, and breweries use spice even when it is very difficult to recognize. (Rochefort, for example, uses a pinch of coriander in their beers, a flavor no one can identify.) Some beers use obvious spice, of course, but even when they do, the intent is to mimic flavors already extant in the beer, not to create a treacly stew.

There are many other characteristics common in Belgian brewing — the use of wheat, oats, and other grains; coruscating effervescence; sourness from wild fermentation — that are typical in the tradition, if not characteristic of it. But the wide variability among Belgium's beers belies the collection of shared features that make them consistent in many ways.

· CHAPTER 14 ·

BELGIAN ALES

or centuries, Belgium was a dark ale country. There was a separate tradition of wheat beers, colloquially known as "white beers," but barley beers were typically amber to brown. Pale lager was late in coming to Belgium, but local breweries, like those in Britain, Germany, and France, scrambled to make sparkling ales to hold on to their customers. Belgium being Belgium, the resulting beers weren't much like pale lager. They were stronger and much more strongly flavored. But they did have wonderful golden hues, bright effervescence, and light bodies. And they became popular fast.

(There is a fascinating irony to the emergence of golden ales. Once, deep amber and brown colors signaled to consumers that a beer was well made — the color was proof they had gone through a long boil. If breweries *weren't* making good beers, they at least artificially darkened them to try to fool customers. When lagers arrived, customer demands shifted, and breweries felt compelled to make ever more clarion, sparkling ales. Within a few decades, breweries felt they had to make certain kinds of golden ales to demonstrate they were of the quality of international lagers.)

So in the twentieth century Belgium began adding to its retinue of amber and brown beers. What emerged was a range of golden beers running from what are sometimes called "Belgian pale ales" (around 5.5%) to midrange ales that don't really have a name to the strong ones of 8 to 10% that are called variously tripels or strong golden ales. (More often, the brewery affixes no style at all to their beer.) Compared to the older, darker ales, they're not that different in the way they're brewed or even in their range of flavors. Indeed, today amber, brown, and pale ales are all made in a similar manner, the styles differing only in the malts used to color them. To understand how these beers are made, we'll turn to the most famous producer of blond ales — Moortgat, which makes the famous Duvel.

EST **Duvel Moortgat** 1871

PUURS, BELGIUM

Duvel is a great example of this style because, like Belgian ales themselves, the beer has gone through a transformation. Duvel dates to the early part of the twentieth century, back to a time when it was an amber ale. In 1970 Duvel Moortgat decided to update its flagship beer to suit modern tastes. They collaborated with the famous scientist Jean de Clerck, who had already consulted with Chimay, Rochefort, and Orval. The formulation they settled on is the modern incarnation of the beer — one of the most influential in Belgium's history.

Duvel's name comes from the Flemish word for devil, and although it goes back to the 1920s, it's especially fitting for this incarnation. With its towering effervescence, which piles a snowy head atop a roiling golden body, this is one of the most beautiful beers in the world. The high carbonation gives it a silky decadence, which leads to that famously rich palette of flavors — slightly honeyed malt to layered ester profile to surprisingly insistent spicy hopping. What you don't detect is the alcohol — the devil in the details — and more than a few people have been seduced by this sumptuous, beautiful beer to drink too much. Thus is the Devil's allure.

Buoyed by the success of Duvel, the brewery was able to begin buying smaller breweries, assembling an impressive portfolio that includes Liefmans, Maredsous, La Chouffe, De Koninck, Ommegang, and most recently, Boulevard and Firestone Walker. Duvel remains the engine that powers the empire, though, and is one of the principal standard-bearers for Belgian beer outside the country. If any beer can stand in for an entire country's approach to brewing, it's Duvel.

BREWMASTER HEDWIG NEVEN

One of the most reproduced beer photographs in the world is an exterior shot of the Duvel brewery, on which is written (in Dutch), "Shh, here ripens the Duvel." The man who oversees that ripening is Hedwig Neven. He has been with the company since 1997 and has been the master brewer for the past decade and a half. He started out studying chemistry but then finished his PhD with the sponsorship of Duvel Moortgat.

Most of the acquisitions have happened since Neven has helmed Duvel. From his laboratory in Puurs, he checks the technical quality of the beer and coordinates activities of all Moortgat's breweries. Whenever Duvel Moortgat acquires another brewery, Neven sets about improving the technical aspects of the process — though he leaves local brewmasters to keep making the beer according to the original recipes. He has also been entrusted with the Duvel brand and has been slowly releasing extensions such as Duvel Single Fermented and Tripel Hop.

Understanding Belgian Ales

Many of the chapters in this book offer special techniques or point to key ingredients as a way of creating authentic versions of traditional ales. The Belgian tradition does include a few interesting quirks — warm rooms, high fermentation temperatures and exotic yeasts, sugar — but sometimes there are no tricks. Duvel is perhaps the best example of any Belgian beer that gross technique will only take you so far. It is one of the few beers that has never really been reproduced, and not because Hedwig Neven keeps his secrets. It's because the brewery has been making this beer for decades and has slowly, slowly fine-tuned all the elements so that a bubbling tulip glass of Duvel looks something like a magic trick.

It's not that any one element is hard to manage; rather, it's when you start stacking them together that they look impossible. Let's start with the attenuation. Just getting the beer as dry as Duvel does is a challenge, but the trouble is that in doing so the brewery lays everything bare. There are no margins for error because everything is revealed. Homebrewers usually have some wiggle room in their numbers. But the art of truly accomplished Belgian ales lies in precision — mash, fermentation, and warm room temperatures must be nailed exactly.

> **It's not that any one element is hard to manage; rather, it's when you start stacking them together that they look impossible.**

All beers depend on balance. Belgian beers often use alcohol strength, carbonation, and attenuation rather than hops to balance sweet bodies and florid ester displays. Darker ales may contain hints of nuts or cocoa to aid in the endeavor, and some yeast strains contribute balancing phenolics. Only a few beers bring hops into the equation, and Duvel is a case in point. It has all the usual hallmarks of a Belgian ale — a silken body whipped by carbonation, a candy-sweet palate, and gentle floral and fruity esters — but it adds a peppery layer that comes from both phenols and spicy European hopping.

The lesson I've taken from tasting and brewing these beers and visiting breweries in Belgium is that the way to perfect them is slowly, variable by variable at a time. First you have to master the individual parts and then adjust them so that they work in concert. You have to find what works and try to reproduce it as closely as possible every time. So far as I know, there aren't any tricks with Belgian ales — you just have to put in the time.

Brewing a Belgian Ale

Let's start with the body. Pale Belgian ales are amazingly lithe beers born of very high rates of attenuation. Duvel finishes out at 1.5° P/1.006, achieving its incredible attenuation through a multistage mash that breaks the malt down into perfectly digestible parts. In many cases you may look at these recipes and think about skipping some of the rests, but that's less advisable here. You want all those enzymes working in your favor throughout the mash.

Neven was a bit vague on the malts he uses for Duvel — not atypical for a Belgian brewer — but says you can achieve that rich golden color with pilsner malts alone. "Typically, a strong blond Belgian ale will use pale malts and an amount of easily fermentable sugars such as dextrose in the brewhouse. The ratio depends on the specificities of the beer you desire." You could achieve a slightly deeper gold with a hint of Vienna or Munich malt. There are always trade-offs; Vienna will give a fuller flavor and will increase the body, sending the beer tripel-ward. All-pilsner malts require longer boiling to achieve deeper colors. In either case, that multirest mash will also help you create that thick, pillowy head. There are some ways to help this along, such as including a touch of Carapils or wheat in the grist, but if you skip a rest, you'll sacrifice some fermentability.

Unusual for most Belgian beers, hops are a big part of Duvel's palate. It only tips the scale at around 30 IBUs, but Duvel tastes bitter. This is a lesson in extreme attenuation and slender malt profiles — and it's what makes hoppy Belgian beers challenging. Because they have so little body, Belgian ales can easily be overwhelmed by bittering hops. Use hops with clean, gentle bitterness — Neven recommends continental hops. Belgians don't do much late-addition hopping; it's just not part of the flavor profile. Indeed, Duvel doesn't add hops at all later in the boil, and it's evident in the beer's stiff, almost Czech-like hop profile.

Gentle but insistent hopping is the secret of Duvel. I don't believe that strongly in secrets, but I do know that we control this balance aspect better than others.

— HEDWIG NEVEN, DUVEL MOORTGAT

Finally, as with all Belgian beer, so much of the process happens after the boil. Duvel goes through a complex process of fermentation and lagering, dropping to near freezing at the conclusion of primary fermentation. It spends time in a warm room for secondary fermentation and then is dropped to around 41°F (5°C) for six weeks to condition. The cold temperatures allow the beer to ripen and also clear, and it's a good technique to adopt for homebrewers who lack filtration.

SCOTTISH YEAST?

One thing Duvel is *not* secretive about is yeast. Theirs, they proudly note, originally came from a Scottish brewery. I have no reason to doubt that, but neither do I think it has much relevance to the yeast the brewery uses today. Scottish yeast is famous for making very clean, ester-free beer. Duvel's yeast, by contrast, is hugely characterful.

This is what happens when yeast takes on "house character," evolving to behave differently (Duvel survives very warm temps; Scots ferment on the coldest edge of the ale spectrum) and produce different flavors. Duvel's yeast may have once been Scottish; today it is very much Belgian.

MALT BILL

9.5 pounds Belgian pilsner malt (77%)

0.5 pound Carapils malt (9%)

1.75 pounds dextrose (15%)

STEP MASH

131°F (55°C) for 15 minutes

145°F (63°C) for 35 minutes

163°F (73°C) for 25 minutes

90-MINUTE BOIL

0.67 ounce Styrian Golding, 65 minutes (5.5% AA, contribution of 12 IBU)

0.67 ounce Saaz, 65 minutes (4.0% AA, contribution of 9 IBU)

0.33 ounce Styrian Golding, 30 minutes (5.5% AA, contribution of 4 IBU)

0.33 ounce Saaz, 30 minutes (4.0% AA, contribution of 3 IBU)

FERMENTATION AND CONDITIONING

Ferment with Wyeast 1388/White Labs WLP570, starting at 68°F (20°C), encouraging it to rise to the upper 70s F (25–26°C) (but stopping before it gets to 80°F [27°C]) for 5 days. If you are using a standard carboy and have no way to control temperature, consider pitching a little warmer (72°F [22°C]), since the yeast activity in 5 gallons won't create the same temperature rise commercial breweries do.

HEDWIG NEVEN

—

DUVEL

PACKAGE

Bottle-condition only. These beers are typically built around serious carbonation levels, so shoot for 4 to 5 volumes. Re-ferment at 75°F (24°C) for 2 weeks, then condition at 40 to 45°F (4–7°C) for 6 weeks. (You shouldn't have to add yeast, as enough yeast will be left over to re-ferment. You just add sugar.) This conditioning period will allow the beer to mature and clarify. Note that many standard bottles are not built for this level of carbonation, so stockpile a collection of thick-walled bottles from such breweries as Duvel and Orval that can handle the pressure.

- Expected OG: 17° P/1.070

- Expected TG: 1.5° P/1.006

- Expected ABV: 8.4%

- Expected bitterness: 28–32 IBU

Notes: This follows a typical Belgian mash, though in some cases brewers might begin with a ferulic acid rest at 113°F (45°C) to boost phenols, either continuing on as written, or skipping the step at 131°F (55°C). Neven notes that the sugar is "typically dosed in the kettle, or even in the cold wort stream." Hop selection is not critical, but you should shoot for spicy, aromatic hops. "Most of the time continental European, Slovenian, and Czech hops can be used, added in multiple stages during boiling." Do not use American varieties if you are shooting for a typical Belgian flavor profile.

NEXT STEPS

This recipe has been groomed to optimize the flavors in Duvel, but the basic approach and process is applicable to most Belgian styles. It will work on lighter pale ales, amber ales, and strong abbey-style ales, as well as standard brown ales that don't use wild yeasts. Belgian brewers use basically the same approach, varying just the recipe: they use a base of pilsner malt with small proportions of specialty malt for color; nearly all use sugar or a lightening agent (corn, for example); they seek well-attenuated beers — if not always as attenuated as Duvel; they don't use many hops. The beers are bottle-conditioned and almost always effervescent; while generally strong (6.5–12%), they can be as low as 3 or 4%.

The differences among these beers rest far more on execution than recipe or method. It comes from yeast selection, dialing in the fermentation and bottle-conditioning temperatures, and levels of attenuation. Many Belgian ales use wheat, and some may use spelt or spices; others might be dark, some might even be hoppy, but the contours of the Belgian ale, whether it's called a dubbel, an abbey, a Belgian pale, or a strong golden, are the same.

OTHER BELGIAN ALES

If you are making basic Belgian ales of any color (pale ales, ambers, browns, dubbels, strong dark abbey ales), the principles don't differ wildly. You are going to use a mashing regime similar to the one listed here (more on that in a moment), you'll be adding sugar, fermenting warm, and doing bottle conditioning. You might alter the mash schedule depending on the attenuation you're seeking. Duvel is made for very high attenuation, but some of these beers have a fuller body. If you're looking for more body, your rests will look more like this: 145 to 148°F (63–64°C) for 30 minutes, 158 to 162°F (70–72°C) for 25 minutes, and a mash out of 167 to 172°F (75–78°C) for 5 minutes. If you're looking to create spicy phenolics, you may want to add a ferulic acid rest at 113°F (45°C) — though many Belgian yeast strains will give some phenolics just by dint of the very warm fermentation.

That leaves you mainly with the question of color and subtle flavors, all of which can be achieved through the grist. I spoke to Kerkom's Marc Limet, who makes an absolutely wonderful dark ale (Bink Bruin) with a rich cacao character and a biscotti-dry finish. Is there any secret to darker ales? Not really, he says. He alludes to the convoluted processes of old, but says that "now you have so many choices in good malts, dark sugars, and other things you can use to brew a dark beer." At one time, breweries may have boiled their beers for 16 hours to make them brown; now they just add darker malts and sugars.

Following are a few guidelines should you wish to make one of these darker ales. Note that where possible, always try to source Belgian malts.

AMBER ALES (5–7% ABV, 15–20 IBU). Until a hundred years ago, the lightest that barley beers got was amber. These are fuller bodied and sweeter than pale ales, generally with a somewhat subdued yeast profile (at least for a Belgian ale). Make an all-malt grist using Belgian Munich for color and pale ale malt.

BROWN ALES (4.5–8% ABV, 18–35 IBU). Slightly different from the dark monastic ales, Belgian browns have a touch of bitterness, either in the form of cocoa or roast, but just enough to balance the beer. Use a grist with some combination of dark caramel sugar, a dark caramel malt (*not* Special B, which will turn it in the direction of an abbey ale), Munich malt, or biscuit malt to build color, sweet flavor, and body. Include a small amount of roasted malt (1–2 percent) to add a hint of roast and drying flavor. Use either pilsner or pale ale malt as the base malt. Yeast character is typically mild (again, for Belgian ales).

DUBBELS (6–8% ABV, 15–25 IBU). Dubbels differ from brown ales in the following ways: they lack any roasty flavors, they are sweeter, and they usually have more yeast-driven flavors. Build color with dark caramel sugar, Belgian Munich malt, and caramel malt (including Special B), and use pilsner as a base malt.

STRONG, DARK ABBEY ALES (9–12% ABV, 20–45 IBU). Strong, dark abbey ales — sometimes called quadrupels — follow the same prescription as dubbels but are brewed to higher gravities.

A NOTE ON SUGARS

There is some confusion about the sugars used to make Belgian ales. Many homebrewers know about Belgian "candi" sugar — it is sold as cubes or rocks of raw-looking sugar. Apparently there was a time when Belgians used this stuff regularly, but now they typically use liquid dextrose or sucrose. (It's why Neven references adding it directly to the cold wort stream.)

When making dark ales, dark sugar is a nearly ubiquitous ingredient, but there's a catch. As Stan Hieronymus describes in *Brew Like a Monk*, this isn't the same stuff you buy at the homebrew store called "dark candi sugar." He explains: "Caramel syrups are sold in Europe, giving brewers a variety of choices not available in the United States. Many American brewers use dark candi (rocks) as a substitute, but while the darkest provide a rummy, unrefined character, they don't come close to replicating the caramelized flavors found in darker Belgian ales." There is at least one company selling this now in the United States (Dark Candi), and you might be able to track down other caramelized sugars from Europe on the Internet.

Pitching Rates

Let's spend a moment talking about yeast. Two things affect the production of flavor compounds: temperature and pitching rates. The higher the temperature, the more "stuff" yeast produces — it's why lagers are cold fermented. For Belgian beers warm ferments are important to producing the esters and phenols that give the beer its character. But there's a point at which yeast starts producing stuff you don't want — solventlike flavors, for example. The yeast strains cultured from Duvel sold in the United States (Wyeast 1388 and White Labs WLP570) are fairly clean and neutral at lower temperatures and need to get into the 70s F (21–26°C) before they start producing fruit and spice.

The harder yeast has to work, the more it will produce that "stuff" as well. Breweries control this by pitching more or less yeast, as measured by millions of cells per milliliter of wort. A rule of thumb is a million cells per mL for every point of gravity on the Plato scale (0.004 of specific gravity). A 10 Plato beer (1.040) would therefore require a pitch of 10 million cells per mL. Underpitching stresses the yeast, causing it to create more esters and phenols. And guess what? Many Belgian breweries pitch at lower rates than breweries elsewhere.

Duvel pitches at 7.5 million cells per mL, which is quite a bit lower than you would expect for a 1.069 beer (though it's also true that the simple sugars Belgians add to their grists make them easier to ferment). By comparison, one pack of Wyeast or White Labs contains 100 billion cells, or 6 million cells per mL in a 5-gallon batch. Even by Duvel's standard, that's quite low, and you should be worried about underpitching too much. Low pitch rates can lead to anemic fermentation, stuck fermentation, high terminal gravity, and the production of higher/fusel alcohols and diacetyl.

Underpitching is risky, and I personally never want to risk sluggish fermentations. If you pitch two packs of yeast or create a starter, your rates will exceed Duvel's. However, if you monitor the temperature closely and make sure it rises to around 75°F (24°C) (and not more than 79°F [26°C]), you should get plenty of yeast character. As with all things, if you're curious about the effect of these techniques, experiment. Underpitching is risky, but there's a reason Belgians do it.

CHAPTER 15

WITBIERS

he twentieth century was not kind to funky Belgian beer styles (see page 142), and following the Second World War, they were dying off in droves. One of the more famous local specialties was brewed in the tiny hamlet of Hoegaarden (pronounced *hoo garden*), a milky-white, acidic ale not wildly dissimilar to lambic. Belgians were turning to industrially made lagers and soda pop, and rapidly dwindling sales forced the last of the Hoegaarden breweries, Tomsin, to shut down in 1957.

Fortunately, it wasn't long before Pierre Celis, a milkman who had once worked at the Tomsin brewery, decided to revive it. He consulted with a retired brewer to create a new recipe in 1966, one that harnessed spicing in place of older, more rustic techniques. It took decades for the beer to find a wide audience, but in 1995, a division within Coors launched a beer that would be renamed Blue Moon. It was lightly wheaty, with a balance of orangey sweetness and a crisp finish. It went from extinction to being one of the most widely brewed styles in the world. In 1960 not a single person on the planet expected Belgian white beer (*wit* or *witte* in Flemish, *bière blanche* in French) to be the best-selling ale in America in the early twenty-first century, but that's exactly what has happened.

EST **Brewery Ommegang** 1997
COOPERSTOWN, NEW YORK

When a group of Belgian beer proponents, including importers Don Feinberg and Wendy Littlefield and officials from the Belgian brewery Duvel Moortgat, founded Brewery Ommegang in 1997, Americans had little concept of "Belgian ale." As importers, Don and Wendy specialized in Belgian beers and had been championing breweries such as Duvel, Rodenbach, and Dupont for 15 years. With Ommegang they built not only a brewery but a mechanism for educating Americans about the Belgian brewing tradition. It was purpose-built to make beer like Belgians do — and look like a Belgian brewery to boot.

By any measure, the endeavor was successful. Ommegang has established itself as one of the most respected breweries in the country, and now Belgian styles proliferate. One of the best examples of Ommegang's influence is saison. Farmhouse ales are now standard styles in many breweries' rotations, but when Ommegang introduced Hennepin in the late 1990s, there was Saison Dupont and not a lot else. It was Hennepin, much more than the Saison Dupont, that introduced Americans to the style. With each release, Ommegang made Americans aware of ambrée, dubbel, Belgian pale, and strong dark ales.

They were not the first to introduce witbier when they released Witte a dozen years ago, but Ommegang brought a sense of Belgian-ness to their version. Few American witbiers spend time bottle conditioning, but Ommegang's witbiers rest in a 75°F (24°C) warm room to finish a secondary fermentation. Along with Allagash (White) and Unibroue (Blanche de Chambly), Ommegang revealed to the world depths not evident in Blue Moon and other earlier examples.

In the past few years, Ommegang has taken further advantage of its sibling breweries — Duvel Moortgat bought out Feinberg and Littlefield in 2003 — by releasing such beers as Gnomegang (with Brasserie d'Achouffe), Spiced Saison (Boulevard), Zuur (Brouwerij Liefmans), and of course Duvel Rustica (with Duvel). Belgian ales are no longer uncommon in the United States, and Ommegang is one of the reasons that is so.

BREWMASTER PHIL LEINHART

Very few people have been inducted by the Belgian Brewers Guild into the Knighthood of the Brewers' Mash Staff — a kind of hall of fame for masters of the Belgian tradition — but Phil Leinhart is one. He has over 25 years of brewing experience, including stops in England and Germany, brewing on systems as small as brewpubs and as large as Anheuser-Busch's. He arrived at Brewery Ommegang in 2007, refining processes, expanding production, and adding many more beers to the rotation. In 2011 and 2016 Leinhart's Witte won the Great American Beer Festival gold medal in the witbier category.

Understanding Witbiers

It's usually not necessary to dip into the distant past to understand beer styles, but with witbier it's instructive. The small town of Hoegaarden, 30 miles west of Brussels, was in the sixteenth century located in a seam between ruling powers — and their tax collectors. This led to a proliferation of local breweries and a style known as Hoegaarden beer. The nineteenth-century brewer Georges Lacambre described that beer this way: it is made "of five to six parts barley malt to two of wheat and one or one and a half of oats." It went through a typically convoluted mashing process before boiling and then was sent to a coolship for spontaneous fermentation. It was served within a few days, while still fermenting. "This beer is very pale," wrote Lacambre, "very refreshing and strongly sparkling. When fresh its raw taste has something wild, similar to that of beer from Leuven."

When Pierre Celis decided to revive this style in the 1960s, he adapted the beer to modern brewing methods, trying to replicate the lactic zing through the use of a crisp, dry yeast and the additions of coriander and bitter orange peel. It was less a re-creation than an impressionistic reimagining. You'd think this would make modern witbiers canvases for broad reinterpretation, but oddly, Celis's blueprint has become an orthodoxy from which few deviate. There's no reason this should be the case, and gradually breweries have begun to experiment with different spicing and more rustic (and sometimes wild) yeasts. For homebrewers it's a style that offers huge possibilities.

Brewing a Witbier

As the name implies, these beers were historically a very pale, milky color. This points to the one aspect of the recipe in which it's important to stay close to historical norms. The zinginess of the palate, the flavors of citrus and spice, the crisp finish — all of these are realms for experimentation, but first we have to make sure the witbier is white and wheaty. Leinhart notes that the "original wits were brewed with 'wind malt,' which wasn't even kilned after germination — just air-dried, so it was extremely pale. Most Belgian brewers use two-row pilsen malt as base for most of their beers. Even standard [American] two-row pale can impart more toasted, malty notes (and color) than I like to see in the style."

You can use either unmalted or malted wheat — and different breweries make different choices — and in amounts up to 55 percent of the malt bill. Either white or red wheat (the color of the seed coat) is fine, but "some say red wheat contributes to a rounder flavor," Leinhart notes. At Ommegang, "we use a combination of hard red wheat flakes (raw) and soft white wheat (malted)." The reason, as Leinhart explains it, has to do with particle size and weight. "Raw (unmalted wheat) has a lot of large, high-molecular-weight proteins. Very high amounts of said proteins can create very large particles in beer, which actually decrease the haze because these particles succumb to gravity and settle out. Some malted wheat can stabilize the haze since the large proteins are partially broken down into smaller proteins/ peptides during the malting process. The haze is more stable because the smaller particles so formed tend to stay dispersed in the beer longer." Oats round out the grist and help add to the cloudy appearance and also a rounder mouthfeel, but should be used in amounts around 5 percent of the grist.

Leinhart follows a mash schedule similar to the one Celis originally used, beginning with a ferulic acid rest at 113°F (45°C). As with weizens, some yeast strains convert ferulic acid to 4-vinyl guaiacol, a phenol responsible for a spicy, clovelike flavor. A ferulic acid rest seems typical, but the main mash temperature ranges all over the board. Leinhart's is very low (144°F [62°C]), while Allagash White is made with a high, single-infusion mash (153 to 155°F [67–68°C]). This starts to get to the flexibility of this ale and how to think about choosing methods to suit the style of wit you prefer.

MALT BILL

---

5 pounds Belgian pilsner malt (56%)

1.75 pounds red wheat malt (19%)

1.75 pounds wheat flakes (unmalted) (19%)

0.5 pound flaked oats (6%)

1 pound rice hulls, for mash bed permeability (optional; at Ommegang they're not necessary)

STEP MASH

113°F (45°C) for 5 minutes

144°F (62°C) for 40 minutes

154°F (68°C) for 15 minutes

170°F (77°C) for mash out (5 minutes)

60-MINUTE BOIL

1 ounce Czech Saaz, 60 minutes (3.5% AA, contribution of 13 IBU)

0.25 ounce Czech Saaz, 15 minutes (3.5% AA, contribution of 2 IBU)

0.3 ounce cracked coriander seed, 15 minutes

0.5 ounce dried bitter orange peel, 15 minutes

FERMENTATION AND CONDITIONING

Ferment with Wyeast 3942, Wyeast 3944, White Labs WLP400, or WLP410 at 70°F (21°C). Rack after primary fermentation (4–5 days), and condition cool for up to 2 weeks.

PHIL LEINHART

—

OMMEGANG

Package

Bottle-condition or keg. Pierre Celis conducted secondary fermentation typical of Belgian ales; Ommegang does as well, but most breweries do not. Bottle conditioning may subtly change the profile of your wit after it goes through a secondary fermentation.

- Expected OG: 11.5° P/1.046

- Expected TG: 2° P/1.008

- Expected ABV: 5.2%

- Expected bitterness: 15 IBU

Notes: Fermentation temperatures may begin as low as 65°F (18°C) or as high as 77°F (25°C). Use higher temperatures to boost production of esters and phenols, lower temperatures for a more neutral beer (and consider how these will interact with your spice choices). The spice suggestions here are low; other sources recommend double or more of the spices. You may also add the spice earlier, after 30 minutes. "This is the way you manage the spice," Leinhart notes. "Some brewers add it earlier, some later." You may want a bolder flavor, so adjust to taste. For a crisper, more tart witbier, use up to 3 percent acidulated malt.

Next Steps

Having addressed the body of the witbier, let's return for a moment to its spirit. Think of a sunny summer day, and imagine what slakes the thirst: a light-bodied, low-alcohol beer that has a hint of sweetness but that relies more on acidity and a crisp finish to temper the enervating heat. To achieve that particular balance, Pierre Celis used coriander, bitter curaçao orange peel, and a dry yeast strain — now the standard for the style.

But others have addressed the spirit of a witbier differently. At Allagash Rob Tod uses a highly attenuative yeast to produce white wine notes and a bone-dry finish. Japan's Kiuchi brewery adds orange juice, nutmeg, and unmalted barley to Hitachino Nest White Ale. Blue Moon uses sweet Valencia oranges rather than bitter ones, Saint Archer White uses whole navel oranges, and a number of breweries have begun to experiment with fresh citrus zest instead of dried peel.

The upshot is this — there are a lot of different routes you can take to achieve something flavorful and zesty. Let's consider three different areas where you might address your attention.

SPICES

The coriander-and-curaçao orthodoxy is hard to shake, but there's nothing sacred about those spices. Indeed, a number of people find that coriander's orange sweetness can work against the goal of crispness — it's an easy spice to overdo. I tend to side with Ommegang's Leinhart: spices are best in moderation, and you want your beer to taste like a beer. That doesn't mean you can't use a number of spices, though. One of my faves is Boulevard's Two Jokers. Imperializing a witbier is a little odd (Two Jokers is 8% ABV), but the spicing is very understated, despite the additions of cardamom, coriander, orange peel, lavender, and grains of paradise. A number of breweries have used lemongrass to great effect, and chamomile, which Randy Mosher promoted in *Radical Brewing*, is now common.

But this is one area where commercial brewing lags behind the work of homebrewers. There are dozens of herbs, spices, and other flavorings that may be harnessed to achieve that special witbier spirit — and homebrewers have been experimenting with them for years. When choosing a spice, consider it in the context of other spice, hop, and yeast selections. If you've chosen to use a ferulic acid rest to promote spicy phenolics, lavender would harmonize more ably than perfumy elderflower. If you're using hops to create the impression of citrus, you might use cardamom or chamomile to add complexity. As you work with different spices, you'll begin to get a sense of what they add, so the combinations will become more intuitive. (See Alternative Witbier Spices, next page.)

 The key with spices is subtlety; they should be well blended into the overall character of the beer and not stick out on their own.

— PHIL LEINHART, OMMEGANG

ALTERNATIVE WITBIER SPICES

Just about everything this side of jalapeño could and probably has been used in witbiers. (And Cigar City actually *did* make a jalapeño wit.) Some do seem more appropriate than others, though. Here are a few recommendations.

Cardamom. This sweetish spice gives Indian food its distinctive flavor (think chai tea). It's extremely potent, so use it sparingly.

Chamomile. Phil Leinhart used this in a double wit and says it "imparted a slightly floral, honeylike quality." It will increase the perception of sweetness as well.

Citrus zest. In typical witbier preparations dried peels are added for a bitter, slightly orange flavor. Using zest instead turbocharges this effect. Grate the peel of one-half to one whole fruit for a batch of beer, and add at knockout. You're capturing delicate essential oils, so you don't want to lose the volatiles. Using limes, Meyer lemon, or other unusual citrus will give it unique flavors.

Elderflower. Back in Lacambre's time there was a French version of witbier known as bière blanche de Paris made with elderflower. It has a heavy, sweet flavor that can suggest fruit such as lychee. It's the flavor in St. Germain liqueur.

Fruit juice. Citrus is a natural choice both for flavor and acidity, but other juices can be added for accents. Acidic fruit (raspberries, passion fruit, pomegranate) will achieve a similar effect while other fruits can mimic esters (peach, grapes, watermelon). Let your fancy be your guide.

Ginger. Becoming more common in witbiers, ginger adds an earthy pepperiness.

Heather. Like chamomile, heather gives a honey-sweet flavor and seems to add viscosity.

Lavender. This is another potent and distinctive spice — add too much, and you end up with a strong, soapy beer. Look for culinary lavender rather than buying stalks at the florist's.

Lemongrass. This is a natural fit with witbier, but it works better when added to the conditioning tank. Heat draws harsher, weedy notes from lemongrass.

Mint. Fresh mint is rich in chemical compounds beyond mouth-tingling menthol (including peppery caryophyllene, citrusy limonene, and piney pinene) and contributes a complex cooling quality.

Orange blossoms. These add a floral orange aroma that will help suggest citrus rather than scream it but are so delicate they should not be added until knockout at the earliest.

Peppercorn. More typical in saisons, white, black, or pink pepper can add not only a spicy kick but also sweetness and aromatics.

Sage. This is an unusual choice, but it works well if you're shooting for something with a hoppier profile. The savory elements of sage harmonize nicely with earthy or tangy hops.

Thyme. Like sage, thyme's association with savory dishes makes it a slight outlier, but used sparingly its earthy, woody qualities can fill out an herbal profile. Consider especially lemon thyme, which has a citrusy flavor.

Yeasts

Without speculating too wildly about Pierre Celis's thinking, one reason to substitute spices for wild yeast would be to mimic compounds produced during fermentation. Standard witbier strains such as White Labs WLP400 and Wyeast 3944 are known as POF+ strains; that is, they have the capacity to convert ferulic acid to the spicy phenol 4-vinyl guaiacol. (The acronym comes from a kind of lager-oriented slur. It stands for "phenolic off-flavor," which represents the prejudice of a lager brewer, where phenols are verboten. But in wits and weissbiers these are hardly "off" flavors.) Other yeasts produce different compounds in differing arrangements, and these can all be harnessed to add complexity to your beer.

I've had great luck with saison yeasts and abbey strains. These kinds of yeasts create wonderful esters and phenols and typically dry beers out to a nice, crisp finish. Good attenuation is important when you're adding spices, which create the impression of sweetness. White Labs WLP585 and Wyeast 3711 are good choices. Abbey strains produce less intense flavors, but when fermented warm do produce a more specifically Belgian character. I'd recommend White Labs WLP530 or Wyeast 3787, and pitch in the mid-70s to 80°F (24–27°C).

Hops

Witbier isn't known as a hoppy style, but as the "white IPA" trend demonstrates, American hops and spices can work well together. It makes sense: the orangey-citrusy layer created by coriander and orange peel is very much in the same flavor family with hops such as Amarillo, Citra, El Dorado, Meridian, Sorachi Ace, and others. The idea is not to add bitterness but to layer in the flavors and aromas these hops produce at the end of the boil. As with other ingredients in the witbier, the key is choosing hop varieties that complement the spices and fermentation characteristics you've selected.

Wild Witbier

If you really want total authenticity, you could also tinker with wild yeasts and bacteria. The nineteenth-century Hoegaarden beers Lacambre wrote about were served young and tart, after a lactic fermentation but long before wild *Brettanomyces* had a chance to become active. You can accomplish something similar by mashing and boiling the witbier as usual but first pitching *Lactobacillus* (Wyeast 5335 or White Labs WLP677). Take regular samples, and taste the wort to assess its level of acidity. When it's where you want it, bring the wort to a boil, cool it again, and pitch with a witbier yeast. This technique allows you the maximum control over acid levels. For even more control, consider kettle souring (page 106).

Block 15's Nick Arzner made a wonderful wild example called Wonka's Wit. His process is to divide the batch and spontaneously ferment half of it. The other half he inoculates with *Lactobacillus*. "When the pH drops to 3.4 (one to two days), I rack in with the [spontaneous batch]." (You *could* use Arzner's approach, but the *Lacto*-only method will give you a more stable, predictable beer. Try it first.)

A different approach is less traditional but produces lovely flavors: adding *Brettanomyces* after fermentation. Because *Brett* consumes sugars left behind following a *Saccharomyces* fermentation, it will continue to ferment after primary. I've had the best luck with *Brettanomyces bruxellensis* (White Labs WLP644), which produces lush tropical esters as it finishes out the beer. If you use a highly attenuating yeast such as Wyeast 3711, it will limit the influence of *Brettanomyces*, giving it just a hint of wildness and great fruitiness.

CHAPTER 16

SAISONS

One of the unexpected successes in the world of beer styles is undoubtedly the saison. According to the beers tracked on BeerAdvocate, since the new century more saisons have been brewed in the United States than all other styles except IPA and pale ales. That's an amazing turnaround — in the 1970s there were only a couple of these still being made in the world. (Most of the other rustic Belgian styles had already died out, too: Louvain wheat ales, Peeterman, uytzets, the old Hoegaarden beers, and more — all gone.)

It's even more interesting because the style has no real standard-bearer in terms of sales. Ommegang's Hennepin may be the closest thing to a "flagship saison," but it's hardly a big seller. Here's another measure of this style's niche status: although it has grown since I visited in 2011, at the time Brasserie Dupont, the most famous maker of saison in the world, was making just 13,000 barrels of beer across all their brands *in total*.

So why are there so many of them now? Brewers love saisons. No style gives a brewer more room to fiddle around, or fewer constrains on what she "must" do; no beer is as expressive or sensitive to the brewer's whim. There are a number of qualities that may be or usually are present, but the only one that's mandatory is lots of yeast character. No other nonwild ale gets more of its character from yeast than a saison, and that's what makes them such fun to brew. Because they have no benchmarks for strength, color, mash regime, or hop schedule (spices may be in the mix, too), this chapter differs from the rest. We'll look at the style generally and discuss some of the different approaches, but it's impossible to offer a "typical" recipe.

EST **Brasserie Dupont** 1844

TOURPES, BELGIUM

Any discussion of saison must begin with the small farmhouse brewery in Tourpes, near the French border, 45 miles southwest of Brussels. Time seems to move more slowly in the countryside here, where the only thing to tell you it's the twenty-first century and not the nineteenth are the cars. The buildings, the irregular fields — they appear timeless. Brasserie Dupont is cut from this cloth, changing only when required by the march of time.

Founded in 1844, the brewery made few upgrades in equipment or process for over a century (though the German army did seize the kettle in World War I to make munitions, forcing Dupont to replace it in 1920). As recently as the 1980s they were still malting their own barley and working with a mash tun that predated the brewery. A fire in the malt house caused them to discontinue that activity, and in 2008 the old mash tun finally gave out. But the brewery still uses its own well water, still fires the kettle with an open flame, still manages a very old yeast strain (one of the most famous in the world, and still makes many of the same beers it has for decades.

What's interesting is that while everyone agrees Saison Dupont is the classic example, almost no one makes a beer like it. Dupont has a strongly mineral quality, and the yeast tends toward phenols. It is hugely effervescent and builds piles of snowy head. The herbal hopping joins with the phenolic yeast strain to create one layer of savory flavors, but these are offset by the vibrant esters that send the beer in a complementary, spritzy citrus direction. It is one of the most layered, complex beers in the world, but it's also very Belgian.

When Americans make these beers now, they tend to veer away from the minerality, the effervescence, and the herbal notes, accentuating esters and attenuation instead. This points to the conundrum of the saison: the classic example is not much imitated yet stands so tall that it can peer over the shoulder of every brewer making his own version of the style.

OLIVIER DEDEYCKER

There are 10 members of the fourth generation at Dupont, but Olivier Dedeycker is the heart of the operation. "My parents lived 500 meters from here, and my grandfather lived here, so we were always in the brewery. All of my holidays were spent here at the brewery." He didn't plan to take up the family business when he went off to college, but it drew him back early on. After graduation in 1990 he started as brewing engineer, working with his famed predecessor and uncle, Marc Rosier, and took over duties as master brewer in 2002.

Beginning in the 1980s, Rosier started adding to the line, and together with Dedeycker expanded it substantially in the 1990s and 2000s. Under Dedeycker the brewery has added a stout and a much-lauded dry-hopped version of Dupont's saison and gone through a major expansion in brewing operations.

Understanding Saison

It really stretches the term to call saisons a "style." They're more like a state of mind. Originally, they were made where the ingredients were produced — on farms, generally on primitive equipment. Even then they weren't really a style. Olivier Dedeycker gave me an overview when I visited Brasserie Dupont. "It was what we call in Belgium *bière de saison*, saison beer, brewed in the winter and drunk in the summer by the people who worked in the fields. So we speak of a beer with a low alcohol content, high bitterness, no residual sugar, so a refreshing beer. At this time they would have beer that was totally different from another one from the next year due to microbiological intervention." Dedeycker doesn't mention it, but the truth is that most of these beers were probably close to undrinkable. Farmers made them rarely, on bad equipment, from ingredients that may not have made the food-grade cut.

What's especially ironic is that now saisons are considered among the most accomplished, sophisticated beers in the world. They are definitely made with certain "rustic" elements (we'll come to those in a moment), but they are also complex, balanced, and bubbling with flavors that make them a favored beer at the dinner table. Because modern brewers have control of brewhouse specifications, they can take those qualities from the farm and turn them into the pinnacle of the brewer's art.

If you survey saisons now, there's *huge* variation. Jolly Pumpkin makes Bam Noire, a 4.5% dark beer with wild yeast. Ommegang's Hennepin is 7.7%, blond, made with standard *Saccharomyces* yeast (though an eclectic strain), and spiced with coriander, orange peel, grains of paradise, and ginger. Saison Dupont is 6.5%, golden, and made with its own strange (but not wild) yeast, 100 percent pilsner malt, fairly noticeable hopping, and very hard water. Boulevard Tank 7 is a booming 8%, also fairly hoppy (using American varieties) but quite pale, made with wheat and corn but a less exotic yeast strain. So to recap: 4.5 to 8%; straw to chestnut; spices or not; wild yeast or not; wheat, corn, or just plain pilsner malt; and hard or soft water. And those are just the ingredients: we haven't even begun to consider brewing methods.

In terms of brewing there are different considerations in both the hot and cold side. Since it is an old farmhouse style, single-infusion mashing is certainly defensible, but step mashes are more common in Belgium now. Many Belgian breweries give their beer a ferulic acid rest to boost phenols. Some breweries mash at low temperatures to increase attenuation, but some want a thicker mouthfeel, so they mash higher (also a consideration if wild yeast is in the mix). On the cold side, breweries follow the lead of their yeast, fermenting at merely warm temperatures — or sometimes letting the mercury rise beyond what any commercial brewery would normally consider reasonable. In the United States, breweries tend to skip the ferulic acid rest and keep fermentation temperatures comparatively low, producing light esters and downplaying phenols.

So what are the parameters of style? In *The Beer Bible* I described five qualities that were often associated with saisons, listed here by an increasing likelihood of being present in any given example:

INTERESTING GRAIN CHARACTER, which could mean a wheat softness, a silkiness from oats, or the nuttiness of spelt. At one time these beers were made with rougher grain grown for food and not optimized for beer brewing. These beers shouldn't taste perfectly smooth and refined, like factory white bread; rather, they should have some flavor and texture, like a handmade whole-grain loaf.

A SPICINESS that may derive from actual spices or come from hops and fermentation. If spices are used, they shouldn't dominate the beer. Rustic ales should be refreshing, not sweet, herbal stews.

A HAZY APPEARANCE that might come from a variety of causes — grains or starches, hop matter, or yeast. When breweries began to be able to make perfectly clear ("bright") beers, it signalled to the customer that there were no infections or quality problems. A bit of haze suggests handmade ales of the prefiltering age.

A CRISP, REFRESHING DRYNESS. Rustic ales were originally used to sate thirsts on hot days, so they couldn't be very sweet or heavy. Effervescence, minerality, hops, and yeast character may figure into the equation. Most saisons have a thin, vinous character that comes from their highly attenuative yeasts.

A PRONOUNCED YEAST CHARACTER, the most important quality in a rustic ale. This one is really nonnegotiable. "Rustic" can almost be read as code for untamed yeasts and the wild, fruity, or spicy compounds they produce. The yeasts need not be wild, but they must be interesting.

One outstanding question: whither the dark saison? As the style was making its ascent, dark saisons were fairly common brewery experiments but are seen less often now. For any beer that emphasizes yeast character, dark malts are a challenge. Roastiness and yeast don't harmonize well; roastiness blots out esters and often clashes with phenolic notes. Where darker saisons work, it's when they use malts such as dehusked Carafa malts that contribute a nutty note and very little roastiness. Think of how dunkelweizens manage to taste chocolaty and nutty — flavors that work well with banana and clove.

Brewing a Saison

Given the broad variability in this range of beers, there are few hard guidelines to offer and no recipe given here. Below are a few notes for each stage of the process.

WATER. Belgian water is typically hard and can provide an interesting flavor element to the beer. Dupont gets its "very hard" water (Dedeycker's description) from a 65-foot well and uses it untreated. It is not a crucial element.

GRAIN BILL. Pale malts are the most typical here. Breweries seem to split between pilsner and Belgian pale malts, and adding a color malt is also common. Never use caramel malt; the flavor and body are not appropriate for this style. It's very common for breweries to use other grains, just as farmers would have done. Any character pickup from wheat, oats, spelt, or even rye malt is perfectly in keeping with this rustic style. To suggest American rusticity, Boulevard's Steven Pauwels uses corn in Tank 7, a practice that seems increasingly common in American saisons.

MASH SCHEDULE. Select a mash schedule appropriate to the type of saison you're crafting. Use a ferulic acid rest (around 113°F [45°C]) for phenol formation. Mash lower for greater fermentability, possibly using a two-step mash of around 145°F (63°C) and 155°F (68°C), or even use a single-infusion mash of 149°F (65°C). Most of these beers are brewed for a thin body and high attenuation, but there's nothing that says they must have that profile. At Kerkom Marc Limet makes a wonderful saisony beer called Bink Blond that has a satisfying cakiness to it, along with a hint of wild yeast. Also keep in mind that if you plan to use wild yeast, it will thin and dry out, so make sure you ferment warm (153 to 155°F [67–68°C]) to give the *Brett* something to munch on.

BOIL. At Dupont Olivier Dedeycker boils his saison for 90 minutes over an open flame, which deepens the pilsner malts to a golden color. There's really no reason to extend it beyond 60 minutes, though, especially if you add a touch of color malt to the grist.

HOPPING. Uncharacteristically, Americans have resisted making hoppy saisons, but there's no reason to. It is a yeast-forward style, but a note of bitterness is not out of place. Even more possibilities are presented by late-boil, postboil, and even dry-hop additions. We have one outstanding example of this type of saison in IV, a saison by the newer brewery Jandrain-Jandrenouille. Stéphane Meulemans and Alexandre Dumont got their start importing hops for Yakima Chief, and when they started their own brewery, they made wonderfully lush saisons rich with American flavor. The harmony between yeast and hop gives a wonderful lychee flavor to IV.

SPICING. For some reason American brewers have gotten it into their heads that saisons can use a bit of touch-up with spicing. This is an issue of preference, but the essence of a saison is yeast character, which is itself spicy (and fruity). Those are the flavors you want to encourage, and spicing should be unnecessary (and in many cases can create clashing flavors or flavors that mask the fermentation flavors).

> When I asked Olivier Dedeycker about adding spices, he offered a very diplomatic reply: "I'm not convinced they are necessary," he said, emphasizing that his saison never uses them.

FERMENTATION. This is, of course, the biggie. It's the only nonnegotiable dimension of the saison. There are a few solid workhorse yeast strains out there, including a version of Dupont's (White Labs WLP565, Wyeast 3724), Brasserie D'Achouffe's (WLP550, Wyeast 3522), as well as the French saison strain from Thiriez (Wyeast 3711). All these yeasts are sensitive to temperature and will produce markedly different compounds depending on how warm you ferment. Dupont's strain doesn't do well at low temperatures and is famous for stalling out at around 1.020. You need to make sure it is well aerated. If it does stall out, it may start again, or you may have to pitch another yeast to finish it out (it will have produced many of the flavors you want already).

Another good choice is the strain from Westmalle (WLP530, Wyeast 3787), which is tolerant to temperatures in the low 80s F (27–28°C) and which, at those higher temperatures, can produce wonderfully saisony character. Saisons are another great beer to use with open fermentation, a process that helps develop yeast-derived flavor compounds (see chapter 8).

Dupont's Process

Dupont begins with very hard water, which Dedeycker does not treat. For Saison Dupont the brewery uses 100 percent pilsner malt in the grist, mashing in at 113°F (45°C). They use an unorthodox method of raising the temperature slowly over the next hour and three-quarters until it reaches 162°F (72°C). They conduct a boil of 90 minutes over open flame, which does deepen the color to gold. Saison Dupont is a comparatively hoppy saison, but Dedeycker deflected my questions about hop variety. He generally hops the beer with Belgian-grown Goldings but does sometimes alter the varieties depending on that year's crop. He uses only two additions, one at the start of boil and one in the last minute of the boil. He has recently begun dry-hopping a version of his saison and uses different varieties each year.

Dupont's fermentation is the most unusual in the world. Dupont has peculiar, squat, square fermenters, and Dedeycker pitches the yeast (a mixture of multiple strains) at 77°F (25°C). I had heard rumors that it derives from a red wine strain (Dedeycker: "maybe"), but it is in any case very old ("from my grandfather's time"). His wife, who holds a doctorate in microbiology, manages the yeast now, and Dupont can reuse it for 100 to 150 generations — remarkable for a mixed strain.

The strain not only likes warm temperatures, it won't finish out properly unless it reaches them. How warm? Dedeycker took me to the control panel so I could see for myself. One read 34°C (93°F), one 35°C (95°F). They will let the yeast get as hot as 39°C (102°F) before intervening to keep it from rising higher. Primary fermentation lasts one to two weeks, depending on the conditions. (It seems that even Dupont finds it finicky.)

They use a different culture for secondary fermentation in the bottle, letting the beer condition in a warm room for six to eight weeks. Re-fermentation is so important to the character of Dupont that they must lay the bottles on their sides during bottle conditioning; otherwise, the beer doesn't taste right. "If we start the secondary fermentation like so" — here he made the gesture of an upright bottle — "we have a totally different beer. The yeast multiplies very differently. We do all the multiplication of the yeast in the bottle; we don't pitch the beer with massive quantities of yeast. We pitch, but just a little bit. It seems to be only a small thing, but the impact on the taste is really big." Underpitching yeast is a good way to stress the yeast and develop esters, and it appears this happens during re-fermentation as well.

A BIT MORE ABOUT YEAST

If the story of Dupont tells us anything, it's that in the case of saison yeast is king. The practice of nurturing a yeast strain that can tolerate such extreme temperatures (15°F [8°C] warmer than in any other brewery I've ever encountered), giving it a specific environment (shallow, square fermenters), and then finishing off the beer with another round of very specific conditions for re-fermentation — all these things make Dupont taste like Dupont.

Homebrewers who treat their saisons the way they treat their IPAs are probably going to find them lacking that certain something that makes the style sing.

Saisons challenge you to break rules: using open fermentation, fermenting warm, using mixed yeast strains. If you're willing to try things at risk of spoiling a batch of beer, you may be rewarded with a truly unusual and spectacular saison.

Beyond regular practices there is the question of wild yeast. Historic saisons were all affected by what Dedeycker called "microbiological intervention" — they were rustic beers made on the farm, and all were inoculated with wild yeasts and bacteria. (In many cases breweries probably spontaneously fermented them.) So it is certainly appropriate to consider adding a bit of funk to your saison.

I don't think there's any right or wrong approach, but consider the nature of saison. They are not principally a wild style; they get their wonderful yeast character from the esters and phenols created by *Saccharomyces*. Those flavor elements are pronounced, but they're not impervious to other flavors. Spice and excessive hopping can occlude them — and so can wild yeasts. One of the best examples of a well-struck balance is the tiny brewery Blaugies, which uses a mixed yeast strain that produces all the lovely florid *Saccharomyces* characteristics you want from a saison strain but is also blended with something wild that, over time, inflects the beer with a drying rusticity.

I have had great success pitching a standard saison strain and running it as dry as possible. My favorite farmhouse strain is Wyeast's French Saison (3711), which goes very dry — 1.004 to 1.006. I then pitch *Brettanomyces* (I've had luck with different strains), which adds a wonderful tropical note but, because the beer is already so dry, doesn't overtake the original strain. You can adopt your own approach (kettle souring, blended cultures of wild yeast with regular yeast, and so on) — which is of course the essence of making saison.

CHAPTER 17

BIÈRES DE NOËL

or most of beer's long history, it was a spiced beverage. The palate was sweet, lightly alcoholic, and often heavy and under-attenuated. The stuff we think of as beer is the historical newbie, made possible only because one particular spice — *Humulus lupulus* — won out over all the rest. In fact, when hops first came along, it took centuries to become the standard because the bitter flavor was unfamiliar and unpleasant to drinkers used to sweet, spiced beverages.

Bitterness did win out, though, and the tradition of spicing mostly died out, but not in Belgium. What's more, it hasn't been isolated to a particular style. Most any beer might have a bit of spice tucked in, either clandestinely, to accentuate native flavors in the beer, or stridently, to take center stage. And once a year Belgium celebrates the winter holiday season with an outpouring of *bières d'hiver (or bières de Noël)* that are more or less *expected* to be spiced. The Belgian use of spice, whether overt or covert, has continued since the prehop era, and there are lots of clues about how to use them. Spicing is not easy, and as more and more Americans dabble in the practice, they could benefit from some tips from the masters.

EST # St. Feuillien 1873
Le Rœulx, Belgium

Though St. Feuillien is named for a saint (and later an abbey) and makes a line of abbey-style beers, it is not and has never been an abbey brewery. In some ways its story is more interesting. Founded in 1873 by a woman, Stephanie Friart, it has remained in family hands since — and is still owned and run by a woman, Stephanie's great-great-niece, Dominique Friart. She left to study literature at the Sorbonne and was living in Paris during a period when the brewery was shuttered from 1977 to 1988. Friart returned to help run the business and has spent the past 15 years building it into one of the most vibrant of the small, family-owned breweries in Belgium.

St. Feuillien's bread-and-butter beers are classically Belgian — strong, bottle-conditioned ales brimming with fermentation flavors. But it is their seasonal Cuvée de Noël that is the most interesting and perhaps most Belgian of all. I typically bring a bottle or two when I visit holiday parties, and the reactions to this ale are never subdued. It's something like rum cake — strong, dark, chocolaty, full of decadent fruit and spice flavors. At least half the people at these parties say they've never tasted anything like it.

In fact, there *is* something like it: the rest of the St. Feuillien beers. Although the brewery is coy about which beers are spiced, there's no doubt that all their beers are *spicy* (and fruity). Tasting notes for Grand Cru sound like booths at a farmers' market: banana, black pepper, lemon, apricot, apple. The Triple has pear and peach. Speciale tends more toward culinary flavors such as chocolate and dates. And . . . is that clove in the Grand Cru, coriander in the Triple, and cinnamon in the Speciale? You can't quite tell whether it's overt spicing or the effects of fermentation. If you try these beers first and then sample the Cuvée de Noël, it all begins to make sense. Spice is a native element in almost every Belgian beer, whether it was added or is a function of the yeast.

BREWMASTER ALEXIS BRIOL

A big part of St. Feuillien's success goes to longtime brewer Alexis Briol. Even before heading off to the famed Université Catholique de Louvain, he apprenticed at Cantillon. Upon receiving his brewing engineer degree, he spent a short time at De Koninck before joining St. Feuillien in 1996. In the 20 years since his arrival, he has overseen the expansion and modernization of the brewery and developed a host of the brewery's core beers, including Triple, Saison, and Grand Cru. In recent years, he has even collaborated with international breweries and begun to experiment with American-style beers — most notably an IPA with Green Flash Brewing.

Understanding Bières de Noël

Belgians spice their beers in a couple of different ways, and both are instructive. In one case the spicing is so delicate you don't notice it. Here the spices act as extremely understated flavor notes and are generally mistaken for fermentation characteristics. In a country where the flavors of fruitiness and spice are expected anyway — because of the yeast — it's easy enough to sneak in actual spices to achieve similar kinds of flavors. It's not even easy to discover which of the beers have spices and which don't, because for Belgian brewers that's the point: You're not supposed to taste the spice. The beer should present itself holistically. The late writer Michael Jackson wrote about a meeting he once had with a spice dealer in Belgium who showed him invoices of breweries not known for spices that were nevertheless buying them, "to demonstrate that he has sold a wide variety of exotica to an equally disparate range of his nation's brewers." So lesson one is: don't let 'em know you're spicing your spiced beers.

In the second case brewers make beers to display spice flavors, and the best examples are the annual Christmas beers that start appearing at the end of November. These are so popular that nearly every brewery makes one — I counted over 100 of them a few years back, and Belgium had around 150 breweries at the time. Among these, St. Feuillien's Cuvée de Noël is one of the best known and a great example of how to make overt use of spices wonderfully palatable while retaining an essential beeriness.

Cuvée is a dark beer, which is a good place to start (many bières de Noël are dark). It has a rich, chocolaty base on which rests a platter of dark fruits — cherry, fig, baked apple, and raisin. The spices are tucked into the spaces between these malt notes, with hints of ginger and cinnamon, as well as flavors that are harder to identify. Clove? Coconut? Or is it vanilla? Even in a spice-forward beer such as Cuvée de Noël, the flavors don't smack you across the face and say, "I am coriander, dammit!" Subtlety is always at play.

Brewing a Bière de Noël

Spiced beers divide people, but done properly, they don't need to. In beer terms spices taste like interlopers: they add a sensory dimension that competes with everything else going on in the beer. To work — whether the spices are barely perceptible accents or the stars of the show — they must relate to the other flavors in the beer. Think of them by analogy. In a musical composition each instrument must communicate with the others in key, rhythm, and harmony. The problem with many spiced beers is that the spices clash with the other flavors like an out-of-key flügelhorn.

On a deeper level, I think everyone who wants to spice a beer should ask the question: am I adding this spice to enhance the flavors of the beer or to cover them up? The spices must work for the beer, not the other way around. This is absolutely critical when you approach your recipe. I speak from experience here. I once became enchanted with the idea of lavender and decided to make a saison. As

I created the recipe, I wasn't thinking about how the lavender would enhance the beer but how the beer would be a dais for all that lavendery goodness. The predictable result was a lavender tincture that completely blotted out the flavor of beer. I've encountered this same problem in countless examples of commercial beers — I pretty much hide when I see a spiced ale at an American brewpub.

Beyond the platitudes, there are some basic practices to keep in mind. The active ingredient in spice comes from essential oils, which degrade over time. Buy only fresh spices. There are good online resources, but since you're going to be buying such small amounts, look for a store that specializes in spice and has a fresh stock on hand. Some sources suggest making an alcohol tincture of spices, but I would caution against this. Spices have dozens of compounds, and if you use them fresh, you'll get a fuller, more complex sense; tinctures intensify but simplify flavors and aromas. The addition of grain alcohol is also detectable in the beer, and to my tongue it reads as hot and often a bit harsh.

Instead, add spices postboil. Alexis Briol calls it "warm infusion," and the idea is "simply to avoid the aroma's evaporation." Those essential oils will volatilize in the warmth, but they won't vent off as they would during the full boil. They also won't extract tannins from the fiber of the plant material, which adds unpleasant harshness to the beer. (If you taste a spiced beer that has a bitter note like black tea and muddy, indistinct spice flavors, you can be sure the brewer boiled the spices good and long.) Whether you're crushing or grating, prepare the spice immediately before you add it — again, to preserve those volatile essential oils.

Briol suggests approaching spices with respect. "Spices are very powerful (much more than hops in some cases). As a newcomer, avoid high quantities; go gradually, and use simple mixes (two or three maximum) at the same time." This is good advice; a single spice already contains many compounds, and they react with heat and fermentation to produce flavors you may not anticipate. Once you start adding other spices, they interact with each other, and then you're dealing with an unpredictable mélange of chemical compounds and organic reactions. Of course, once you find combinations that work, you can begin adding in other spices. There's no limit to the number you can use, but build up as you go.

(It would be absolutely wonderful if someone had spent a decade or two studying the way spices work in beer, but no one has. While brewers can give general advice, there's no manual for how to use spice — you have to chart that landscape yourself.)

SPICES AND YEAST

Finally, and counterintuitively, Briol says that when using spices, "you need a yeast that produces not a lot of aromas." This may be a surprise to many brewers, but while I'd add a caveat, it's a good place to start. When using characterful yeasts and spices, you may have an "uncanny valley" effect — spice flavors that taste close to, but not exactly like, fermentation flavors and vice versa. They are near enough to seem like a good idea but far enough to compete. You see this quite often in spiced saisons, which are very often much less than the sum of their parts.

The yeast is already so characterful that the addition of spices only muddies the flavor; too many pieces in the orchestra, to go back to our metaphor. Think of characterful yeasts as additional spicing — you can use them, but make sure you have your base spices down, go cautiously (that is, ferment on the cool side to inhibit ester and phenol formation), and be prepared to find flavors that don't quite harmonize in the end.

MALT BILL

9 pounds Belgian Vienna malt (52%)

5 pounds Belgian 50 EBC amber malt (29%)

1.5 pounds Belgian 120 EBC caramel malt (9%)

1.5 pounds Belgian Special B malt (9%)

5.5 tablespoons burnt sugar syrup (added in the boil) (2%)

STEP MASH

Mash in at 113°F (45°C)

131°F (55°C) for 15 minutes

163°F (73°C) for 30 minutes

172°F (78°C) for 5 minutes

60-MINUTE BOIL

0.5 ounce Tettnanger, 55 minutes (5.0% AA, contribution of 7 IBU)

0.33 ounce German Tradition, 55 minutes (6.0% AA, contribution of 5 IBU)

5.5 tablespoons burnt sugar syrup, 55 minutes

0.75 ounce Spalt Select, 15 minutes (6.0% AA, contribution of 6 IBU)

¼ teaspoon licorice juice

ALEXIS BRIOL

—

ST. FEUILLIEN

Spice Infusions

Turn off the flame, and let steep for 5 minutes:

1 gram (¼ tsp) cinnamon powder

0.5 gram (⅛ tsp) chamomile

1.5 grams (⅜ tsp) curaçao orange peel

0.5 gram (⅛ tsp) bourbon vanilla bean (*Vanilla planifolia*), whole or chopped, either grade A or grade B. Use about one-quarter of a 7-inch bean.

Fermentation and Conditioning

Ferment at 68° to 72°F (20–22°C) until 4° P (1.016) with Wyeast 3787 or White Labs WLP530, then rack and condition for 2 weeks at around 44°F (7°C).

Package

Bottle-condition only.

- Expected OG: 23° P/1.096
- Expected TG: 4° P/1.016
- Expected ABV: 10.5%
- Expected bitterness: 18 IBU

Notes: Three of the malts Briol suggests are specific to Dingemans. These choices are not critical, but he is attempting to build color, body, and aromatics into the recipe. Burnt sugar is a specific type of sugar that differs from other dark sugars; if you can't find it at your homebrew store, look for a substitute at specialty stores that sell Caribbean ingredients. I searched high and low for licorice juice (or liquorice juice) and never found it. Substitute a half teaspoon of dry licorice.

NEXT STEPS

A few notes on the above recipe. Briol actually offered a couple of variations, the other a simpler version of the one detailed here. The grain bill was composed of pilsner and 100 EBC aroma malts in a 4:1 ratio. The mash and hop schedules were identical. In place of the four spices, he suggested just a half teaspoon (2 grams) of coriander. Both recipes are fairly typical of the kind of base beer you'd find in a bière de Noël.

Whether you're making the simplified or more elaborate version, the thing that really leaps out is the spicing: Briol calls for *tiny* amounts. Looking around at standard homebrew recipes offered by other writers, you'll find recipes with an order of magnitude more spicing. I think you could safely double these amounts without worrying about overdoing it (or even more than that). But don't. Start here, and pay attention to the results. You learn a lot more about spice when you can barely taste it than you do when it dominates the palate. In these minidoses your beer won't taste spiced — but it will have tastes added by spice. In small amounts the spices inflect other flavors more than offering their own unmistakable flavors. It's the reason the "spicy" flavors in St. Feuillien's beers hint at spice without offering definite evidence of their presence.

Once you discover the power of *suggesting* spice, then you can begin to use a heavier hand and let them come out of the shadows. In terms of ingredients spices are the most elusive to work with; you'll be many batches in before you begin to feel confident you understand spicing amounts and resultant flavors. That's another reason to start out at the low end and use rich, flavorful styles of beer that stand on their own.

Working with Spices

The first spice question that leaps to mind is, how much? And it's not a terrible one. But a couple of other questions should be asked first: what kind? and when? As a category, "spice" is broad, and it includes flowers, herbs, barks, seeds and pods, roots, fruits, and buds — and each one is more or less susceptible to the effects of heat. As a related corollary, think about whether the spice is fresh or dried. Where a spice may come in either form, you have to decide whether you want the greener, brighter flavors from the fresh version or the deeper dried versions. Also keep in mind that fresh herbs contain water, so are heavier than their dried counterparts. Add 1.5 to 2 times as much of them as you would dried herbs.

The answer to the type question will give you a sense of how to approach the next question, when to add the spice. Flowers, herbs, and fruits contain delicate volatile oils that will be destroyed by prolonged heat. Barks and seeds (cinnamon, nutmeg, peppercorns, and so on), conversely, may require heat to pull flavor out of their woody wrapper. Heat puts compounds in solution more quickly (boiling water makes coffee in minutes; cold water takes hours) but also does violence to them.

This is intuitive to the homebrewer, because it's the same process that happens with hops. This is the reason Briol only conducts warm infusions. In most cases it's safer to do warm infusions or add the spice in the last 1 to 5 minutes of active boil. But even this may be too much if what you're really after are the most delicate, aromatic elements from a spice. You don't make tea by boiling the herbs. You steep them. There's a lesson there.

The decision about quantity is tough because the strength of each spice differs. The brewer Doug Odell once gave advice I've found indispensable: make a tea and assess the potency of the spice you plan to use. Do it the way you would any tea; bring water to a boil, and then do an infusion, steeping for 5 minutes. This will at least give you a sense of the relative strength of the spices and give you a starting place. You can also blend your teas to see how the flavors work together. From there follow Briol's advice and use tiny amounts to begin with, steadily increasing them as you go along.

Finally, for fresh spices rich in essential oils, consider "dry-hopping" them. The same principle is at work. Adding hops during conditioning preserves the essential oils and produces the most vivid aromas. The delicate oils in flowers and herbs are consumed in the heat of the kettle, muting their expressiveness. After primary fermentation, dose your beer with herbs and flowers for a day or two, and then taste the beer. If you begin with a small infusion, you can always add more before packaging.

The Good, the Bad, and the Unusual

All brewers know a few go-to spices: coriander, orange peel, cinnamon, and vanilla. In the meantime, here is a (very) incomplete tip sheet.

Elderflower, hibiscus, jasmine, orange blossoms, rose petals. Flowers are delicate and subtle, but they can really add a lot to a beer. While floral scents sometimes remind people of soap, hops also sometimes remind people of flowers — so using blossoms can add an interesting, relatively familiar flavor to the mix. Definitely don't add these to the boil. Steep them briefly for 1 to 3 minutes or add to the conditioning tank.

Cardamom, grains of paradise, pink peppercorn. When people say they don't like spiced beers, they usually mean *overspiced* beers. Using cardamom and grains of paradise (which are in the same family) is a great way to overspice a beer. They're both extremely potent and also quite specific in their flavor. It's hard to use them as nuance, and their flavors are so particular, they usually distract. Pink peppercorns, which aren't related to true pepper, aren't as strong but have a very particular flavor that dominates beer. We're purely in the realm of the subjective here, so your mileage may vary, but be careful when using these spices.

Sagebrush, spruce, juniper. Most of the spices typical in beer come from Europe or Asia (dating to the period of European colonialism). But North America has a few great offerings as well. A program called "Beers Made by Walking" in Oregon and Colorado has uncovered some wonderful foraged ingredients. In particular, western sagebrush (*Artemisia tridentata*), spruce (*Picea sitchensis*), and juniper (*Juniperus communis*) have been used to great success. Sagebrush gives beer a tangy, savory flavor; spruce a sweet, tart, honeylike character; and juniper something like culinary (not soapy) lavender. We've only scratched the surface, but these hits suggest there may be many more out there.

Part 5

French & Italian
TRADITIONS

—

*I*f you start ticking off the great European brewing nations in your mind, France clocks in — by dint of the *bière de garde* style alone — perhaps eighth. Italy likely doesn't rate at all. Italy and France have so much going for them artistically and gastronomically that beer seems at best a marginal consideration. (This is true inside those countries as well as out.) In reality, though, Italy's new breweries may be Europe's most vibrant and eclectic, and France is not far behind.

Of the two, France's tradition is much older, being centered in the region around Lille, which is snuggled very near the Belgian border. Brewing dates back to a point in history prior to the creation of Belgium, when control of the region was traded among various European kings. Barley, wheat, and hops have been grown there for centuries, and Lille was one of the main centers of ale brewing in a band that ran east through Brussels and Cologne. It remained a major center until the early twentieth century, when lagers began to insinuate themselves into the French palate. Then came World War I, with a major front that cut right through this area and effectively wiped out French brewing. By the time the breweries were rebuilt following the two world wars, lager had become the default position in France, and ale breweries had to conform to modern preferences.

Italy never really had a beer culture. Austrian control of central Europe stretched at times into Italy, and lager brewing gained a small foothold with such breweries as Peroni (1846) and Moretti (1859). These breweries made the same types of light lager that proliferated throughout the world in the late nineteenth and early twentieth centuries, and there was nothing uniquely Italian about them.

The revival came first to France, in the 1970s, when breweries like Duyck (Jenlain), Castelain (Ch'ti), and La Choulette reintroduced ales — sort of. Their beers, which borrowed a name common before the world wars, bière de garde, are more closely related to bocks than anything else. They were malt focused, strong (6 to 8% ABV), and lagered. And popular. They helped steer the French back toward ales, making them more receptive to Belgian styles and eventually sparking a renaissance of small breweries that now make a broad range of more typical ales. They run the gamut from English- to American-style ales but lean toward rustic Belgian varieties and often incorporate local fruit, herbs, and spices.

Italy's new breweries didn't get started until just a couple of decades ago, in 1996, but they quickly developed lineages with distinctly Italian contours. Now they make fruity, hoppy lagers; balanced, complex sour ales; and hoppy ales that are lushly flavorful. They have been inspired by Belgium principally, but they have also borrowed from the United States, England, and Germany. What links Italian and

French beer producers is a love of food and a philosophy that instinctively creates beers to accompany local cuisines. If the hallmark of American brewing is intensity, in France and Italy — no matter what the style — it is complexity and balance.

Hallmarks of French and Italian Beers

Unlike many of the more famous brewing regions, these qualities may seem at times ineffable, but give them careful attention and you will begin to see how truly accomplished the beers from these two countries are.

RICH, NOT INTENSE, HOPPING. French hops are not well known to Americans, but they have been used to great effect to add an herbal quality that works as well with traditional bières de garde as spiced wheat ales. In Italy there's a whole lineage devoted to hoppy beers ostensibly in the American mode, except that the fruity, vibrant flavors are always more balanced and less intense.

GENTLE MALTS. When you think of the French love of bread and pastry, it's not surprising to learn that French malts are possibly the world's best. They make delicate, billowing base malts that are so soft and flavorful that bières de garde remain balanced even with almost no hopping. Italians also prize softer malts, generally eschewing crystal malts in favor of rounder base malts.

BALANCED TARTNESS. Both French and Italian brewers have embraced farmhouse ales that are only brushed by wild yeasts. But it is the Italians, using their knowledge of winemaking, who make the most accomplished tart ales in the world. When I traveled through Belgium, brewers there kept mentioning this to me — and it turned out to be exactly right. Italian wild ales are balanced by other flavors and never dominated by overly sour notes.

SUBTLE USE OF SPICE. French and Italian breweries seem to use spice in the brewery like they do in the kitchen — instinctively and gently. They also have a proclivity for local spices that give their beers a native taste.

This list could continue on, though the elements become ever more subtle — and this underscores the nature of the beers from these two countries. They are constructed of many subtle flavors rather than relying on any one. Yeast esters, water hardness, dry hopping — any of these elements may also contribute to the overall success of a beer, but they are like extra voices in a choir. Before you make a French or Italian beer, think of ways to add a pinch of flavor here and a pinch of flavor there — these styles depend on many small contributors to achieve their overall fullness of flavor.

CHAPTER 18

FRENCH BIÈRES DE GARDE

mericans have long slotted French bières de garde in with Belgian saisons in a single catchall category of "farmhouse ales." This is wrong, both historically and stylistically. The rustic beers made in farmhouses across the Nord-Pas-de-Calais did once very much resemble the rustic beers across the border. In the early twentieth century, lagers were beginning to replace farmhouse beers, and then came the First World War, which cut a swath directly through the heart of that brewing region. When local brewers were finally able to begin to reconstitute brewing decades later, after the Second World War, the lineage of rustic ales had been severed.

When breweries started up again after the wars, they largely took up the low-alcohol lagers that were popular with industrial workers. When breweries finally returned, ever so tentatively, to ales, they made products that used lagers as their reference point, not the old funky farmhouse ales. They were elegant and smooth, lagered to a burnished refinement. (In French *garde* means roughly what lager means in German — "to keep or store.")

Duyck was the first to make such a beer, with their popular brand Jenlain. It created the template for the modern bière de garde, and breweries such as La Choulette, Castelain, and St. Sylvestre began making similar versions. Bières de garde are typically strong, from 6.5 to 8.5% and very much malt forward. Some may have a trace of hops, but none has anything approaching insistent esters. Indeed, modern bières de garde are so much like lagers that they have much more in common with bocks than they do saisons.

EST **Brasserie St. Germain** 2003

AIX-NOULETTE, FRANCE

The little town of Aix-Noulette has barely four thousand souls but has long been an important location in the heart of the French brewing region. Long before brothers Stéphane and Vincent Bogaert joined Hervé Descamps to found St. Germain in 2003, Aix-Noulette was home to the Brasme brewery, which at one time made around two hundred thousand barrels of beer. An old tin Brasme sign hangs in the tasting room at St. Germain, and when Stéphane begins to tell the history of his brewery, he goes back much further, recounting the history of brewing in Nord-Pas-de-Calais, the rise of modern bière de garde in the 1970s, and, gesturing at the sign, the importance of their predecessors. Even beer people don't really think of France as a beer country, but Descamps and the Bogaerts mean to change that. "Everybody [in France] thinks Belgium when you say beer," Stéphane explains. "In this region we are not so famous compared to Belgian breweries — but the history is the same." To bring the focus back on local ales, St. Germain shows how truly French beer can really be by sourcing all their ingredients from the fields around the brewery. (There are very few places on earth where that's possible.) That even includes sugar from local beets (don't tell the English breweries), as well as chicory — a local specialty — and rhubarb. There are some limitations, though. Although France has some of the best barley and wheat in the world — no surprise in a country famous for its *boulangeries* — there are only a handful of local varieties of hops, though St. Germain is getting good at working with this narrow range.

And what looks like a limitation to the brewery has the effect of tasting like house character. While many of the classic bière de garde producers make beers with almost no hop flavor, St. Germain looks for a richer balance. Something about the local terroir produces rustic, herbal hops (similar to ones grown 40 miles away in Belgium), and in my favorite of the St. Germain beers, Page 24 Réserve Hildegarde (in two versions, pale and amber), the hops add a delicate flavor somewhere between lemon rind and wildflowers. Bières de garde are not powerfully flavored beers, and neither are St. Germain's. But they are the most characterful of the traditional types, and the closest to the American palate.

Understanding Bières de Garde

Saisons and bières de garde are often clumped together in a category only a marketer could love — "farmhouse ales." It's wonderfully evocative but doesn't tell you anything about the beer. And anyone who's sampled saisons such as Blaugies's and Dupont's as well as bières de garde such as Ch'ti, Jenlain, and La Choulette can attest to this: they don't *taste* anything alike. They do share a common history, but the lines diverged nearly a century ago. The reason is war and its aftermath.

When you drive around the countryside near Lille, you see cemetery after cemetery — the dead, buried near where they were killed in the horrible trenches of World War I. The battlefields are scattered throughout this region. The day I visited St. Germain, we were greeted by folks from Brasserie Castelain and ate lunch near a cemetery of Canadian dead. What the First World War didn't destroy, the Second helped finish off. By 1945, 90 percent of the French breweries had been destroyed.

When ales started coming back to the Nord-Pas-de-Calais, they bore a striking resemblance to the beers that replaced them — and looked nothing like the saisons across the Belgian border. Although most modern bières de garde are ales, they are big, heavy beers, from 6.5% up, and always focus on a velvety smoothness. Cold fermentation and lagering help bring this about, and the resulting beers, burnished and malt scented, are so soft you can't perceive the sometimes mighty alcohol cosseted within the malty folds.

Brewing a Bière de Garde

The classic bière de garde is a light-amber beer (*ambrée* in French) of around 7% alcohol, though there's actually a family within the style. Alain Dhaussy of Brasserie La Choulette believes this is a holdover from the nineteenth-century ales that were boiled for hours. Blonds and browns (brune) are also common — though blonds are a postwar innovation. From a sensory perspective the most important element is malt, and if you can source French grain, you'll get a more authentic profile. I find French malt and wheat to be redolent of a bakery; it even seems pillowy on the tongue, like a nice baguette. Specialty malts give ambers a toasty or caramel note and browns notes of dark fruit, toffee, or brown bread (and never roast).

Most of the bigger names in bières de garde make their beers with nearly no hop character. Since so many of them date back 30 years or more, this seems to be an artifact of the flavorless lager age, and as tastes evolve, some bières de garde are getting spiced with a delicate layer of herbal hops. Buy a bottle of Saint Sylvestre Gavroche or Duyck Jenlain Ambrée or La Choulette Ambrée and see how they manage to make big beers (they're all 7.5% plus) palatable, with next to no hopping. They're big, bouncy beers, generally quite thick bodied, yet they are eminently drinkable. The balance is between alcohol and malt, not malt and hop. When breweries such as St. Germain do add grassy hops to the mix, they're an accent to this typical balance point.

According to tradition, the essence of bière de garde is lagering, even though the effect is subtle. It creates the smooth balance the style is known for. It is so subtle that some breweries lager only for 2 to 3 weeks (St. Germain), though others still conduct crazy-long lagering (Castelain goes for 6 to 12 weeks, depending on the beer's strength). Cold lagering has the effect of creating clarion beers, and this is another important benefit (bières de garde should never have a rustic cloudiness). Some people, when tasting bières de garde, find fruity elements (tasting notes often mention peach, dates, grapes), but these usually come from the malts, not the yeast, and I harbor a theory that the slow lagering helps encourage them. (This is only a theory.)

BIÈRE DE GARDE

VINCENT BOGAERT,
STÉPHANE BOGAERT,
AND
HERVÉ DESCAMPS

—

ST. GERMAIN

MALT BILL

9.5 pounds French pilsner (84%)

1.75 pounds Munich (16%)

STEP MASH

If possible, start with 95°F (35°C) water and raise to 145°F (63°C)

145°F (63°C) for 25 minutes

165°F (74°C) for 35 minutes

Sparge at 169°F (76°C)

80-MINUTE BOIL

0.75 ounce Brewer's Gold, 60 minutes (9% AA, contribution of 23 IBU)

0.33 ounce Brewer's Gold, 30 minutes (9% AA, contribution of 8 IBU)

0.5 ounce Goldings, 5 minutes (5% AA, contribution of 0–5 IBU)

FERMENTATION AND CONDITIONING

St. Germain recommends fermenting with Safale S-04 yeast, a strain from Whitbread, at 75°F (24°C). (Wyeast 1099 or White Labs WLP017 are good substitutes.) Lager as cold as possible (down to freezing) for 3 weeks.

PACKAGE

Bottle-condition or keg after lagering.

- Expected OG: 14° P/1.057

- Expected TG: 3° P/1.012

- Expected ABV: 5.5%

- Expected bitterness: 30–32 IBU

Notes: The most unusual element of this process is the very high mash rest at 165°F (74°C). This is designed to preserve unfermentable sugars that give bière de garde its smoothness. "Bières de garde are mostly sweet and not too hoppy," Stéphane Bogaert says. "It can help in having a more rounded beer with a strong body. The difficulty is to have a nice balance between maltiness and bitterness." Two rests at 145°F (63°C) and 165°F (74°C) are unusual — but so is a bière de garde.

Bogaert recommends Castle Malting's 25 EBC Munich, but substitute any 10L version you can find (French and Belgian are the best). The hops used at St. Germain are actually grown locally. Since you're not going to find the Brewer's Gold and Goldings that grow around there, you can substitute French varieties. Strisselspalt is the classic French landrace hop, but newer varieties Triskel and Aramis are available. The suggested yeast will create noticeable fruitiness at 75°F (24°C) — a quirk of St. Germain's house character. If you want a more neutral palate, ferment colder or try White Labs WLP072 or Wyeast 1007. It's even kosher to use a lager yeast when making bière de garde (Wyeast 2112 is a good choice).

NEXT STEPS

St. Germain offers a relatively low-alcohol formulation for bière de garde. This recipe scales up without many difficulties. For an 8% bière de garde, shoot for about 45 IBUs to keep the balance point in the same place. You can vary the color by tinkering with the pilsner/Munich blend. La Choulette uses medium amber crystal and a tiny dash of black malt to add color. For bigger bières de garde, add a week for lagering at a minimum.

There is a way to bring a bit of the past into modern bières de garde without changing their character. It is suggested by La Choulette's Alain Dhaussy when he noted to me that "the use of special [crystal] malt gives more color and a more or less pronounced taste of caramel to recall the long cooking of the beginning of the century." But of course, you can also achieve this with the "long cooking" that was typical of breweries 150 years ago. Boiling wort will eventually darken it. Laymen call this "caramelization," but the wort is actually going through a Maillard reaction as it deepens in color.

If you start with pilsner malt, it will take several hours to deepen it to amber. Along the way, though, the wort will pick up flavors you can't get any other way: sweet berry and honey notes along with rich, portlike ones. Interestingly, the process doesn't result in caramel flavors. Long boiling also has a pronounced effect on the feel of the beer. It creates a thick, velvety texture, one very much in keeping with modern bières de garde.

If you attempt a longer boil, there are two things to keep in mind. First, you'll need to start with a lot more liquid if you want to end up with 5 gallons. How much? That's hard to guess and depends on the dimensions of your brew kettle, heat intensity, ambient humidity, and other factors. Some homebrew algorithms use 14 percent per hour as a standard evaporation rate. At that rate you'd need to start with 9 gallons of wort to end up with 5 gallons of beer for even a 4-hour boil. But those calculations start looking very different if your evaporation rate is only 10 percent. Of course, all of this is going to affect your gravity as well. My recommendation is to start modestly and add water back to the boil if needed once you're within spitting distance of the end.

The other consideration is hops. According to Lacambre, nineteenth-century brewers regularly boiled their wort with hops for the duration of the boil. (Of one long-boiled beer, he wrote, "The taste is far from being very pleasant indeed, for it is bitter, harsh, and somewhat astringent." After a marathon boil with hops, I don't doubt it.) I'd skip that. Gigantic Brewing makes a beer each year called Massive! that they boil for 9 hours. They hop as you would any beer, with the bitter charge going in with an hour left in the boil. Given the heightened sweet flavors and heaviness that comes from the long boil, you can start with 90 minutes left in the boil without adding unnecessarily harsh flavors. Ninety-minute hops have a slightly sharper quality, as though they've embedded their lupulin claws more deeply into the beer.

"SPECIAL FLAVOR"

In his famous account of mid-nineteenth-century French and Belgian brewing, *Traité Complet de la Fabrication des Bières*, Georges Lacambre described his encounter with the *bières brunes des Flandres*:

> Boiling of these beers is longer and stronger than *uytzet*: commonly the boiling of these beers is 15 to 18 and even 20 hours in many breweries. The aim here is especially to color the beer, as well as [adding] stability and the special flavor that the wort gains by this long boil.

(TRANSLATION BY RANDY MOSHER)

Long boils were very common in Belgium and France at the time. Especially in Flanders, where Lacambre found this beer, drinkers prized long boils. A 9-hour boil will turn a beer made with pilsner malt ruby; one can only imagine what happens after 20 hours. The flavor is distinctive as well, and while some unscrupulous brewers stained their worts with the mineral lime, they couldn't counterfeit that "special flavor" any other way.

CHAPTER 19

RUSTIC FRENCH ALES

s we saw in the previous chapter, the modern tradition of French bière de garde was a reboot of an older, more rustic beer dating to the early twentieth century, also called, confusingly, bière de garde. That earlier line may have been severed, but memory of it was not. As Belgian saisons — themselves barely rescued from extinction — began to revive themselves across the border in Belgium, brewers such as Thiriez and Brasserie Au Baron wondered about France's farmhouse history. Was there a way to reconstruct the French farmhouse tradition without just importing it wholesale from Belgium?

The result was a melding of old and new. The French tradition of laying down strong ales in a manner similar to lager had become a point of national pride (there was even talk of an *appellation d'origine contrôlée*), and this element is a fixture of brewing in the Nord-Pas-de-Calais. What changed was the emphasis on yeast character and a more florid flavor palette. Rustic French ales are fermented warmer with wilder yeasts than traditional bières de garde to produce layered flavors of esters, phenols, and funkiness. French brewers have also rediscovered their love of herbs and spices, as well as rustic grains. These hybrid bières de garde are not as offbeat as Belgian saisons; they still aim for the smoothness and balance of the older ale-brewing tradition. They have taken a middle way, a road that may well lead to the future.

EST **Brasserie Thiriez** 1996
ESQUELBECQ, FRANCE

Like many folks in Lille, in Nord-Pas-de-Calais, the heart of the French brewing region, Daniel Thiriez found his way to beer through the bières de garde that started gaining popularity in the late 1970s. His parents were pilsner drinkers — typical for most of the twentieth century — but when Thiriez tried Duyck's Jenlain, his understanding of beer changed. It planted a seed in his mind that grew over the 11 years he worked as a human resources manager at a local company. In the mid-1990s, he began to wonder whether he could make a living brewing characteristically French farmhouse ales, with a Belgian twist.

"My idea was very simple: Northern France has a long tradition about brewing, and most people enjoy beer very much, but there were few traditional remaining breweries (Jenlain, Choulette, Ch'ti), and the bière de garde style was sort of limited, with smooth, rather strong and malt-oriented beers. So I was convinced that the style, combined with the Belgian saison style, could offer different beers: drier; more drinkable; more balanced between cereals, yeast, and hops; lower alcohol; more bitterness. I also had the influence from some British ales and bitters (even though local people do not appreciate [them])."

He found a rustic little building that had been a brewery in Esquelbecq and began working on the formulation for a beer with those qualities. The most important step was finding a yeast strain. Thiriez's came from the Institut Meurice in Brussels, which maintained a large collection. He worked with the director at the time, Alain Debourg, to find exactly the strain that would bring Thiriez's vision to life. The one he settled on is familiar to American brewers and homebrewers — it's known as the "French Saison" strain at Wyeast (3711). That choice was propitious; not only did it make Thiriez the leader of the "new" bière de garde tradition, but it helped create an entirely new palate in France.

Understanding Rustic French Ales

If rustic French ales are just a move back toward older forms of farmhouse ales, aren't they just a version of the Belgian saison? Yes and no. Brewers such as Thiriez admire the Belgian tradition enormously. Indeed, the French are enamored of the beers of their smaller neighbor, sometimes to the exclusion of their own ales. Thiriez cites saisons, abbey ales, and gueuze as his central influences.

But brewers of the Nord-Pas-de-Calais see themselves as very much part of the French tradition. Even when they don't brew classic French bières de garde, brewers acknowledge their debt to them. Hence rustic French ales are typically lagered (or garded) at cool temperatures. This has the effect of smoothing the beers and softening the edges. The French seem more interested in hops than the Belgians as well. Together, the slightly less vivid yeast expression and more insistent hopping place them closer to the American palate. If you're looking for the "French" in a saison, experiment with lagering times. Thiriez recommends a relatively short period, but aging a month or more will produce subtly different results.

Thiriez's range includes a line of hoppy, characterful farmhouse ales. In addition to sporting herbal bouquets, they are earthy and etched with a tracery of lemony-to-lavender esters and just a hint of wild funk. They seem the very definition of "farmhouse" but feature approachable flavors that give them broad appeal. Breweries in the United States have agreed, and although everyone acknowledges Dupont's primacy in the world of saisons, Thiriez's are actually the kind of rustic beers American brewers more often emulate. When you see a "saison" on the menu at your local brewery, it may owe a greater debt to Thiriez than to Dupont.

THIRIEZ'S YEAST

Daniel Thiriez is a name known to very few Americans, yet he has nevertheless had substantial influence on American brewing. His yeast was the source of Wyeast's 3711 strain, one of the first commercial saison strains available, and one that brewers love for its familiar citrus esters. It has changed somewhat since it was cultured by Wyeast, and Thiriez points out that it is hugely attenuative, unlike his. (Some brewers have seen their saisons approach 1.000 terminal gravity.)

He nevertheless recognizes it. "Some flavors may be rather close," he acknowledges. As Americans have developed a taste for saison, they are more attracted to the esters that are like those in the 3711 strain than in Dupont's much funkier phenolic yeast.

Brewing a Rustic French Ale

Rustic French ales form a continuum, not a style. Three things to consider are strength, color, and hop use. The classic French ales are amber or *"ambrée,"* but you also find blonds and browns. Traditional bières de garde are strong (6.5–8.5%), but rustic ales are occasionally less so (some are as low as 5%). Finally, rustic ales typically exhibit at least some hop character and may be quite bitter. Other variations include the additions of spice or mixed yeast strains that include *Brettanomyces*. The one thing that links all these various elements together is lagering followed by bottle conditioning.

This recipe for rustic French ale is similar to Thiriez's Blonde d'Esquelbecq. France is home to some of the world's best barley and wheat, and Thiriez recommends using it if you can find it. (It's so good, even Germans sometimes use it.) He is less finicky about using French hops, but you might consider substitutions if you can find them; French hops display a unique herbal terroir that accentuates the Frenchness of these ales.

> ## MALT BILL
>
> 10.5 pounds French or Belgian pilsner malt
>
> *Or*
>
> 9.5 pounds French or Belgian pilsner malt (91%)
>
> 1 pound wheat malt (9%)

STEP MASH

113°F (45°C) for 15 minutes

144 to 147°F (62–64°C) for 45 minutes

162°F (72°C) for 20 minutes

80-MINUTE BOIL

1.5 ounces Brewer's Gold, 60 minutes (6% AA, contribution of 30 IBU)

1 ounce Czech Saaz, 10 minutes (4% AA, contribution of 5 IBU)

FERMENTATION AND CONDITIONING

Ferment with Wyeast 3711 at 72°F (22°C) for about 5 days. Cool to 54°F (12°C) and condition for 2 weeks; finish out with a week at around 40°F (4°C).

PACKAGE

It's best if the beers go through a secondary fermentation in the bottle at room temperature. This is the classic presentation, and the secondary fermentation will substantially change the beer's ester profile.

- Expected OG: 14° P/1.057
- Expected TG: 2.5° P/1.011
- Expected ABV: 6.5%
- Expected bitterness: 35 IBU

DANIEL THIRIEZ

BRASSERIE THIRIEZ

Notes: Thiriez recommends French spring barley for the pilsner base malt. He prefers French-grown Brewer's Gold hops and Strisselspalt from Alsace for the ambrée (see Next Steps). Since these are hard to source, substitute English Brewer's Gold for the French and Mt. Hood for Strisselspalt, with adjustments to proportions depending on alpha acids. (If y.ou can source any French-grown hop varieties, consider those as well. Thiriez is much impressed with Alsace-grown Triskel and Aramis.)

After the initial fermentation, ABV will be around 6.1% but will rise to 6.5% after secondary fermentation in the bottle. Because the 3711 strain is so much more attenuative, I've had some luck slowing down fermentation by racking after it has dropped to 1.015. Because the esters develop early in fermentation, you don't lose much character by hitting the brakes at 1.010.

NEXT STEPS

If you want to try a classic French amber, Daniel Thiriez suggests these substitutions. For the malt bill, 75 percent pilsner malt can be combined with 12.5 percent light caramel (50–60 EBC/25–30 L) and 12.5 percent medium caramel (100–120 EBC/50–60 L), *or* 10 percent Vienna or biscuit malt along with 7.5 percent each of light and medium caramel. Mash and hopping schedules are the same, except Thiriez recommends Strisselspalt in place of Saaz for aroma. The target IBUs are 25 rather than 35. He does not personally use spice but suggests bitter orange peel, coriander, or cinnamon "in very limited quantities" to accentuate the flavors.

One of the typical amber bières de garde will taste especially smooth because of the caramel malts and long lagering time. With a rustic interpretation you're going to add some yeast character that will nudge it in the direction of a saison. Keep in mind that caramel malts and rustic yeasts don't harmonize especially well; start fermentation at 68°F (20°C) to inhibit the formation of esters and phenols. This is not an easy beer to brew well, but it makes for an absolutely wonderful autumnal tipple if you can pull it off.

CHAPTER 20

ITALIAN LAGERS

Superficially, Italian lagers may resemble their forebears to the north. They have the same colors and names, and their labels may even have the same Gothic scripts favored by Bavarian breweries. But put them to your nose and tongue for analysis, and you find subtle aromas of orange blossom, say, or rose — and possibly more than just a few hops. They taste fuller and richer and contain narrow shafts of fruit flavors.

Like Americans, Italians had no national tradition to hinder them, so they freely borrowed not only from Germans and Czechs but selected practices from the English and American repertoire as well. But the thing that makes these beers so characteristically Italian is their luxurious balance, a fact that is highlighted perfectly when these beers come into play at the dinner table.

EST Birrificio Italiano 1996
LURAGO MARINONE, ITALY

It is not often that you can find a single source for anything, but when you write the history of Italian lagers, you start with Birrificio Italiano. Modern Italian brewing dates back only to 1996, when two pioneers began the two lineages that now characterize it. The ale line was founded by Teo Musso, and it was Birrificio Italiano's Agostino Arioli who cut the path to lagers.

When he was about 20, Arioli began homebrewing ("because I was a lazy student," he jokes). As his hobby became more serious, he followed his interest to Germany where he took classes that would help him as a brewer. He bounced around learning the trade in Germany, England, and Canada before opening Italiano. His first beers leaned heavily on his original German influences, but he didn't stop there.

His most famous beer, Tipopils, is characteristic of his multinational approach. "I [had] visited some English brewers and studied some more about English cask beer. I knew that they were using dry hop in the cask. I thought, why don't I do this with my Tipopils?" The finished product is something like a German kellerbier crossed with an English cask ale. It is intensely aromatic, full, and rich — one of the best pilsners made in the world. That's not just idle praise, either; it was an enormously influential beer, creating a standard for Italian lagers that many other breweries follow. And not just in Italy: Matt Brynildson readily cites Tipopils as the inspiration for Firestone Walker's Pivo Pils.

Understanding Italian Lagers

In my travels throughout the beer country in the north of Italy, I kept encountering beers that were amazingly balanced, no matter what the style. The hoppy beers were not too hoppy; the sour beers were not too sour. It is not a characteristic that the brewers even seemed aware of. Eventually, after much prodding, I got Arioli to ponder this a bit, and what he came up with was instructive. "These beers are beers you drink with your senses more than with your brain. *Birra da meditazione* — meditation beers. When you drink a meditation beer, you really *think* about it. 'This taste reminds me of flowers; this taste reminds me of the food my aunt used to prepare me.' So you're really thinking about the beer."

With lagers this means tweaking and pulling until you've extracted a bit of extra flavor from each element of the beer, always making sure to keep them in balance. I think this comes from the Italians' instinctive sense of flavor. To use a food analogy, the Italians make beers that are like sauces simmered for hours with a complex blend of herbs and spices, not blazing preparations dominated by chili peppers.

Arioli agrees that it is a strong possibility. "In Italy we grow up where you can spend *hours and hours* discussing food. The whole family, we can discuss food for a long time. 'This is better; last time was worse. It's overcooked, or it's too rare.' Really, we talk about food a lot. We care a lot about food. So this probably automatically requires us to brew beers that can fit with our sense of what is pleasant, what is balanced."

Italians are attracted to many of the same kinds of beers that Americans are, but the approach is not toward extreme flavors. Italian lagers follow the inclination of American lagers toward more flavor, but only to a point. If there are hops, they are not too bitter or aromatic; if there are esters from warmer fermentation, they don't become a distraction. Think about all the possible elements that contribute flavor and amp them up a bit over the German approach — but all together, in a kind of symphony.

These beers are beers you drink with your senses more than with your brain. They are *birra da meditazione* — meditation beers. When you drink a meditation beer, you really *think* about it.

— AGOSTINO ARIOLI, BIRRIFICIO ITALIANO

Brewing an Italian Lager

Italians don't put down beer the way Germans do, by the liter. They prefer beers that are a little stronger, a little more flavorful, designed to be savored. At Birrificio di Como Andrea Bravi says, "I don't drink a lot of beer — maybe one glass or two. So it should have a good body and be strong." Arioli agrees. "When we are talking about lager, especially pils beer, Italian beers are more hoppy, more fruity, and also a bit more malty." Tipopils certainly fits this description, but so does another of Arioli's lagers, Bibock — an assertive, slightly smoky dark bock brimming with flavor.

Arioli's approach seems to be to start with a German model and trick it out. Tipopils has drawn so much attention for its dry hopping, but it has other characteristics that make it distinctive. I think the most important element is fermentation temperature. "We ferment at higher temperatures, and this makes a certain difference," Arioli says. While it's typical to ferment in the middle 40s F (7°C), Arioli goes higher, as much as 10°F (6°C). The coldest he ferments is around 52°F (11°C). We know that higher fermentation temperatures produce more esters, but I think there may be more going on than that.

Arioli also dry-hops during primary fermentation with Tipopils. There may well be more happening with the biochemistry than just ester production — the hoppy character he gets is certainly unusual. It's richer and more integrated, *deeper* somehow, than in any other lager I've tried. He dry-hops at very low levels (30 grams/hectoliter in primary, 70 g/hL during maturation) but nevertheless gets massive character.

Arioli is also far more attentive to pH than other brewers I've spoken to — and he likes it low (more on that in Next Steps.) He starts with a low mash pH and suggests adjusting your sparge liquor to a pH of 5.5. I was surprised by this, so he suggested an experiment. "If you adjust pH at the beginning, watch the results. Split your wort using natural pH versus adjusted pH." He added, "Beginning fermentation pH is really important," and he shoots for 5.1. I must have looked a little skeptical about this, but he smiled and joked, "Most homebrewers love suffering, so this is the right way to do it."

MALT BILL

8 pounds pilsner malt (99%)

2 ounces CaraMunich II malt (1%)

STEP MASH

126°F (52°C) for 10 minutes

151°F (66°C) for 30 minutes (until iodine negative)

171°F (77°C) mash out

Note: Mash pH should be 5.2–5.3; sparge liquor should be pH 5.5. See notes for more.

75-MINUTE BOIL

0.75 ounce German Northern Brewer, 60 minutes (8.0% AA, contribution of 22 IBU)

0.5 ounce Perle, 45 minutes (8.0% AA, contribution of 13 IBU)

1 ounce Hallertauer Mittelfrüh after flameout (4.0% AA, contribution of 0 IBU)

0.25 ounce Saphir after flameout (3.5% AA, contribution of 0 IBU)

FERMENTATION AND CONDITIONING

Ferment with a standard lager yeast at 52°F (11°C) for a week — Wyeast 2206/2308 or White Labs WLP830/WLP833 are great, or the strain of your choice. Dry-hop during primary with 0.25 ounce Saphir or Hallertauer Mittelfrüh. Mature for 3–4 weeks at 32°F (0°C). During maturation, dry-hop with 0.6 ounce Saphir.

PACKAGE

Keg is best, but "re-fermentation in the bottle is not a catastrophe."

AGOSTINO
ARIOLI
—
BIRRIFICIO
ITALIANO

- Expected OG: 11.5° P/1.046

- Expected TG: 2° P/1.008

- Expected ABV: 5.0%

- Expected bitterness: 30–40 IBU

Notes: To achieve a low mash pH, Arioli adds lactic acid. You could use lactic or phosphoric acid or substitute 5 percent of the pilsner malt with acidulated malt; use a pH meter or strips to assess the pH. Arioli also encourages a pH of 5.1 at the start of fermentation, which may require another acid adjustment. "Fresh yeast is critical. Do at least one starter; two is best." Do not rack more than once. Arioli, fastidious about oxygen, says, "If you transfer from one carboy to another, evacuate with CO_2." (I guess he thinks you *really* want to suffer.)

NEXT STEPS

The recipe above is fairly straightforward — if unusual — though Arioli would encourage you to experiment with malt and hop types as you wish. What I found fascinating with the recipe was Arioli's insistence on acidifying everything as he went along. For most of the recipes in this book, I traded e-mails or sometimes phone calls with the brewers, but Arioli and I discussed this over pints of Deschutes beer when he visited Portland in 2015. That allowed me to witness firsthand just how committed he was to this pH issue. So let's do some unpacking.

In the main, pH is one of those details that affects beer subtly; the chemistry more or less takes care of itself, which is why brewers were able to make beer long before they ever heard of a hydrogen ion. But different pHs can affect the way a beer feels and tastes, so adjustments in one direction or the other do affect the finished beer. In the mash, proteins and starches are broken down into simpler molecules by specific enzymes — and those enzymes work within different optimal pH ranges: glucanase (5.0), protease (4.5–4.7), and amylase (5.1–5.8). Water has a pH of roughly 7.0, but grains lower the pH within the mash. Brewers shoot for a pH that averages the effect, somewhere between 5.2 and 5.6 — and most mashes will naturally fall within that range.

There are a couple of reasons to pay attention to mash pH. Some malts, such as Munich malts or adjunct malts, are enzymatically weak and need higher pH. Decoction mashes should start out with a somewhat higher pH, 5.4 or above, because boiling the mash during the process will lower the pH. Higher mash pH also helps extract color (which ain't great when you're making a pilsner).

On the flip side a low-pH mash (5.2 or 5.3) has several benefits. It improves the efficiency of the process, lowers wort viscosity (which improves filtration), improves haze stability, and increases attenuation — all important in the commercial brewery. More important for the homebrewer are these advantages: low pH is believed to result in better flavor (more rounded and soft, yet crisp and characterful), a more pleasant bitterness, and denser, more lasting foam.

Arioli makes it a point to lower his liquor's pH for sparging as well. Why? Because higher pH may extract tannins from the husk of the grain, giving the beer a harsh astringency (which, in slight beers like pilsners, can be observable). Tannin solubility is affected by both high temperatures (which is one reason to sparge around 170°F [77°C]) and water alkalinity. Below a threshold of 6.0, water won't extract tannins. Arioli's suggestion of 5.5 ensures no tannins are extracted.

In the kettle the central effect of pH has to do with iso-alpha acid solubility and its effect on the flavor of the beer. The higher the pH, the more acids are extracted. Many brewers feel that the bitterness from higher-pH worts is harsh, though. The same reaction that causes tannins to be extracted in high-pH sparges is at work with hop acids, so it makes sense. (A lot of what brewers believe, from the effect of first-wort hopping to low mash pH to low kettle pH, is based on impression, however. Brewers also felt high cohumulone hops contributed to a harsh bitterness — but when tested, researchers at Oregon State University found no correlation between cohumulone levels and the perception of harshness.)

Finally, during fermentation, yeast naturally reduces the pH of its environment (that would be the beer) while raising its own internal pH. The biochemistry of the way yeast works means that this difference (higher pH inside the cell, lower pH outside) makes it easier for yeast to take up maltose, resulting in a healthy fermentation. This is the moment Arioli suggests adjusting the pH experimentally — dividing the wort into an amended, low-pH batch and leaving a portion at its native pH.

Final comments: Keep in mind that pH is affected by temperature, and all the values listed here refer to room-temperature pH. There are various ways to test for pH, from relatively expensive meters to cheap paper strips, with predictable advantages and disadvantages to both. If you're deeply nerdy and a lot smarter about chemistry than I am, John Palmer and Colin Kaminski get into water chemistry in very fine detail in *Water: A Comprehensive Guide for Brewers*.

Chestnut Beer

For centuries and probably millennia, Italians have eaten chestnuts; whole surely, but often ground into flour from which they made bread and cakes. Chestnuts served as a kind of backstop during hard times, when famine or war put the wheat harvest in jeopardy. It makes perfect sense, then, that Italian brewers would think: "I wonder if you could make it into beer?"

You can. Grown throughout Italy, chestnuts are put into the service of any number of beer styles. Lagers, though, because they are more malt friendly and subtle, serve as the best platform for this kind of beer. Chestnut trees are in the same family as oaks, and the nuts are starchy like acorns. Their effect on the beer is as much tactile as anything. The texture is thick and silky — almost oily — a bit like oats. The flavor can be roasty or smoky depending on the way the chestnut was prepared, and I sometimes detect the earthy flavor of root vegetables beneath the more obvious notes.

Andrea Bravi at Birrificio di Como made a chestnut lager called Birolla. He sampled several different flours before settling on the one he liked best, one in which the chestnuts were roasted over beech and that is tinged with smoke. "First I mash the chestnuts at 75°C (167°F) because the starch has to become gelatinized. Then we add the malt and water to get a good saccharification [preparing a typical lager]. In Italy people all have individual preferences, so I do milled chestnut, but someone else will use roasted chestnut, some others boiled chestnuts, some raw chestnuts — so, a lot of different beers."

You can use raw, boiled, or roasted chestnuts to make one of these. (They're gluten-free, and some breweries use them in place of wheat flour.) The flour is probably the easiest, and Italians make it for export. It's not cheap, though, so experiment with a pound or two. Follow Bravi's instructions about mashing, letting stand for an hour, and then adding to a traditional lager mash. I have found no information on the amount of sugars available in chestnuts, but it stands to reason that it's less than barley — your final gravity may be approximate.

CHAPTER 21

ITALIAN ALES

*I*talian ales fork into two traditions, but the tines are not especially far apart. The first and oldest was founded by Baladin's Teo Musso, who cribbed very heavily from the Belgian playbook. At Baladin Musso makes ales that could easily sneak into a Belgian café unnoticed: witbier, strong dark ales, Belgian pale ales, and saison. His beers go through warm fermentations and spend a time bottle-conditioning in a warm room. Musso's approach informed breweries that came afterward, and Italy for a time looked like a region of Belgium.

But eventually, the vibrantly hoppy beers of the United States exerted an influence on Italians. They shifted from a largely yeast-focused approach and started accentuating hops, and soon "IPA" and "American pale ale" began to appear on beer labels. They, too, were vibrantly hoppy — but they weren't exactly in the American mode. Italian IPAs were lighter in color and body, dry, and not so bitter. They were marked more by esters than are American hoppy ales, sometimes intensely so, and the flavors were different: berry, bergamot, rose, apricot. By twinning the Belgian tradition of expressive yeasts with the American tradition of expressive hops, they managed to invent a native tradition all their own.

EST **Birra Toccalmatto** 2008
FIDENZA, ITALY

Before he imagined opening a brewery, Bruno Carilli worked in the food industry doing logistics and purchasing. When I asked him to describe his background, he recited that first bit with a kind of melancholy. His career took a turn when he started working for the brewing giant Carlsberg (in Italy), sparking his interest in beer. (Here his tone of voice took an upbeat turn.) While he was there, he learned a lot about hops — the relevance of which will soon be evident — and started homebrewing as well.

This gathering interest coincided with the Italian beer renaissance and led Carilli to leave the corporate life and open a little brewery in the town of Fidenza in Parma in 2008. Unlike some of the first-wave breweries that preceded him, Carilli didn't have to experiment with different styles to find his voice: he came into brewing knowing exactly what kind of beers he wanted to brew. "I have always loved the hoppy beers," he said, pointing to a lineup that includes seven

American-style pale ales or IPAs. His first beer, not by chance, was called Re Hop (King Hop) — the label shows a regal hop creature dressed in an ermine robe.

Many Italian breweries are now doing hoppy ales, but a few, such as Carilli's, Milan's Lambrate, and Birra Del Borgo in Borgorose, have not only mastered the art of hops but have given their beers a wholly original twist. They are not derivative American knockoffs. Carilli, in particular, gets a distinctive house character in his hoppy ales that suggests tropical fruits with an Asian twist. He's even able to do this with his saisons, another passion of Carilli's. He experiments broadly, blending American, German, and South Pacific hops to create his fruity concoctions, which are unlike any beers you'll find in America.

Understanding Italian Ales

When American homebrewers began going pro back in the late '70s and early '80s, they had no template to work with. They were trying to figure out the beers even as they were making them. That was a major liability early on — a lot of the first microbrewed beer was pretty bad — but it came to be a huge asset. Freed from national tradition, they could pick and choose the techniques that seemed valuable. Italians were in exactly the same boat, with one exception — they could also crib from the now-extant American tradition.

Carilli agrees. "Our fortune is that we have no tradition, so we are quite free to experiment." In his case, the three major elements of his beer come from three different national traditions. His original brewery resembled an English kit and was outfitted to handle post–kettle hop additions. He likewise regularly uses an English yeast strain (as well as the Chico 1056 strain so many Americans use).

But he also has a warm room, and every one of his beers gets a secondary fermentation there — even lagers. This is a big clue to how the Italians squeeze more fruit from the hops; they accent the fruitiness with esters. But unlike the Belgians, who regularly use sugar to thin out the body of their beers, most Italians use all grain. This means the malt base more easily supports a heavy load of bitterness. Finally, Carilli has an American's love of hops, though he was ahead of most Americans by expressing that love through flavorful and aromatic late additions.

All of these collude to make hoppy ales that are lightly sweet, fruity, comparatively less bitter than American examples, and very aromatic. One of Carilli's favorite words is "extreme," and he sounds a lot like gung ho Americans who make hop tinctures and face-melting IPAs. But his beers aren't actually extreme in the least.

They're full of flavor and aroma, but they're soft and harmonious. This is typical for the Italian approach, where balance is a reflexive habit.

Brewing an Italian Ale

Think of brewing an Italian ale as using components from Belgian, English, and American traditions. Italians start by approaching the malts from a Belgian or German perspective; that is, rich base malts as the foundation of flavor. Carilli makes no secret of the influence American beers have had on him, but there is one thing he doesn't love. "I only use pilsner malts in my beers. I don't like so much caramel in the beer, so much body." This is typical. Italian ales may have color, but they don't have the density of some American IPAs nor the sometimes sticky crystal-malt sweetness. He takes a continental approach to adding color, using Vienna, Munich, or other noncrystal malts.

> **Italian ales may have color, but they don't have the density of some American IPAs nor the sometimes sticky crystal-malt sweetness.**

Next, Italians brew with simple step or single-infusion mashes. They're looking for fermentability and a bit of flavor. I was surprised to find a wood-clad English kit at Toccalmatto (they have since expanded to a bigger, more modern brewhouse). Carilli brews a bit like an English brewer, too, adding an infusion of hops in post-boil. This has become an American approach as well, but the Italians were often more influenced by British brewers and tumbled to this approach more quickly than Americans did. They hop like Americans, focusing on flavor and aroma additions later in the boil, and then regularly dry-hop during conditioning; again, like Americans.

Fermentation and conditioning are where the Belgian influence comes in. The main difference between Italian hoppy ales and American versions is the way Italians use esters to boost fruitiness. Carilli uses an English strain, and I suspect this is common; the ester profiles are more like English than Belgian strains. Carilli puts his beer through a secondary fermentation in the bottle, and this further enhances those esters that result in such sensual, fruit-forward beers.

Carilli was so busy during the writing of this book that he was unable to offer a recipe, so I've based the following on the information I collected when I visited Toccalmatto a few years back.

STEP MASH

146°F (63°C) for 35 minutes

162°F (72°C) for 20 minutes

60-MINUTE BOIL

0.33 ounce Citra, 60 minutes (11.0% AA, contribution of 12 IBU)

0.33 ounce Galaxy, 60 minutes (14.0% AA, contribution of 16 IBU)

0.25 ounce Citra, 15 minutes (11.0% AA, contribution of 5 IBU)

0.25 ounce Galaxy, 15 minutes (14.0% AA, contribution of 6 IBU)

0.25 ounce Sorachi Ace, 15 minutes (11.0% AA, contribution of 5 IBU)

0.5 ounce Galaxy postboil (14.0% AA, contribution of 4 IBU)

0.5 ounce Amarillo postboil (8.5% AA, contribution of 3 IBU)

0.5 ounce Sorachi Ace postboil (11.0% AA, contribution of 5 IBU)

FERMENTATION AND CONDITIONING

Ferment with Wyeast 1968 or White Labs WLP002 at 70°F (21°C) until you reach terminal. Rouse yeast after terminal, and let sit for 2 more days to absorb diacetyl.

Optional: Dry-hop with an ounce of Amarillo, Citra, or Galaxy, or a blend equaling 1 ounce.

ITALIAN ALE

BASED ON RECIPES DESIGNED BY BRUNO CARILLI

PACKAGE

Bottle-condition only, at room temperature for at least 2 weeks.

- Expected OG: 15.3° P/1.062
- Expected TG: 3° P/1.012
- Expected ABV: 6.6%
- Expected bitterness: 55–60 IBU

Notes: Use acidulated malt to soften hops. This hop blend incorporates some of the varieties I kept hearing about at Italian breweries, but obviously, it's no more definitive than a blend in any American IPA. I included the controversial Sorachi Ace because it is a key hop in Carilli's flagship Zona Cesarini — as is Citra. The use of a postboil infusion in either a hop back or whirlpool addition is mandatory. The yeast strain suggested is Fuller's — different from the one Carilli uses — because it is lightly fruity but also reliable.

NEXT STEPS

I haven't had a chance to experiment too broadly with the myriad combinations offered by the different fruity yeast strains and hops available (a task that gets harder by the month as new hop varieties come on the market). Finding that precise blend of ester and hop oil could become a person's life work — though what pleasant work it would be. Nevertheless, you can get fairly far down the road just using fruity yeast strains — and don't foreclose the option of turning to Belgian yeasts — vivid hop blends, and bottle conditioning.

For Italians, the blending of traditions continues with hops. It fascinated me to hear how Italians regularly blended not only American and South Pacific hops but classic German varieties as well. This is part of that lack-of-tradition thing; Italians see no reason Hallertauer can't be used in combinations with New Zealand and American hops. (Even among Americans, who have developed their own firm views of the "right" way to brew, this is a heterodox approach.) Blending terroir is another way Italians manage to pull unexpected flavors from their hop additions. Hallertauer and Tettnang were in rotation a few years back, and I wouldn't be surprised if some of the new varieties, such as Hallertauer Blanc, Hull Melon, and Mandarina Bavaria, are now getting a workout.

SOUR AND WILD ITALIAN ALES

In addition to ales that trace their influence to California and Belgium, and lagers that look north to Bavaria, Italy has a third important brewing tradition: tart, barrel-aged beers. But if these appear similar to those made elsewhere in the world, don't be fooled. This vein of Italian brewing takes its cues from the local art of winemaking. Not only did Italian breweries begin using Italian wine casks to age their beers, they began to take lessons directly from vintners, making beer that is as sophisticated as any made in the world.

As with all beers Italian, those made with wild yeasts prize balance above intensity; they are nuanced, refined, and with their restrained acidity, excellent with food. That last point is the key to why, even after such a short time, Italians were turning out some of the best sour barrel-aged beers in the world. They already understood what a balanced beverage could do at the dinner table, and they had winemakers, vineyards, and wine barrels close at hand.

The best example of how this process unfolded is with Valter Loverier at LoverBeer. Before starting his brewery, he began speaking with winemakers in his native Piedmont. It is common for vintners to use the wild yeasts on the skins of grapes to ferment their wine, and this gave Loverier an idea. Why not use those same yeasts to inoculate beer? That's what he did once LoverBeer opened: he pitched grape must from Barbera d'Alba grapes, and put the batch into a wine foudre. The grapes not only inoculated that batch of wort but seeded the foudre with local yeasts and bacteria. Now the other batches of beer that spend time in that vat also pick up a little bit of Piedmont. "This is the philosophy of the brewery: to join, to have a fusion of the old recipes of the Flemish area, sometimes forgotten, with Piedmont winemaker's, and so we use wood, fruit, grapes." (This process is described in Part 7, Brewing Wild.)

Few have taken it as far as LoverBeer, but Birrificio Del Ducato, Birra Del Borgo, Birrificio Montegioco, Torrechiara (Panil), and others all make excellent, wine-barrel-aged sour beers.

Part 6

American TRADITION

e're witnessing something in the beer world as rare as the birth of a new indigenous language: the emergence of a new national brewing tradition. Like languages, brewing traditions mostly die off. They didn't used to be fused with entire countries but more often with regions or even single towns. In the nineteenth century dozens of indigenous brewing traditions could fairly be said to exist, but they were done in by the modern world — communications, industrialization, nationalization. In the twentieth century dozens died, and no new traditions took their place. In fact, the last one to emerge was the faceless, pan-national lager-brewing tradition that caused the death of so many of the others. The idea that a new tradition might develop organically would have seemed implausible — perhaps unthinkable — four decades ago.

What is national tradition? It's a cultural institution, invisible, yet strangely powerful. Like other cultural institutions, it is created and perpetuated by inter-action and familiarity. If you cross the border between Bavaria and Bohemia on a train, the landscape doesn't change; the climate and soil doesn't change. And yet the food in a Czech restaurant does not resemble German food.

When I first started reading about beer, I was amused by descriptions of how Belgians, admiring stouts and Scottish ales, decided to brew them at home — and promptly made Belgian ales that only vaguely gestured in the direction of the orig-inal styles. Brewing, for a Belgian, means strong, dry beers that go through second-ary fermentation in a bottle. It's just how you brew — you wouldn't dream of not making beer that way. All the great brewing countries have a distinctive approach that does not resemble the approach of even neighboring countries. Like cuisines, brewing traditions tend to stay within national borders.

Lo and behold, Americans have one, too. When Americans started brewing nonindustrial lagers 30-odd years ago, they imitated the beer styles brewed in Europe; many of which still serve as a decent counterfeit for the originals. But where the real change has happened is in America's embrace of hops and the sub-sequent ways we've adapted our brewing to cater to them. We think about hops differently from the way any other country ever has, we use them differently, and, in the true test of national tradition, our techniques are now influencing breweries elsewhere.

Although there's some dispute on exactly when all of this started, I credit Ken Grossman and Sierra Nevada with striking the note that has reverberated ever since. He laid the basic template in 1979 when he created the brewery's Pale Ale, a beer that bore all the hallmarks of the American style: an ale designed so that all the other elements of the beer served to highlight the fresh, electric flavors of American hops. It borrowed a bit from the English tradition but deviated in key ways. At 5.6%, it was quite a bit stronger than English ales; it was a bit hoppier than English ales and, because it used local hops, tasted quite a bit different; finally, Grossman used a neutral yeast that didn't contribute any fruitiness, leaving the caramel malts and Cascade hops to do all the talking.

Even more important, Sierra was miles ahead of the rest of the country in 1981 when they released their seasonal Celebration, the first modern American IPA. It's amazing to me that this beer doesn't get more attention for how much it anticipated what would ultimately become popular more than 20 years later. Even 35 years later it is remarkably current: a robust 6.8% beer with 65 bitterness units (unimaginable in 1981) and iridescent with those spiky, citrusy, piney flavors that are now the hallmark of American brewing.

Developing a Tradition

Americans trudged through the 1980s and most of the 1990s essentially looking to Europe for inspiration. It wasn't until near the end of the 1990s that hoppy ales became popular and the rest of the country caught up with Sierra. The first wave of hoppy beers leaned heavily on bitterness, and there was an unfortunate race to see who could pack the most IBUs into a beer. By the mid-2000s, breweries were starting to discover the pleasures of hops added later in the boil and conditioning tank, which both added tons of flavors and helped balance the high levels of bitterness.

Over the next decade the evolution continued, and bitterness slowly gave way as late-addition and dry hops came to characterize American beer. It has become such a prominent feature of American brewing that "hop bursting," a practice homebrewers popularized in which *no* bittering hops are used, is now a regular commercial practice. In the mid-2000s America's hoppy ales started impressing foreign brewers, and now "American-style" beers are made by small craft breweries all over the world.

This is something new in the world. In my survey of the historic sources, no country has ever focused so intently on late– and post–kettle hopping. Ever since hops were incorporated into brewing, there have been bitter beers. But because hops came along as a way of managing spoilage, that bitter charge has always been primary. British breweries have been dry-hopping for decades, but building beers around the intense flavors and aromas of hops is a style for which I have found no precedent.

Now Americans have been doing it long enough, and have gotten so adept at it, that it's hard for them not to think about goosing a beer by adding late-addition hops. I'm about as orthodox a homebrewer as you'll find, but I have been infected by this habit myself. A saison? Well, I think, it would certainly be great to have some nice citrusy accents to the beer. A German lager? Isn't it really in the spirit of these beers to add a bit of delicate aromatics by dry-hopping? A Belgian dubbel? Hmm, perhaps just a hint of pepper from a nice whirlpool infusion. This is the culture at play, the national tradition, and I am no more able to resist it than the Belgian who puts his Scottish ale through the warm room.

Of course, it's not entirely about hops. There are a few other key hallmarks of American brewing, so let's run through the main points.

TWO-ROW PLUS SPECIALTY MALTS. The four major European brewing countries lean very heavily on base malts to build the flavor profile of their beer. Americans have a recipe-based approach that starts with neutral two-row malt as "sugar" (the fermentables) and uses specialty malts for flavor and color. This is unusual, and no other country does it.

CRYSTAL MALT. Although use of crystal is tapering off, it has long been a key flavor marker for American ales (another legacy of Ken Grossman). Other countries use caramel malts in small proportions, but Americans use them to contribute both body and a distinct caramel flavor to their beer. The body helps buffer bitterness, and the caramel harmonizes nicely with the flavors in American hops. However, as Americans rely more and more on late-addition hops, crystal malts are being de-emphasized — but not eliminated.

NEUTRAL YEASTS. The most popular strain of ale yeast in the United States, by far, is the Chico strain (Wyeast 1056, White Labs WLP001, Safale Fermentis US-05), which ferments well and gets out of the way so the hops can shine. Guess which brewery "Chico" refers to? (Sierra Nevada.)

STRENGTH AND INTENSITY. American beers have traditionally been stronger and more intense (whether they're hoppy, tart, or malty) than beers elsewhere. This was partly because brewers and drinkers were unsophisticated; as the market matures, flavors are coming more into balance. It is nevertheless likely that, relative to other countries, Americans will always favor strength and intensity.

AMERICAN HOPS AND LATE-ADDITION HOPS. As already discussed, these are by far the clearest marker of place. There is a worldwide move toward hop breeding, and breweries are moving in the direction of individualizing their beers with specific combinations of hops. This trend is aided by the focus on late-addition and dry hops, where the flavors and aromas of these new varieties are most expressive.

America is not at the terminal point of its evolution, but it is past the midway point. Drinkers and brewers are in agreement about the basic contours, and we'll just have to wait and see where the ride takes us. Wherever the American tradition ultimately settles, it will revolve around lively hop flavors — and a style of brewing new to the world.

· CHAPTER 22 ·

HOPPY ALES

ity the poor IPA, a beer type invented in another country and another time. Now the name is being put into service to describe an almost comical range of beers: double and triple IPAs; session IPA; Brett IPA; red, white, and black IPAs; Belgian IPA; fruit IPA; tart IPA; even India pale lagers. As absurd as these names are (black India pale ale and India pale lager being especially Dadaesque), they point to a very real phenomenon. An entire national tradition has developed in the United States around the use of electric American hops, and the best we've been able to do so far in naming it is attaching "India" or "IPA" to the title. Linguistically it's absurd, but stylistically it has a clear logic.

Moreover, this national tradition is still evolving. Hoppy American ales began transcending niche status 20 years ago, but those beers were very different from the ones we know today. The '90s hoppy ales were brewed to gale-force bitterness. Breweries built these beers around citrusy American hops (the classic C-hops, which should now be granted some kind of hall-of-fame status along with Goldings, Hallertauer, and Saaz) and substantial crystal malt additions. That model is now seriously on the wane, replaced by a philosophy that prizes hop aroma and flavors far more than bitterness. If you're reading this book, you probably already know about these trends.

What you may not know is how radically this is changing the way breweries make these beers. Hops have always been used in the brewhouse primarily for their bitterness; this not only balanced malt sweetness, but it had the additional virtue of protecting the beer against infection. What we know about hop utilization is based on the way they have always been used — at the start of boil, with minor additions later on that add "incidental" bitterness.

Breweries are now flipping that, adding scant amounts at the beginning of the boil and getting most of the flavor, aroma, and, yes, bitterness, from late or postboil additions. In a modern hoppy ale of 50 IBUs, perhaps only 10 percent of the bitterness comes from the first addition. The rest of the bitterness comes from those later additions, which add further layers of flavor and aroma to the beer — flavors and aromas that have never appeared in beer before.

Breakside started life as a little brewpub in the outlying neighborhood of Woodlawn back in 2010. Both the neighborhood and the brewery have changed a lot since then. The original brewery contained a tiny three-barrel kit and was entirely hands-on. Brewer Ben Edmunds's beers, at turns experimental and traditional, soon became popular enough to demand a production facility, which opened in 2012.

In Portland Edmunds is known as an alchemist. At any given time Breakside will have a number of experimental beers with everything from lychee to fennel pollen to spruce tips alongside classic pilsners, kölsches, and stouts. What has lately drawn the most attention, however, is Breakside's raft of hoppy ales, starting with the flagship IPA, which in 2014 scored a gold at the Great American Beer Festival. Edmunds and his team of brewers started stacking in other hoppy ales like cord wood: Wanderlust IPA, Lunch Break India Session Ale, India Golden Ale, La Tormenta (a dry-hopped sour), as well as a host of seasonal and one-off hoppy ales. (In a typical year Breakside makes 85 different brands of beer.)

Portland was on the vanguard of modern hoppy American ales as the profile migrated from bitterness to flavor, and Breakside remains on the cutting edge. Their La Tormenta, released in 2013, revealed how lactic sourness could complement tropical hop flavors. Breakside's emphasis on whirlpool and dry hopping has also given them a leg up on making sessionable hoppy beers, which are becoming one of their signature types. Breakside has gone from being an obscure, remote brewery to setting the pace for the trends in American brewing.

BREWMASTER BEN EDMUNDS

Edmunds's interest in brewing developed when he was living in Colorado, where there was great outdoor fun during the daytime but less to do at night. He started homebrewing and was surprised by how much it "clicked" (his word). Pretty soon he was enrolled at the Siebel brewing school and studying in Chicago and Munich. With his second degree in hand, he headed to Portland, found a job as assistant brewer at Upright, and before long ran into the folks planning to open Breakside. They hired him as their first brewer, and he has overseen every batch brewed since.

Understanding Hoppy Ales

There's no reason to spend a lot of time discussing these beers — they are the clear favorite among American homebrewers, who know them well. The one thing I would emphasize again is the now-mandatory importance of very rich, vivid hop flavors and aromas. These define the style. Bitterness is no longer a necessary element in these beers (as such products as Deschutes' Fresh Squeezed IPA show), but lush hop flavors and aromas are.

When I spoke to Edmunds, he made an interesting additional point, and I think it's relevant when we consider national tradition. Ingredients matter. You could make a perfectly executed Czech pilsner, but if you used Mosaic hops, it wouldn't be appropriate for style (however tasty it might be). In a similar vein Edmunds believes American hoppy ales have become so well established that they need a marker of place as well. In his mind that means the classic American C-hops, plus Amarillo and Simcoe. "If you're not using one of those, you might have an awesome hoppy beer, but it will lack an element of familiarity." This is one brewer's rule — one that other American brewers routinely violate — but it is part and parcel of a developing tradition in which rules are increasingly observed.

If you want to make a hoppy American ale, it behooves you to use some classic hop to anchor the flavor in familiarity.

— BEN EDMUNDS, BREAKSIDE

Brewing a Hoppy Ale

When he's brewing a hoppy ale, whether an American amber or red ale, a pale ale, or any variant of IPA from session through triple IPA, Ben Edmunds approaches it the same way. He actually had to describe the thinking to me a couple of times before I grasped what he was saying; it is both simple and radical. "To make a successful hoppy ale, the bottom line is you have to start with a very clear flavor profile of your hops in mind and work backward. Everything stems from the hops."

For Edmunds this means starting with a standard hop schedule — one he uses for every hoppy ale — and sticking with it. Breakside follows this blueprint: the first addition at 60 minutes (start of boil), then at 10 minutes, and finally at whirlpool. Edmunds doesn't think it matters too much whether the late addition comes at

20, 5, or 1 minute from the end of boil — but he does think it makes sense to stick with one formula. And here's the part that seemed so radical to me: he builds his IBUs starting with the whirlpool addition and works backward from there. And he always uses the same amount of hops in the whirlpool, no matter what their alpha acids.

At Breakside that means 1.5 pounds per barrel, which would be 4 ounces per 5 gallons. He typically uses a "soft" hop such as Citra, Galaxy, Mosaic, Amarillo, or El Dorado in the whirlpool, and they steep for roughly an hour. During that time the temperature drops from boiling to about 180°F (82°C) and, contrary to what some people think, contributes substantial bitterness. Most bitterness calculators assume very low utilization, but at Breakside they get about 12 percent, or half what you'd expect if the same hops had been added at 60 minutes.

Once he calculates the bitterness on the whirlpool addition, Edmunds moves to the 10-minute addition. Again, he uses a consistent amount — roughly 1 pound per barrel (2.667 ounces per 5 gallons), though he may adjust slightly up or down if the alphas look out of whack. For the 10-minute addition, he likes "punchy" hops — varieties with a little zing — such as Cascade and Centennial.

Only at this point, once he's added up the bitterness contribution from the 10-minute and whirlpool additions, does he round off the bitterness he needs with a 60-minute bitter charge, and it's always small, contributing between 5 and 10 IBUs. He's often not even looking for bitterness from this charge — just good kettle performance (causing trub to form and preventing boilover). The bitter charge can be really tiny. "I made an IPA today on the three-barrel system where the 60-minute addition was 1.1 ounces," he told me, laughing.

This is, he says, the way most brewers now think about their hoppy ales. "In all formats, the old model of the hop schedule is almost entirely outmoded," Edmunds says, referring to old hop schedules where the bulk of the hops go in at 60 and 30 minutes. "Frankly, it's not a secret, but all the brewers who make these award-winning beers — everyone does it. Those 60-minute hops are basically for kettle performance."

BUILDING BACKWARD

To emphasize the lesson of this approach: Edmunds builds his bitterness backward, starting with the whirlpool. This is an extraordinary development in brewing. Many brewers over the centuries have made beers that emphasized hops. But it is an American innovation to use these giant loads of hops late in the boil to create not only bitterness but intense flavors and aromas. Nowhere in the historical record have I found this approach.

Edmunds approaches the grist with a similar mind-set, building a recipe that uses some body-building malts, crystal malt, and dextrose in addition to base malts. Stronger beers will use more dextrose to boost alcohol and attenuation, while lower-alcohol and darker beers will use more color malts and crystal malts. Edmunds uses crystal malts for "back-end sweetness," not the heavy caramel and dark-fruit flavors and recommends always using crystal of 40 lovibond or lower in hoppy ales — except in the case of hoppy red ales, when he does use 60L crystal and a small amount of other dark crystal malts.

Yeast selection is not a critical element — Americans overwhelmingly favor neutral, clean yeasts — but even here there are considerations. The central issue is not ester production, but flocculation, which affects dry hopping. In Edmunds's experience the presence of yeast changes the expression of hop aromas. "With higher-flocking strains, we find that you'll get stronger dank, oily, and juicy notes than in the presence of more yeast. Midflocking strains (such as White Labs WLP001 or Wyeast 1056) are what most of the brewers who pioneered American hoppy ales use, so the most classic dry hop aromas were created using these strains. If it's familiarity that you want — lots of citrus, tropical, floral, and fruity notes — use a medium flocculator." Finally, lots of yeast in suspension "dulls the pungency of hop aromatics."

Again, no one has researched these effects. "The theories range from the idea that there is a biotransformation of hop oils in the presence of yeast to the idea that there is some biophysical mechanism by which yeast pulls hop oil out of beer," Edmunds said.

THE QUALITIES OF BITTERNESS

We don't know a lot about bitterness. We know that an IBU is a chemical measurement of a given amount of iso-alpha acids dissolved in beer. We have some sense of the way isomerization happens during a boil, and how this affects the measurement. (Hop's alpha acids must be isomerized — their molecular structure rearranged — to go into solution and add bitterness to a beer.) What we don't know is how the use of hops affects the *perception* of bitterness. Several studies, for example, have demonstrated that using first-wort hoping (adding hops to the kettle during lautering) creates a "smoother" bitterness. What does that mean? We don't know — it's a subjective, albeit measurable, judgment.

The sense of bitterness is confounded by the additional perception of hop flavors (aromas and tastes), which track as "hoppy" to the palate. Until a decade ago, breweries had never brewed in the way Edmunds describes here, and scientists hadn't studied what happens chemically when you add immense amounts of hops postboil. If the subjective sense of bitterness can be altered merely by using first-wort hopping, surely there's a big difference in late-wort and post–kettle hopping. Even well into the second decade of the twenty-first century, we still don't have the science to help describe these effects.

MALT BILL

8.5 pounds two-row American or
Canadian malt (73%)

1 pound light Munich (9%)

1 pound 20L crystal malt (9%)

1.2 pounds dextrose/corn sugar (10%)

SINGLE-INFUSION MASH

152°F (67°C) for 45 minutes

60-MINUTE BOIL

0.25 ounce Amarillo, 60 minutes (8.5% AA, contribution of
7 IBU)

2.6 ounces Cascade, 10 minutes (7% AA, contribution of
22 IBU)

4 ounces Citra in the whirlpool, letting stand 45 minutes
(11% AA, contribution of 50 IBU, possibly)

FERMENTATION AND CONDITIONING

Ferment cool (65 to 70°F [18–21°C]) with a low-ester
American ale strain such as Wyeast 1056 or White Labs
WLP001. Twenty-four hours after primary fermentation
is complete, rack to secondary and begin dry-hopping
with 4 ounces of a blend of Citra and Comet hops. Let
stand for 3 days. If possible, rouse the hops each day to
keep them in contact with the beer; if it's not possible,
Edmunds suggests adding a second and even third dry
hop of the same volume each day. Rack, and chill for
a week.

BEN EDMUNDS

BREAKSIDE
BREWERY

Package

Bottle or keg. Because perishable hop flavors and aromas are central to these beers, they don't last long. "Do everything in your power to keep oxygen out of the beer." Edmunds recommends evacuating kegs with CO_2 and notes that bottle conditioning will extend the life of your beer somewhat.

- Expected OG: 15° P/1.062

- Expected TG: 3° P/1.013

- Expected ABV: 6.4%

- Expected bitterness: 70–80 IBU

Notes: Edmunds recommends treating your water with at least 100 ppm calcium and a 5:1 or greater sulfate-to-chloride ratio. You may also use a bit of acidulated malt to lower pH (no more than 3 percent). Dry-hopping amounts will vary depending on gravity. For low- to mid-gravity beers, use 3 to 4 ounces. With higher-gravity IPAs, bump it up to 5 ounces. For high-gravity double and triple IPAs, you can use up to 10 ounces of dry hops (!). Note that the IBU figures here are extremely provisional.

When Edmunds began tweaking his recipes a few years back, he did it entirely by taste, which is how he ended up using so few hops at 60 minutes. Start with this recipe, and then, like Edmunds, begin tinkering — and ignore the IBU values. Think carefully about bitterness and IBUs, and disregard the calculators that tell you there are no IBUs in the late-addition and whirlpool hop additions.

Next Steps

My discussions with Ben Edmunds have led me to conclude that we're in need of a serious rethinking of hops. The way Americans use hops has changed the way we think about them. For the last thousand years, hops' principle purpose has been bittering, which was often a proxy for microbial protection. As a result, every beer style on earth had used the bulk of the hops early in the boil. Everything we know about hops and bitterness stems from this approach.

To the extent researchers have looked at hops (and they haven't done much), they've looked at the bittering end of things. But because Americans are now using the vast percentages of their hops late or after the boil, the effects are even more mysterious. We know something about alpha acids and isomerization, and we know a little about the four main oils in hops — beyond that, it's all guesswork. Since brewers are using these hops in real time, they need to understand how the different varieties affect their beer. We don't even yet have the language for different categories, so breweries are making it up as they go along.

Hops researcher and professor Tom Shellhammer has been looking into some of these questions at Oregon State University. In an earlier study he and his team looked into whether cohumulone levels affect a hop's bittering "harshness" or not. For decades it was assumed that higher cohumulone levels made a hop unpleasant, and this belief led breeders to choose emergent strains with low amounts. But nobody had ever tested it. Shellhammer did. The results? The differences were subtle, but when the researchers "did pick up a difference and could describe it, the *high* iso-cohumulone hop had more desirable attributes. It was less harsh and medicinal, [and had] finer, more fleeting bitterness."

He's currently at work on a study looking into whether a hop's oil content has any effect on dry hopping. It's an effort to figure out what makes the technique effective. "If you're going to use hops for dry hopping and make a consistent product batch to batch, should you as a brewer hop based upon the mass of hops, or the oil content of the hops — or based on something else?" His early results have so far found no correlation between oil content and a hop's ability to give beer those rich, aromatic notes brewers prize. We are still in the dark ages of hop knowledge — and If there's anything good about that state of affairs, it's that things are only going to get more interesting as we go forward.

PUNCHY OR SOFT?

As we talked about hop varieties and their use at different points in the brewing process, Edmunds kept calling some of them "punchy" and others "soft." He struggled a bit to explain what he meant, but the terms themselves do much of the heavy lifting. Hop varieties behave differently from each other, a phenomenon brewers have intuited for decades. Some hops seem more aggressive, while others are gentle. It's not really a matter of intensity — Amarillo is as flavorful as Cascade — but the "feeling" that accompanies the flavors differs.

For Breakside this means a lot of American hops can be clumped into these two groups: soft hops (Citra, Galaxy, Mosaic, El Dorado, Amarillo) and punchy ones (Cluster, Cascade, Centennial, Columbus, Chinook, Simcoe, Comet). A few don't fit into either category: Edmunds offers Nelson Sauvin and Equinox as two that have elements of both. These categories may — probably will — evolve. Breakside may eventually discard them. But they illustrate how brewers think about hop varieties as they use them in the brewery.

That leaves it up to the brewers to suss out the qualities of hops that make tasty beers, and Breakside has some additional advice:

LIMIT THE NUMBER OF HOP VARIETIES you use to five at the most, with three or four being ideal. Once you add too many different hop varieties in, the flavors become muddy, indistinct. This is obviously a preference, and many breweries use seven or eight varieties. I've found it to be good advice, especially as you're learning which hops do what to your beer. Limit your variables.

ON THE OTHER HAND, USE MORE THAN ONE. Some single-hop beers really work, but not many. Most varieties lack the complexity to give you a lush presentation of different flavors.

DON'T BLEND THE HOPS ON HOT SIDE ADDITIONS but instead devote one hop to each addition. There are a couple of reasons for this. Again, blending makes it hard to isolate which flavors you like and may create those generic "hoppy" flavors. But Edmunds also believes hops work better or worse at different times. "Over time, we've learned which hops we like better as kettle hops, which ones we like better as whirlpool hops, which as dry hops. Comet, only a dry hop. Amarillo, El Dorado, Citra — great whirlpool hops. Centennial and Cascade we like better as a 10-minute hop." It's fine to add a blend of varieties during dry hopping, and Breakside typically uses two or three varieties to get complex aromas.

PLAN TO DRINK THE BEER QUICKLY. This is perhaps more important to a commercial brewery, but every homebrewer should understand it, too. These kinds of hoppy American ales are the least stable beers a brewer can make. "You have 20 days of brewery freshness, and then it begins to degrade. If you bottle-condition, you might buy yourself a week. But by day 30 you're dealing with a fundamentally different beer than you had at day 1. When you're building these beers you should know what that beer will taste like at day 30." What's especially interesting is that hop varieties change at different rates, and some wear better than others. Using their Wanderlust IPA as an example, Edmunds says, "the first 15 days is all Mosaic." It goes through an awkward adolescence; then "around day 30 the Amarillo starts to come forward, and it becomes this new beer. When you have that beer from days 30 to 45, it has a little bit of tropical dankness, but essentially all that Mosaic character is gone, and it becomes brighter [and expresses] citrus peel, marmalade."

SCALING UP OR DOWN. Every beer Edmunds makes, from his session IPA to triple IPAs, starts with this basic formulation: 70 to 85 percent base malt (typically US or Canadian two-row; possibly some UK malt blended in); 10 to 15 percent body-building malt (includes Munich, Vienna, flaked grains, aromatic/honey malt, dextrin malts); 0 to 10 percent dextrose; and 0 to 10 percent crystal malt (in rare cases he's used up to 25 percent body-building malts). Crystal malt is good for balancing punchy hops and isn't necessary when all you're using are soft hops. The sugar is useful in bringing a clean finish and giving hops a platform for expression but should only be used in beers that are 14° P/1.057 or above.

Session IPAs and triple IPAs shouldn't be mashed at the same temperature. Drop the mash to 150 to 152°F (66–67°C) for high-gravity beers, and use 10 percent dextrose unless you want a chewier beer. For session IPAs skip the sugar and raise your mash temperature to 155°F (68°C) or higher. When Harpoon Brewery made its session IPA, Take 5, brewer Steve Theoharides used pale and body-building malts and then pushed the mash temperature to the limit. "We really pushed the upper limit on our mash temperature. We're pretty high — around 160, 161°F (71, 72°C)." It was a temperature he'd never reached before, and when it came time to brew on the 120-barrel system, he confesses, "My teeth were chattering a little bit." You can't argue with the results, though. "Now we get something that attenuates to 65 percent, which is remarkable, especially for such a low-ABV beer," he says. (Harpoon Take 5 IPA, like Breakside's IPA, relies on late-addition hops. In fact, there are no bittering hops at all in Take 5.)

From there you follow the hop schedule no matter what beer you're making: start with 3 to 4 ounces in the whirlpool, another 2.5 to 3 ounces at 10 minutes, and just enough of a bitter charge to inhibit boilover. This part never changes, though for very light beers you have to be mindful of the alpha acid percentages in the hops you choose. "If you want to make a beer with really high alpha aroma varieties, great — but don't try to make a session IPA that way," Edmunds cautions. "Because either you're not going to use enough hops (because you don't want to get the IBUs too high) or you'll get your IBUs too high from using too many high-alpha hops."

Working with Fruit, Belgian Yeast, and Acidity

Hoppy American ales have ranged well beyond just a continuum of strength and color — they are now made with spices (white IPAs), fruit, Belgian yeasts, and even *Lactobacillus* and *Brettanomyces*. These are built the same way but require a bit of extra care and handling.

FRUIT IPAS. These are so expensive that professionals don't make them very often — which make them great for homebrewers. Edmunds advises you to look at what the fruit adds beyond fermentables and flavor — sweetness, body, and astringency — and adjust your recipe accordingly. You will obviously want to use hops that harmonize with the flavors, and there are many fruity varieties that do so. A touch of acidity will give fruit structure and make the aroma and flavors pop, so consider adding just a bit of malic, tartaric, or lactic acid — like winemakers do.

DRY-HOPPED SOURS. This is a fairly recent entry to the canon, and an impressive one. Moderate your alcohol to 5 to 6.5 percent ABV, and keep your IBUs as low as you possibly can. Use kettle souring to produce a cleanly acidified wort that is only moderately tart (see chapter 10 for instructions). This is a hard style to make, and Edmunds says you should master kettle souring before you try it. Dry-hop with "soft" varieties such as Citra, Amarillo, El Dorado, and Galaxy — and don't use spiky ones such as Simcoe. "Hop selection is key," he says.

BRETT IPA. There are a couple of ways to make this beer: pitching with *Brettanomyces* and serving fresh, or dry-hopping an aged *Brett* beer. If you're pitching *Brett*, it will be bitterer than you're used to over time. Build in body and malt sweetness with rye or crystal malt so the beer doesn't bottom out as the yeast munches away. *Brett*-pitched beers end up drier, so tone down hop and water profile and build in body. If you're dry-hopping an aged *Brett* beer, add hops to the conditioning tank just before packaging.

BELGIAN IPA. Edmunds points out that the first wave of these beers tended to focus on phenolic yeasts and hitched them to "dank" hops such as Simcoe and Amarillo. As breweries continued, they switched to yeast strains with lower phenolics and higher ester profiles and chose soft, tropical hops to accentuate the fruity yeast notes. Edmunds also recommends that you choose a yeast that has medium flocculation, because the yeast will change a beer during dry hopping. "Too little or too much yeast in suspension will really change the flavor," he noted.

American hoppy ales are the most individual and customizable style brewed today. When Edmunds and I spoke about them, he pointed out that there are definitely other approaches — making chewy IPAs with high finishing gravities, mash hopping, and mid–kettle hopping. There are few ironclad orthodoxies, and if I'd chosen to speak with Vinnie Cilurzo at Russian River, the methods would look different.

Indeed, while one needs to take note of all these elements individually, it's also important to consider them collectively. The success of a beer always rests in the harmony of the different elements. And here there are no hard rules. Lower levels of carbonation will provide softer hop aromas, but higher levels will give a greater perception of aroma. Increasing mash pH will decrease the utilization of hop acids, allowing more hop character without bitterness — but will lower brewhouse efficiency. Body affects the perception of bitterness, so a thicker or thinner body will affect the way you balance your hops. With each of these decision points, there is no right answer, but they will go a long way to determining the success of your beer.

One thing I take away from Edmunds is that, particularly *because* American IPAs are so customizable, it's good to develop a blueprint yourself and work within it. It eliminates some of the randomness of dealing with so many ingredients and techniques and helps you hone your approach and find your own IPA "voice."

CHAPTER 23

FRESH-HOP ALES

et us consider the fresh-hop beer. A seemingly simple beast, it is made from the addition of undried hops rushed sun-warm from field to kettle (or tank). These hops suffuse the beer with qualities unavailable to the brewer using dried hops: vivid, almost electrified, perfumy aromas and flavors as intense as ripe fresh-picked fruit or flowers. When they work, fresh-hop ales are among the most satisfying beers in the world. When they don't, they can taste vegetal or even evoke overripe compost. Ten years ago, breweries didn't fully understand how to use fresh hops, but they have learned a lot in a decade. It is one of the styles most available to the homebrewer — or at least the homebrewer with a backyard trellis — and can become a joyful event on the annual brewing calendar.

EST 𝔇ouble 𝔐ountain 𝔅rewery 2007

HOOD RIVER, OREGON

Double Mountain was founded in 2007 by two seasoned veterans from the brewing industry, Charlie Devereux and Matt Swihart — then the head brewer at nearby Full Sail in Hood River, Oregon. The brewery rests along the banks of the Columbia River, in sight of its namesakes Mounts Hood and Adams. But it's also roughly equidistant from the hop fields in Yakima and the Willamette Valley, and this is the more important geographical fact.

Double Mountain has unusual facility with *Humulus lupulus*. Matt and his team of brewers hand-select their hops and know how to coax enormous flavor and aroma from them — and although they make a broad variety of different styles, it is the hoppy beers for which they've become famous. The brewery's regular line consists of three IPAs and a hoppy kölsch. If you have a chance to visit the brewery, you might witness brewers sending one of these beers to a large hop back, filled halfway with whole hop cones. I saw a batch of Hop Lava IPA flow from the kettle, and — no kidding — the wort turned green in the device.

About the time Matt was founding Double Mountain, fresh-hop ales were becoming an annual mainstay among Washington and Oregon breweries. He was one of the first brewers to dial in the process for extracting the most potent flavors and aromas from a fresh hop — the secret is judicious use of conventional kilned hops — and he shares his process here.

BREWMASTER MATT SWIHART

Swihart got his professional start as an aerospace engineer. A love of home-brewing sent him on a path that led to the Siebel Institute and then to a series of breweries. He finally landed at Full Sail Brewing in 1994, ultimately becoming head brewer before leaving to start Double Mountain with Charlie Devereux. "When we started the brewery," he told me, "we had only one thing at the top of our mind. The beer had to be about the beer. We wanted to make beer that we would drink and be delighted with when we walked into a pub. Simple."

Understanding Fresh-Hop Ales

One of the most important considerations in a fresh-hop ale comes before you fire up your hot liquor: when to harvest hops. It's important to make sure you leave them on the bine long enough to produce the essential oils that will make your beer pop. Hop researcher and Oregon State University professor Tom Shellhammer, who is currently doing research on the effect of oils in dry hopping, explains that unlike alpha acids, which are stable throughout the growing life of a hop, oils increase. "At the beginning of the summer, there's hardly any oil in the plant, and it just keeps going and going and going throughout the season."

Once the hops are ready, it's time to brew. "It is imperative to loosely pack your undried hops and get them into a kettle within hours of harvest," Matt explains. "The high moisture and oil content at harvest also start to break down and physically compost once the vine is cut. In Hood River we are about 90 minutes from Sodbuster Farms, so we send our truck about the same time as mash in. The hops arrive back at the brewery typically minutes from use in the first brew." When I've made fresh-hop ales at home, I've harvested them after mashing in for maximum freshness. (See Growing Your Own Hops, page 246.)

Brewing a Fresh-Hop Ale

Across the Pacific Northwest, where hundreds of these beers are made each autumn, the variation in base beer is small — a basic pale ale with few malt flavors or fermentation notes to compete with the glorious flavors and aromas of the fresh hops. From there it's all about hop usage.

"We use the wet hops in a couple of locations," Swihart says in describing his process. Double Mountain makes two standard fresh-hop beers, Killer Red and Killer Green. They are similar ales, stronger (both above 7% ABV) and more bitter than standard fresh-hop ales. "We still use dried hops in the kettle for bitterness but add a dry-hop bag stuffed with fresh hops late in the boil for flavor. Where the Killer beers get most of their character is when we add the largest charge of wet hops to our hop back. This maximizes the flavor/fresh-hop aroma into the wort with minimal chance of picking up bitterness. It allows us to use 4 to 5 pounds of hop per barrel and get the flavor we want.

"We've then dry-hopped with traditional hops and/or also dry-hopped with wet hops on various years. I found the most pleasing Killer beers to have a little of both. With that method, you can have the best of both worlds, using various forms of hops (pellets, wet hops, dried cones) to make the best beer possible. Our usage is roughly 4 pounds per barrel wet hop and about 0.5 to 1 pound per barrel traditional hop."

FRESH-HOP ALE

MATT SWIHART

—

**DOUBLE
MOUNTAIN
BREWERY**

9 pounds two-row pale or pilsner malt (93%)

3 ounces Carapils or honey malt (2%)

5 ounces 60–80L caramel malt (3%)

3 ounces 120–130L caramel malt (2%)

SINGLE-INFUSION MASH

153°F (67°C) for 45 minutes

60-MINUTE BOIL

0.5 ounce kilned Warrior, 60 minutes (16% AA, contribution of 32 IBU)

0.5 ounce kilned Warrior, 30 minutes (16% AA, contribution of 25 IBU)

3 ounces fresh hops, 20 minutes

1–1.5 pounds fresh hops in the hop back (yes, *pounds* — see notes)

FERMENTATION AND CONDITIONING

Ferment with "an estery yeast with high attenuation." Matt suggests Wyeast 1028 (London Ale), Wyeast 1762 (Belgian Abbey II), or Wyeast 1272 (American Ale II).

Dry-hop with 1–1.5 pounds fresh hops for 5 days at 70°F (21°C) at the end of fermentation. Cool after conditioning to drop yeast, package in keg (ideally) or bottle.

- Expected OG: 13° P/1.053

- Expected TG: 2° P/1.008

- Expected ABV: 5.8%

- Expected bitterness: 50–55 IBU

Notes: You'll notice immediately that the recipe calls for pounds of hops, not ounces. This isn't a misprint; it's because of the high moisture content of fresh hops. Swihart notes, "Kilned hops are anywhere between 9 and 13 percent water. Fresh hops are 80 to 85 percent water, so although they are higher in oil content, you really do need a ton of them for the correct effect. We use five to seven times more fresh hops by weight than standard hops on any beer." Matt recommends Perle, Brewer's Gold, Sterling, Bullion, or Cascade for fresh hops, but "honestly, best quality supply wins over variety." He urges brewers to "drink soon, drink often."

NEXT STEPS

Breweries have experimented with different styles — lagers, saisons, dark ales — but these invariably interfere with the perception of the fresh hop. Now most breweries make a very basic pale ale and vary fresh-hop additions to create original flavors. Many breweries have come to believe that hop oils are paramount. Not only should you harvest hops later but consider using high-oil varieties.

Gigantic Brewing's Van Havig emphasizes this point. "I think it really all lies in hop choice. The higher-oil hops seem to make better fresh-hop beers. This makes intuitive sense, of course." Many of the highest-oil hops are proprietary American varieties such as Citra, Amarillo, and Simcoe (not always available to homebrewers), but classics such as Centennial, Nugget, and Crystal also have excellent oil content.

Many brewers are reluctant to use fresh hops in the boil at all. Havig says, "I think boiling extracts things you don't want and potentially drives off oil." He uses fresh hops only in the hop back, a method also favored at Deschutes, which makes some of the best fresh-hop beers available. Cam O'Connor (now with Crux Fermentation) says, "We're looking for juicy in-your-face hop aroma and flavor without a lot of vegetative flavors. Hop Trip and Chasin' Freshies are both made [this way]."

Other brewers go further and suggest keeping the hops away from heat entirely, only using them during conditioning. Vasilios Gletsos, now at Hill Farmstead, elaborates. "When I moved to Portland Brewing, I didn't have the flexibility to use fresh hops on the hot side [the kettle], so I devised a plan to add them in secondary/conditioning tanks. We did this as whole flower breweries do: stuffed into mesh bags and tied to the bottom of the vessel. This gave the best 'fresh squeezed' flavor I have ever gotten from fresh hops. A beautiful mix of peach fruit cup with a touch of tea."

If you do use this technique, don't leave the hops in too long. O'Connor says, "Forty-eight to 72 hours seems good before racking it off, which limits contact with the vegetal matter that may be contributing to [unpleasant] flavors."

Growing Your Own Hops

I have a nearly perfect canopy of leaves over my backyard, so I've had to rely on the kindness of strangers (and friends) for my own fresh hops. It's a shame, because hops are easy to grow and make for a lovely harvest. Although some sources say hops grow best north of the 35th parallel (north of many Southern states and Texas), that's not really true. Commercial crops may grow better in the long days of the Pacific Northwest, but home farmers have been pulling fine crops from their backyards as far south as Florida.

Hop rhizomes — roots that look something like ginger — are widely available and inexpensive; consult your local homebrew shop or do an Internet search. One of the challenges in home hop cultivation is knowing which varieties will express themselves well in your local climate and soil. Even hops grown in different climates in the Pacific Northwest (Yakima and the Willamette Valley) are different, so hops will definitely behave differently in North America's varied climates. If you plan to dry your hops and use them conventionally, consider a versatile hop that you can use in many recipes. If you're using them principally for fresh-hop beers, varieties with a proven track record are Cascade, Crystal, Centennial, and Nugget.

For the best yield make sure your hops have room to climb. Hop bines can grow to 20 feet, and they strive to go *up*. They don't need elaborate structures — a simple wire is adequate — but they won't grow well horizontally. Also make sure you don't plant them under shade; hops need direct sunlight and lots of it. Once you get the hops into the ground, don't expect a full harvest the first year — it usually takes another growing season before they produce fully.

Mature hops are dry and papery to the touch but still springy when squeezed. Never wait until the petal edges begin to turn brown. At harvest they should be sticky and aromatic and show visible traces of lupulin (yellow powder). Hold the hop in both hands, and split it vertically along the spine. When the hops are ready, it will split easily, and you'll see heavy lupulin deposits and get an intense aroma.

CHAPTER 24

BREWING WITH CORN

When we cast our eyes to other countries, we look with fondness at unusual practices and ingredients. No one questions why brewers use rye in Finland and Russia, wheat in Europe, rice in Asia, or sorghum in Africa. Indeed, the use of local grain is one of the hallmarks of national tradition, one we admire elsewhere. Why then do Americans so despise their own native grain?

There's nothing wrong with corn. Many Americans are unaware that it is a common ingredient in Belgian beers with pedigrees as august as Rodenbach. Like any other ingredient, it can be put to malign use, but it can also be harnessed to add interest and character to a beer and, importantly, a bit of local flavor here at home. More important, in the last great flourishing of American brewing in the late nineteenth and early twentieth centuries, it helped give character to pilsners, cream ales, and some forgotten beers such as American weissbier and Kentucky common ales.

The great irony is that over time its association with mass-market lagers gave corn the reputation of being something cheap and industrial. In a time when local ingredients are being feted, though, corn should be enjoying a renaissance among brewers as *the* American ingredient. It is time to rediscover our national grain and rehabilitate its reputation.

EST # Fullsteam Brewery 2009
DURHAM, NORTH CAROLINA

The craft beer movement is now old enough that former prejudices are being reexamined, and fortunately, a few breweries have begun to reclaim corn. One of the leaders is Durham's Fullsteam Brewery, which considers using local ingredients a part of its mission. Its founder, Sean Lilly Wilson, has a goal of using 50 percent local ingredients in all his beers by 2020. That's a challenge when you consider that most of the nation's barley fields are far to the north, and the hop fields are even farther away. The region's focus on local produce makes this goal realistic, though; local growers have already been coaxed into producing barley and hops. And in the most interesting experiment with local ingredients, "yeast wranglers" have been hard at work trying to find a native strain of *Saccharomyces* to use as the house yeast.

The brewery is well known for its beers made with local persimmons, basil, and sweet potatoes, but Fullsteam is also a big champion of corn. Locally sourced grains (both barley and corn) are used in El Toro, a cream ale, and corn adds a wonderfully light snap to Paycheck Pilsner. There's a comfort and familiarity in both of these beers that comes from a hint of corn on the palate. It tracks as very slightly sweet and, given corn's association with Southern cuisine, recognizably local. When he founded Fullsteam, Wilson said, "We earnestly wanted to explore what it meant to craft distinctly Southern beer." Turning to corn was one obvious way to communicate that goal.

BREWMASTER BRIAN MANDEVILLE

Like many professional brewers, Mandeville started as a homebrewer, a passion he pursued for a decade before going pro. While his interest in brewing grew, he worked as a political campaign field organizer — he has a degree in political science — radio station director, and distribution manager for the *New York Times*.

Eventually, his love of beer led him to Virginia's O'Connor Brewing in 2011, and then to Fullsteam in 2015. Along the way he augmented his knowledge by studying at Siebel and picking up a certificate in brewing technology. One of his big interests at Fullsteam is incorporating local ingredients and particularly the work on isolating a strain of native *Saccharomyces* to use in the brewery.

Understanding Corn

Corn's principal use, since German immigrants figured out how to deploy it in concert with protein-rich American six-row barley, has been to lighten beer. You don't taste it in many corn beers because the brewer doesn't want you to: he's using corn as a way of adding fermentable sugar without adding body — that's why it's invisible in Belgian beer. The idea that corn should conceal itself behind the flavor of barley is a remnant of two different prejudices, one by European brewers who think of barley as the "proper" flavor and one by Americans who associate corn with the dilution of flavor by industrial breweries.

But it's also possible to use corn to add flavor, particularly in light-bodied pale ales and lagers. "Corn is a fantastic ingredient," says Fullsteam's Mandeville. "It can be used to give a beer a slightly drier mouthfeel and in the right amounts can add a layer of pleasant cornlike flavors and aromas." You most commonly see corn used in pre-Prohibition lagers and cream ales, but it works wonderfully as a way of signaling the New World. That's exactly what Steven Pauwels used it for when he made his American farmhouse, Tank 7, and it seems especially appropriate in rustic ales.

Brewing with Corn

The second brewery I toured in Belgium was Palm's, in Steenhuffel. When we got to the brewhouse, I encountered a vessel I'd never seen before: a cereal cooker. Typical in Belgium, it was created to gelatinize corn, readying it for the enzymatic activity that will break down starches into sugars when added to the main mash. This is a time-consuming process, and while it's possible for homebrewers to do cereal mashing (see Cereal Mashing, page 254), there's a much easier solution.

Here's Mandeville: "The easiest, by far, is to use flaked corn (malted, flaked, or torrefied [puffed] versions). In this case the cereal has already been gelatinized and can be added to the mash of even a single infusion brew with great success."

You can also use this product at the commercial scale, as Fullsteam does in Paycheck Pilsner. It's even possible to use popcorn.

"You read that correctly," Mandeville joked to me. "I said popcorn. The process of popping it will gelatinize the corn, and it will be mash ready. The trick to this is that you need popcorn without *any* additives: no oils, butter flavoring, or other strange things." When you see the word "torrefied" applied to grain, this is what they're talking about. (I haven't heard homebrew nerds kidding about "torrefied corn" at the theater, but they could.)

> **After Thomas Morgan's first batch of American weissbier, members of his homebrew club in Ohio all went home and started working with corn to see what they could come up with. Morgan shipped me out a 12-pack containing the group's effort, and the range of flavors was impressive.**

Corn can make up any percentage of the grist, though when added as a lightener in commercial breweries, it typically doesn't exceed 20 percent. A few years back homebrewer (and University of Dayton professor) Thomas Morgan began experimenting with revival recipes taken from a classic old text by authors Robert Wahl and Max Henius called the *American Handy-Book of the Brewing, Malting, and Auxiliary Trades*. He started with a beer they called American Weissbier, a 30 percent corn beer based on Berliner weisse. Replicating the nineteenth-century standards, he used 50 percent six-row barley and 20 percent wheat along with 30 percent corn. He described it as "delightful and refreshing" but said, "the corn is there, but not as much as I would have thought." This illustrates why corn is used in industrial breweries — it can easily disappear in front of your eyes. Morgan was intrigued by corn's potential and continued experimenting.

The lessons of that experiment support my own conclusions. (You can read about them at Morgan's blog, *What We're Drinking*.) Morgan found that the corn contributed only fairly subtle flavors of sweetness and corn. The effect on body and mouthfeel is more pronounced. Corn lightens as expected but also gives a beer a clean, crisp quality that seems almost lagerlike (no wonder it was used in cream ales). But because it also contributes to the perception of sweetness, a beer made with corn will finish crisply but leave a kiss of sugar behind. This is that comforting, familiar quality I described, and although subtle, it adds a nice dimension to these beers.

ISN'T CORN AN "ADJUNCT"?

At this point my position on corn's legitimacy is probably coming through loud and clear, but it's worth acknowledging that corn and rice have until recent years been as popular as a GMO salesman at an organic food convention. They fall into a category Americans call "adjuncts," which also includes sugar and other cereal grains. In the early days of craft brewing, Americans were motivated in large part by wanting to bring quality and craftsmanship back to brewing. They rejected anything that smacked of industrial shortcuts, such as using "fillers" in beer to boost alcohol cheaply. This reflected an element of naïveté, since many of the traditional beers of Europe are made using wheat, corn, and sugar, but it was an important statement of purpose for the times.

When the trade organization representing craft breweries formed, it held the use of adjuncts in contempt, codifying this view. The Brewers Association wrote that a member must "either [have] an all-malt flagship (the beer which represents the greatest volume among that brewer's brands) or [have] at least 50% of its volume in either all-malt beers or in beers which use adjuncts to enhance rather than lighten flavor." It didn't seem to occur to the organization that corn might be an expression of American identity and heritage.

In 2014 the Brewers Association acknowledged its mistake. "The revised definition recognizes that adjunct brewing is quite literally traditional, as brewers have long brewed with what has been available to them." The new definition no longer mentions adjuncts or carries the bias against their use. It's probably time to retire the concept of "adjunct" altogether. Beer can be and has been made of a range of local grains native to the region, and the idea of calling some of them adjuncts reflects nothing more than unexamined chauvinism.

CORN BEER

**BRIAN
MANDEVILLE**

—

FULLSTEAM

— **MALT BILL** —

6.75 pounds American six-row malt (90%)

0.75 pound flaked corn (10%)

SINGLE-INFUSION MASH

152°F (67°C) for 60 minutes

60-MINUTE BOIL

0.5 ounce East Kent Goldings, 60 minutes (5% AA, contribution of 11 IBU)

1.25 ounces East Kent Goldings at whirlpool/hop back (5% AA, contribution of 9 IBUs)

Ferment with a clean American ale yeast like Wyeast 1056 or White Labs WLP001 at 68°F (20°C).

PACKAGE

Keg or bottle.

- Expected OG: 10° P/1.040
- Expected TG: 2.3° P/1.009
- Expected ABV: 4.0%
- Expected bitterness: 20 IBU

Notes: You can adjust the grist to suit your interests, going up to 30 percent corn and substituting some portion of the six-row malt with two-row. Six-row malt has more enzymatic power than two-row, which is useful in converting the corn — although, as Mandeville notes, "modern two-row malt should be able to handle it just fine." This recipe was designed to be used in conjunction with a cereal mash, which is described on page 254. If you do a cereal mash, everything else in the recipe remains the same.

Next Steps

It's worth taking a moment to mention American six-row malt, which is a natural dancing partner for corn. Two- and six-row barleys are distinguished by the way they grow on the stalk; six-row barley grows in a tighter pattern around the stalk and therefore each seed is less plump than two-row seeds; two-row seeds are flared out to each side of the stalk, giving them some room to fatten up.

A century ago the difference between the two varieties was marked, and the husky, high-protein, and lower-starch six-row was substantially inferior. It did have the benefit of having greater enzyme content, which helped convert the starches in corn, which lacked enzymes. (This is why they worked well together.) Beyond that, the higher protein content can lead to a haziness in the beer, and the thicker husk can create astringency on the palate. Again, both of these issues are mitigated when corn is used as part of the grist.

We don't tend to think of "tradition" when we're talking about the old practice of using six-row malt and corn together. They are often counted as compromises to the "right" way of brewing — an industrial sop to the bottom line. Think about it another way. From the perspective of a Bavarian lager brewer, there's nothing right about the way Belgian saison or English cask ale is made, either. They violate many of the tenets of Reinheitsgebot — and are just philosophically very different beers. American beers made with six-row and corn are no more "wrong" by this formulation than other traditional European ales.

What's more, they constitute an important tradition in American brewing. Most of the old nineteenth-century beer styles grew out of this tandem, and they create a typical "American" set of characteristics. Experiment with the ratios, maybe even throwing wheat (a great American standard) into the mix.

The final step for a classic American taste is hop selection. Mandeville uses Goldings in El Toro, and he recommends them in this recipe. But if you are looking for a throwback hop, consider Cluster, the grandfather of American hop varieties. The variety was dominant at the end of the nineteenth century (96 percent of all hops) and well into the twentieth. Many of these old American hops were originally European varieties crossed with American (or Canadian) wild hop varieties. They were strident, sometimes harsh hops that give sharp bitterness, a characteristic black currant flavor, and sometimes a note critics refer to as "cat piss." (Delightful!)

Hops tend to drift over the years, taking on characteristics of nearby varieties, and modern Clusters do not exhibit especially objectionable flavors. Clusters do retain a rough-hewn, rustic quality that is another signal of local tradition. Other old-school American hops you might try are Galena, Brewer's Gold, and Comet.

Cereal Mashing

Most homebrewers will not bother to conduct a cereal mash on their corn; it's just too damn much trouble. But some homebrewers will want to try it anyway — maybe *because* it's too damn much trouble. If you find yourself in that latter category, Brian Mandeville has you covered. Here are his instructions.

To understand the procedure, it may be necessary to understand some of the science behind what cereal mashing does: gelatinization. Gelatinization is the swelling and disorganization of starch granules after being heated in water. There are several indicators that we look for to determine when we have successfully gelatinized the grain we are working with. Generally speaking, you will notice the swelling of the individual kernels, an increase in the viscosity, increased translucency, and an increased solubility. Anyone who has made corn grits before should be familiar with these signs, as this is the same process that changes hard grits into a creamy delicious dish. Now to the process.

Begin by milling your cereal adjuncts (you will want to mill them to about half the size of your standard crush for brewing; preground corn grits work great for this process). Now add 10 to 20 percent of your milled base barley malt (this base malt will be the source of some needed enzymes).

Add hot water to this grain mixture (50 percent of your total mash water) in your kettle. It is useful to stir this mixture because it sticks easily and can form into a kind of grit cake that is neither pleasant to eat nor does it make good beer.

Begin to heat up your kettle and bring the mixture to the appropriate gelatinization temperature for the cereal adjuncts you are working with. Each kind of grain (from oats to corn) has an optimal temperature range at which this occurs. For corn we're looking to hold the mixture between the low 140s F (60–62°C) and as high as the mid-160s F (73–74°C). You will now want to hold the mixture there for 30 minutes, continuing to stir to avoid scorching and sticking.

Now raise the temperature of your mash until you achieve a mild boil (keep an extremely close eye on it during this stage of the process, as cereal mashes have a tendency to boil over very quickly). You will want to boil the mash for another 30 minutes. This is when the signs of gelatinization that were mentioned earlier should become the most evident.

Meanwhile, in your mash tun dough in your remaining grist and water (the other 50 percent of your total mash water). You will need to preheat your mash tun with hot water, but you can use room temperature water to dough in the remainder of your grist. Don't worry too much about your mash temperature at this stage; we will be using the hot cereal mash to dramatically increase the mash temperature.

After it has boiled for 30 minutes, move the hot cereal mash into your mash tun with your cold mash, and mix vigorously to achieve an even temperature. Some additional hot or cold water may be needed to adjust your temperature.

Continue your conversion phase, recirculation, and sparge as you would normally for the rest of the mash.

Part 7

Brewing

WILD

If you wanted to boil the entire enterprise of modern brewing down to a reasonable definition, it would be this: activities meant to rid breweries of wild yeast and bacteria. The first great innovation in brewing history was malting grain; the second great innovation was hopping. Then in 1857 Louis Pasteur brought brewing into modernity when he described the process not just — or even primarily — of fermentation but the process of infection. That was the third and final innovation.

Here's how he put it in *Etudes sur la Bière* (*Studies on Fermentation*): "How is it that the use of ice and yeast operating at a low temperature [in lager brewing] so greatly facilitates the preservation of our beer and enables us to secure such striking advantages? The explanation is simple: the diseased ferments, which we have pointed out, rarely appear at a lower temperature than 10°C [50°F] and at that temperature their germs cease to be active."

Wild brewing — the activity of courting feral yeasts and bacteria and trying to harness them to produce something tasty — is a remnant of the time before Pasteur. It is a weird and dangerous activity, and more than a few commercial breweries have failed to corral those wild yeasts and keep them out of nonwild beer.

> **Wild brewing — the activity of courting feral yeasts and bacteria and trying to harness them to produce something tasty — is a weird and dangerous activity.**

For the homebrewer, however, it's nowhere near as risky. We often brew alfresco anyway, so there's no real brewery to infect. If you do find your porter has taken on a musk, it's cheap and easy enough to dump the plastic and rubber parts of your equipment and replace them. And since homebrewers are by nature curious, it is a wonderful way to run some fascinating experiments.

There are a couple of downsides. Commercial-scale wild brewing still does exist in parts of Belgium and Germany (and, increasingly, in the United States), but makers of lambic and tart Flanders ales rely heavily on vat aging. Nature-inoculated beers take a long time to develop, and they require the presence of low levels of oxygen to sustain their microbiomes. Wood is porous, and oxygen slowly seeps into the beer — a critical ingredient to the development of wild ales. Furthermore, it's not just the presence of oxygen, but the right amount of oxygen. Wine barrels, with their thin staves and large surface area, expose beer to more air than large vats with thick staves and a smaller volume-to-surface ratio. (See Barrel Aging, page 54, for more.)

As a consequence, the practices of breweries making wild ales are the least adaptable to the home brewery. Rodenbach has tuns as large as 65,000 liters (over 550 barrels, or 17,000 gallons); lambic makers regularly use foeders 10 times the size of a wine barrel. Even if you bought a wine barrel and managed to fill it with wild-inoculated beer, it would be difficult to manage because wine barrels are so small by comparison (though Cantillon ferments and ages in wine barrels). Anything smaller will just expose the beer to too much oxygen. For small-scale projects we have to look elsewhere, using the wisdom of the old masters only as a guide. Fortunately, there are a few work-arounds.

What Is Wild Ale?

But before we get to those work-arounds in the following chapters, let's consider wild ale. What exactly are we talking about? There's a nebulous category that runs the gamut of everything from Berliner weisse and gose to lambic. The tart ales of Flanders, funk-tinged saisons, a catchall category of "wild ales," obscure or mostly obsolete styles such as Lichtenhainer and Münster altbier (never mind adambier and jopenbier) — all of these have either been ruled in or out of the group from time to time. For the purposes of this book, let's think of wild ales as having these characteristics.

WILD YEAST. There's a whole category of beer made with acidification by *Lactobacillus*. Lactic fermentation can be conducted with laboratory yeast within a few days (see Kettle Souring, page 106). It produces a clean, citrusy tartness. It's a reliable way to make a beer, one that's reproducible batch after batch. Let's exclude this kind of beer from the mix. For a truly wild ale, wild *Brettanomyces* must be present. During alcoholic fermentation, *Brettanomyces* produces an entirely different flavor profile, one more complex and varied. It is responsible for that unexpected balsamic note in tart Flanders ales and the tropical fruit notes in lambics. It can also give a beer a dry, leathery quality along with that famous "barnyard" funkiness, and even produce acetic acid. All of this is categorically different from the flavors you get from a lactic fermentation.

LONG MATURATION. As Crooked Stave's Chad Yakobson has ably demonstrated, *Brettanomyces* is capable of producing fairly straightforward primary fermentations. We're more interested in what *Brettanomyces* does after many months — or a few years. *Brettanomyces* has the capacity to consume sugars that regular *Saccharomyces* cannot, and in the long period of activity, it continues to produce those flavor compounds that increase the complexity of a beer. Young wild ale — lambic, say — tastes markedly different before it ages, thanks to this process of slow maturation. It's a flavor profile that can't be imitated by other processes or sped up.

NATURAL INOCULATION. Pitching a strain of *Brettanomyces* and letting it work on a beer for a couple of years is adequate to meet the definition of wild ale. But if the beer is inoculated naturally through ambient yeasts and bacteria (spontaneous fermentation), it definitely is. As we'll see in chapter 26, there's a reason to try to use nature to inoculate your beer. Each location on the planet has a unique mix of yeast and bacteria, and those organisms express themselves in the beer. Spontaneous beer made in Portland, Maine (Allagash) doesn't taste like the stuff made in Tillamook, Oregon (De Garde); Dexter, Michigan (Jolly Pumpkin); or Brussels (the lambic breweries).

There are only two chapters in this section, and the first, Tart Flanders Ales, describes the process of using laboratory-cultured wild yeasts and bacteria. This chapter contains a discussion about the process of making a beer like those of Rodenbach or Verhaeghe, but it applies more generally to pitched "wild" cultures. The second chapter, Spontaneous Ales, describes different ways to work with natural inoculation, aging, the use of fruit, and blending.

• CHAPTER 25 •

TART FLANDERS ALES

The northern and especially western part of Belgium has long been the home of brown ales. Although pale beers have slowly made incursions into the market for these ales, they are still common there, and some of the most famous — Westvleteren, St. Bernardus, Rodenbach — are still under healthy production. Even new revivalist breweries like De Dolle and De Struise have taken up the tradition. For the most part most of the modern brown ales are no longer kissed by wild yeast, but there are a few exceptions. Rodenbach, Verhaeghe, Liefmans, Bockor, and others continue to make round, fruity, and, in particular, tart brown beers like their ancestors did.

Efforts to replicate these beers outside Belgium have largely been failures. Getting the right balance among the elements is difficult, and many American results have been punishing rather than pleasant. In Belgium the beers are wood-aged, and many use yeast strains once obtained from Rodenbach, which used to spontaneously ferment its beer. The elusive balance they achieve rests on a triangle of flavors: rich with fruity esters, a bit sweet, and tart with an acidity that often presents as a distinctive balsamic note.

They are sometimes known (thanks mainly to the writer Michael Jackson) as the "Burgundies of Belgium," and while there's no mistaking them for wine, there is something in the balance of the elements that evokes their deep, vinous flavors. (And if you ever have a guest over who believes he doesn't like beer but loves red wine, hand him a bottle of Verhaeghe's Duchesse de Bourgogne and smile.) These beers are very hard to replicate at home, but it can be done — if you know a few of the key secrets of "mixed fermentation."

EST pFriem Family Brewers 2012
HOOD RIVER, OREGON

Josh Pfriem (rhymes with "team") is one of the most methodical brewers I've ever met. A native Seattleite, he fell in love with good beer while he was studying business marketing in college. That love led to homebrewing, and homebrewing led to an epiphany. "After that first batch of homebrew, I knew I wanted to open my own brewery and be a brewmaster."

He stuck with the business marketing major, but after graduation pursued brewing. He started at Wasatch Brewing (Utah), then moved to Chuckanut

(Washington), and finally ended at Full Sail (Hood River), learning at each stop. Because of the laws in Utah, he learned great discipline making flavorful low-alcohol beers at Wasatch, then learned how to make high-quality, balanced lagers at Chuckanut. Finally, he felt he needed to understand large-scale production brewing, which made Full Sail a good capper to his on-the-jobs brewing education.

Despite this varied experience, the beers of Belgium exerted a special gravitational pull on Pfriem's interests. Before starting at Chuckanut, he and his wife spent several weeks touring the country on their bikes. "To experience those beers fresh, the vibrancy, the finesse, how well the beer paired with food — it was amazing." When he opened pFriem in 2012, he already had a strong idea of the kinds of beers he wanted to make — European, food-friendly beers with an accent on Belgian styles.

But even more, he knew he wanted to make slow, barrel-aged beers like those he tried in Brussels and Roeselare. From the very start his vision for pFriem Family Brewers included a barrel-aging program, and some of his first batches were beers that would become lambic-style and Flanders-style tart ales. When he debuted Flanders Red two years after the brewery opened, he told me, "These are the beers I founded the brewery to make."

Despite the fact that this was their maiden release, pFriem Flanders Red is one of the most accomplished examples of this type of beer made outside Belgium. It captures that rare triangle of flavors — esters, acidity, and sweetness. I was not surprised to learn that he approached the beer the same way the Belgians did, using mixed fermentation.

Understanding Tart Flanders Ales

People have been trying to catalog the styles of Flanders for a long time. Writing in the 1850s, Georges Lacambre clustered the dark beers of the region together out of convenience, acknowledging that they came "in a number of varieties. . . . It varies greatly from place to place and sometimes in the same locality; often in the same town there are not two brewers whose beers are the same." The one thing they shared, their color, was actually a proxy for a brewing method: extremely long boil lengths. The standard was 10 to 12 hours for the famous beers of Mechelen, and in West Flanders they were longer — sometimes an astonishing 20 hours.

More than a century later, the writer Michael Jackson divided them into two types: "oud bruins" (Liefmans-like beers) and Flanders red ales (Rodenbach-like). But this is both too expansive and also too limiting. There are some notable differences between these two models, but why stop at just two? Bockor and Van Honsebrouck make brown beers that get their color from lager mixed with spontaneously fermented ale. Bavik makes Petrus, a similar beer that uses brown ale instead of lager. De Dolle Brouwers boil their brown for three hours — echoes of the past — to encourage Maillard reactions.

Verhaeghe and Rodenbach have vinegar/balsamic notes and pure, sharp tartness. Bockor (Bellegems Bruin) has a similar nose but is smoother and lacks the sharp acetic sour of Rodenbach. De Dolle is a huge, deep beer with a dry, austere finish. Liefmans has a sweet-and-lactic-sour character that is less complex but more comforting. Bavik's Petrus Oud Bruin is woody and bitter but has a nonbalsamic vinegar note that penetrates the palate. These beers are, just as beers of old, different in their own ways. It makes no sense to divide them — as in Lacambre's day they are all singular ales.

Collectively, they compose a range of beers that have a loose affinity. They use different methods of mixed fermentation and aging to create layered, complex beers that use malt sweetness, ester production, and tart, wild flavors to balance one another. When he approached his own version of this type of beer, Josh Pfriem did not try to emulate a particular example. He used his own New World method of mixed fermentation that borrowed from Rodenbach, added the element of wine-barrel aging, and created a beer with a light acidity, bright cherry esters, and a gentle cosseting of natural sweetness.

It is very much in the vein of the old examples, but not a replica. If you are a homebrewer approaching this difficult style, it's worth keeping this in mind: your practices and techniques are liable to produce a beer unlike those of Rodenbach or Liefmans — but that doesn't mean it won't be authentic. Your goal should be to produce a beer with the triangle of flavor, one that is balanced and tasty, not necessarily a replica of one of the famous brands.

Brewing a Tart Flanders Ale

Let's start with Rodenbach, which by any measure is the undisputed king of the category, and work our way back. Founded just after Belgian independence in 1836, Rodenbach didn't become the brewery we know until a third-generation family member, Eugène, returned from England, where they were making vat-aged porter. In 1872 he began collecting wooden vats — foeders — to age his beer the way the porter brewers did. Over time the brewery dug out 10 vast cellars underneath the brewery, where 294 foeders now sit. And it is in those cellars — not in the shining, state-of-the-art brewery — where Rodenbach is truly made.

The essence of Rodenbach's process is this "mixed fermentation" I've referenced, and here's the brewery's master brewer, Rudi Ghequire, describing it: "In our process we work with a yeast culture with eight different yeast strains and also a little bit of lactic bacteria. During the first week we have an alcoholic fermentation from the yeast cells, and after one week the lactic bacteria take over. During the lagering time [four to five weeks] we reduce the yeast cells in the beer by precipitation, and then we send a nearly bright, young beer to the wood. The big difference between spontaneous fermentation and mixed fermentation is with spontaneous you send *wort* to wood and we send young *beer*. Beer has an alcoholic protection, so it is less risky. When you reuse yeast from spontaneous fermentation, you have arrived at 'mixed fermentation.'"

The key here is that Rodenbach brews a beer first, then sends it, fully fermented (and acidified by *Lactobacillus*), to the wood. This means there's only limited sugars available for consumption by the wild yeast resident in the foeders. In the two years that beer sits ripening, those microorganisms will both add acidity (pH in the foeders can drop to 3.2) and dry the beer out (some foeders will produce beer that is 98 percent attenuated).

Even more important are the development of fruity esters that give the beer so much of its character. This makes Rodenbach somewhat similar to a Berliner weisse, where the *Brettanomyces* metabolize acids into esters. Like Berliner weisse, Rodenbach does not have an overtly *Brett*-like palate; rather, it's the interaction of the yeast and bacteria that produces the critical esters. After aging, Rodenbach blends aged lots back with fresh, green beer (67 percent aged stock in Grand Cru, 25 percent in regular Rodenbach). The esters harmonize with the young beer to give Rodenbach its balancing sweetness.

Wyeast offers a version of Rodenbach's complex yeast strain (3763, Roeselare Ale Blend), and many commercial breweries have used it to ferment wort — almost always a disaster. The wild yeasts and bacteria turn the beer into a chemical stew. Josh Pfriem follows Rodenbach's lead and starts out making a standard beer before adding the funk. He makes a beer that will feed the complex biochemistry to come, not one that tastes particularly good at birth. "None of the beers are attractive to drink before they go into the barrels — they're sweet and flabby. But that's what we want. It's not about what it tastes like going in, it's what it tastes like at the finish. We do high mash temperatures, and we build some big dextrines and proteins, stuff for the bugs to chew on. It's a low-IBU, very Belgian-y base to start with." This is the trick, whether you're using the Roeselare strain or pitching your own wild yeasts.

Pfriem mixes a precise cocktail of cultures, and he wants *only* those cultures. Because it's going on wood, he tries to keep the environment as sanitary as possible ("We treat it like pilsner"), purging the barrels of oxygen before filling them with the beer. "We remove the yeast from the beer before it goes into the barrels, and then we're inoculating with a culture of *Lactobacillus*, *Pediococcus*, and *Brettanomyces*." Wyeast grows it up, and they pitch a blend of the three "at the rate of a liter per wine barrel." Pfriem doesn't have the luxury of being able to work with either an old yeast strain that came from spontaneous ferments nor 100-plus-year-old foeders. When you're working from scratch, you have to add your own bugs.

It's a very old style of brewing, and understanding these kinds of beer requires thinking differently. Ghequire left me with a coda that can serve as a North Star for making tart Flanders ales. "The production method that we use is conservation by acidification or acidity. You have to go back in time to when people didn't know the healthy work of hops. They found another method to preserve the beer, and that was conservation by acidity. So they stored the beer on wood, and it became a very acid beer after a period . . . because [in an acidic environment], bacteria don't grow so fast."

THE TASTE OF CHERRIES

One of the most fondly regarded beers by people of my vintage was cherry-infused Rodenbach, which returned in 2016. Cherry is such a perfect addition because the vinous esters already give a hint of it. Cherry seems to be a natural fit for these kinds of beers — Liefmans (Kriek) and Verhaeghe (Echt Kriekenbier) both make versions of their regular beer aged on cherry.

It's easy to implement. Choose cherries with rich colors and full taste. Since you'll be using plenty of souring microorganisms in the beer, you don't need sour cherries for acidity — though of course they work well, too.

Add whole cherries to the carboy at a rate of half a pound to 1 pound per gallon for the final 6 to 12 months on the wild yeast and bacteria. There's no need to crush the cherries; the wild yeast will consume them whole. The pits will add an additional layer of tannins, which in these beers has a cinnamon/spice quality, which is itself a great note.

MALT BILL
10.25 pounds Gambrinus pilsner malt (93%)
6 ounces Weyermann CaraFoam malt (3%)
4 ounces Weyermann Cara Aroma malt (2%)
1.5 ounces acidulated malt (0.9%)

SINGLE-INFUSION MASH

154°F (68°C) for 60 minutes

70-MINUTE BOIL

0.67 ounce German Tettnanger, 60 minutes (4.5% AA, contribution of 10 IBU)

FERMENTATION AND CONDITIONING

Ferment with Wyeast 3538/3787 or White Labs WLP530/WLP540 at between 65 and 70°F (18 and 21°C). Make sure the wort is well oxygenated (25 parts per million, ideally). Rack beer after primary fermentation, and cold condition for 2 weeks (keeping beer as close to 32°F [0°C] as your equipment allows). The beer should be around 3° P/1.012 at this stage.

Rack to a clean carboy, taking care to leave behind as much flocculated yeast as possible, and let rise to room temperature. Pitch a culture of wild yeast and bacteria: Wyeast 3763 (Roeselare) or 3278 (Lambic blend) or White Labs WLP665 (Flemish Ale) or WLP655 (Sour Mix 1). Let mature for 18 to 24 months.

PACKAGE

Bottle-condition only, shooting for 3.5 volumes of carbonation.

- Expected OG: 15° P/1.061
- Expected TG (base beer): 3° P/1.012

JOSH PFRIEM

—

PFRIEM FAMILY
BREWERS

- Expected TG (after aging): 1.3° P/1.005

- Expected ABV: 7.4%

- Expected bitterness: 10 IBU

Notes: Pfriem suggests treating both mash liquor and wort with a gram per gallon of calcium chloride (CaCl$_2$). Hop type is not critical, so use any low-IBU variety available. If you want to use an actual wine barrel, find a barrel "that has seen at least two turns of wine." (Wood character is not appropriate to this style.) Pfriem makes his own blend of wild cultures, and you can, too, but lab blends are best as a starting place.

NEXT STEPS

It's important to start out with a good base beer that has, as Pfriem puts it, "stuff for the bugs to chew on," but this style really depends on those 18 to 24 months in the carboy. The purpose of wood aging is not only to inoculate the beer but to feed it a slow, steady diet of oxygen. For Pfriem this means leaving his casks alone. "We stay out of the barrels. If you get into it, you're going to get more [oxygen in]. You'll develop acetic acid, but we try to keep it as minimal as possible. We want the other microbes to live well." Wood is the ideal vessel to strike this balance, and Pfriem acknowledges that "it's hard to make such a dynamic beer without aging in an oak barrel."

But it's not impossible. Using wood products is discussed in the Old Ale chapter, though the intention here is different. In the case of wild ales, you're not trying to add a woody flavor, but make sure that slow drip of oxygen seeps into the beer. I recommend a small amount of oak cubes; they have less surface area than chips or spirals, which means they'll release oxygen the slowest. Use just 2 ounces, added at the start of aging. You can buy different types, and I recommend a medium French oak. French oak has a less aggressive oaky flavor, and a medium toast will reduce the woody flavors of light toast without getting into the smoky flavors from dark-roasted wood. To further remove some of the flavor-causing oils, boil the cubes for 10 minutes and then let them dry fully before adding them.

Josh Pfriem starts with a standard all-*Saccharomyces* base beer, but if you want to try something closer to Rodenbach's process, try the technique described by Matthias Richter in the gose recipe. He pitches a 1:1 ratio of *Saccharomyces* and *Lactobacillus*. Use one of the same strains Pfriem recommends (Wyeast 3538/3787 or White Labs WLP530/WLP540) and combine with *Lactobacillus* (Wyeast 5335/White Labs WLP677), fermenting at 70°F (21°C). You can also use the alternate kettle-souring technique described in chapter 10.

Blending

One of the secrets to professional brewing — and a necessity in brewing beers with wild yeast — is blending. Each wooden vessel becomes its own ecosystem, and a batch of Rodenbach that comes out of Foeder 133 will not resemble Foeder 132's beer, even if they were made from the same base beer. Rodenbach is made by blending many different foeders together into a mother blend that contains the typical elements expected in that beer.

Lambic is almost always blended as well, though with a different goal. When blending lambic for a gueuze or other blend, blenders are looking to create layers and layers of complexity in a beer, not match flavors from previous batches. At Cantillon Jean Van Roy starts by tasting his older lots first. "It depends on my old beer. If I have a mellow lambic with some soft beer, I can work with two- and one-year-olds with mild character. If I have an old beer with [sharp] character, I have to find other types of beer. Each blend is different."

You have to plan ahead, but blending is a great way to work with homebrew, too. If you have two or more carboys of wild ale, it allows you to compose a beer with the strongest elements of each (while concealing unwanted elements). When blending, think in parts (1 ounce, or a shot glass), and start composing with your different lots. Start with equal blends, and then begin layering in more parts from beers you want to accentuate.

It's even worth considering keeping a batch of beer around that doesn't seem particularly good, because in very small amounts it may add a great deal to a blended beer. At Solera Brewery, not far from pFriem, Jason Kahler describes how he adds a hint of acetic acid from an otherwise unpleasant batch. "I really like a touch of acetic acid, and I have a keg of very hard, acetic beer just to top off a beer. Even just 6 ounces of hard beer in 5 gallons can bring out *so* many different flavors — but not make it taste acetic, either."

· CHAPTER 26 ·

SPONTANEOUS ALES

 **Y**east is everywhere. It lives on, in, and around just about everything on the planet. There are more than 1,500 different species of this single-celled fungus, and their ubiquity made it possible for humans to begin making beer long before they domesticated and started malting grain. In much of the world, people still make rudimentary old beers the way our ancestors did, letting the ambient yeasts and bacteria turn grain-steeped water into traditional beer, such as African *umqombothi* (from sorghum), South American *chicha* (from corn), Russian *kvass* (from rye), and Asian *handiya* and *huangjiu* (from rice).

But in the brewing countries of Europe, much safer domesticated yeasts have displaced all but a few tiny remnants of commercial beers made by spontaneous fermentation, and these — all located in Belgium — were on death's door by the 1990s. Then a funny thing happened. Craft brewers began to rediscover the thrill of brewing with feral microbes, and now there are dozens of breweries openly courting wild yeasts and making a new generation of spontaneous ales. More than a handful are even devoted to making mostly or exclusively spontaneous ales. A couple of decades ago, people weren't even sure whether it was possible to make these beers outside Belgium, but now we know that not only is it possible but that, depending on a brewery's location, they can be exceptionally accomplished.

The processes used to make the most famous wild ales — lambics — are beyond the ability of most homebrewers. Those are vat-aged beers, and the smallest vessels they use, wine barrels, are too big for all but the most avid homebrewer. But the basic process of fermenting wild is tailor-made to small-scale brewing and is one of the few approaches where homebrewers can meet or exceed the quality of the pros. Even more alluring, fermenting wild beers at home reflects the terroir of the backyard, meaning that no two of these beers will taste the same.

EST **Solera Brewery** 2012
PARKDALE, OREGON

It's safe to say that Solera has one of the prettiest locations of any brewery anywhere. When you walk out the back door of the brewery, where picnic tables have been scattered around a grassy field, you stand at the foot of Mount Hood, Oregon's tallest mountain. Just beyond this alfresco dining room is an orchard of fruit trees, and Hood watches over it like a curious giant. Founder and brewer

271
SPONTANEOUS ALES

Jason Kahler could sell cans of Natty Light and people would come just for the view. Remarkably, though, he serves some of the best beer in the United States. Kahler has developed a communion with both wild yeast and the fruit that grows in the surrounding valleys (the latter collects the former), and his wild ales, saisons, and weissbiers bear the mark of this relationship.

Kahler named his brewery after a process he developed as a homebrewer, one borrowed from a technique developed in Spain and Portugal to age wine and sherry. In brewing it's a method of preserving an ecosystem of wild cultures in a vat of beer. Other breweries also use it (notably New Belgium), but Kahler discovered it accidentally when he was blending his own homebrew. It wasn't until later that the word "solera" appeared in his vocabulary — and became a regular part of his brewing routine.

Kahler got his start as a homebrewer in the mid-1990s. That led to a job at Fitger's Brewhouse in Duluth, Minnesota, and then to a more technical education at Siebel. He arrived in Oregon in 2000 to work for a winery, where he became interested in blending. He was still homebrewing, and that was when he began experimenting with the solera project. Eventually he went on to work at Full Sail, Walking Man, and Big Horse, breweries all located in close proximity to Parkdale.

He didn't get to practice much funky brewing at those breweries, so he continued to do so at home — and it was a central focus of Solera when he founded the brewery in 2012 with John Hitt. Many brewers are gun-shy in the presence of untamed yeasts, but Kahler seems to relish having them around. "You can get *Brettanomyces* from the laboratory, and you can get *Brett* from the air," he says. "I love *Brettanomyces*, I love *Lactobacillus*, *Pedio*. They're all there in the air; you don't *need* to buy them." And even more: they give Solera's beer the flavor of the place, a quality of terroir. For a brewery situated where Solera is, it's an understandable impulse.

Understanding Spontaneous Ales

Many people think we only recently learned how yeast works, after Louis Pasteur described it in 1857. That's not entirely true. While brewers didn't know it was caused by tiny fungi, they understood the mechanics well enough. Any homebrewer will realize why: after fermentation the bottom of the carboy is covered by an inch of white stuff. At Bamberg's Schlenkerla, master brewer Matthias Trum put it this way: "*Zeug*, which is 'stuff,' was the German word." He added that managing the *zeug* was even a job at the brewery, handled by the *hefener* (yeast man). "The hefener's job was to harvest the yeast from the batches, to press out as much remaining beer as possible, which was sold at a low price to the poor, and then the yeast was added to the next batch."

So even hundreds of years ago, making a beer without adding yeast was unusual. Brewers used a device called a coolship — a broad cooling pan — to cool hot wort. Most breweries used it in conjunction with such other devices as drip chillers, and they pitched their yeast as soon as they could get it to the right temperature. But lambic makers in the region near Brussels left it in the coolship overnight and in the morning transferred it straight to vats, where it would slowly ferment and ripen over the course of years. It was one of the last traditions of spontaneously fermented beer left in Europe.

That's still how lambics (and a few other Belgian beers) are made. Once they put the boiling wort in the coolship, brewers stand back and let nature take its course. What follows is a strange and wonderful dance of microbes captured by that pan of cooling wort. They each contribute different flavor and aroma compounds to the beer, and they each act at different times. Apiculate yeasts and *Saccharomyces* (regular, but wild, ale yeasts) are the first to act, and within a few days they add enough alcohol to make the solution somewhat sterile. *Pediococcus* bacteria become active after about four months, and they create lactic acid, making these beers tart. The last major actor is *Brettanomyces*, which will begin adding fruity esters within weeks, and then continue to ferment complex sugars for years.

CHARACTERISTICS

Spontaneous ales are recognizable by their complexity, tartness, and funky flavors, but their differences are surprising. *Brettanomyces*, in particular, is an amazingly diverse yeast. Some strains produce fruity compounds (depending on the strain, they might taste like mango, cherries, or lemon). Some are decidedly funky or leathery, others softer and rounded. Even in a tiny region, such as the Payottenland of Belgium, the microbes vary from one brewery to the next. Jean Van Roy, who now runs things at Cantillon in Brussels, told me he'd seen laboratory analyses of the different lambics. "They make a picture of the *Brettanomyces* in each lambic. They analyzed lambic from seven, eight different breweries. All the pictures are different."

Jason Kahler echoes Van Roy and points out that when you pitch lab-grown *Brettanomyces*, you're not getting this region-by-region variability. "You're not embracing your terroir — which I'm a big fan of. You should just embrace what you have." Wild brewing is, unlike any other kind of beer making, a product of place, making these beers irreproducible anywhere else. They lend themselves to blending, to the use of fruit, and to slow aging. Among connoisseurs, lambics and especially gueuze (a blend of different lambic vintages) are often considered the best beers in the world. And while the brewer and blender play important roles, it all comes down to the action of those unique local microorganisms. Boon's doesn't taste like Cantillon's or Girardin's, which don't taste like Allagash's or Solera's — or what you'll produce if you use this technique at home.

Brewing a Spontaneous Ale

There are two important elements in brewing spontaneous ales: inoculation and aging. Inoculation is variable and uncontrollable. It not only depends on the location of inoculation, but the season and ambient temperatures. In Belgium lambic is only made between November and March. There are too many microbes in the summer air, and the wort stays too warm for too long. Even within the season lambic makers watch the weather and select days when the temperature will be what they like. "The best temperature for me is around 0° Celsius [32°F]," Van Roy says. He continues, describing how cool the inoculated wort should drop overnight. "The goal is to reach between 18 and 20°C [64–68°F] tomorrow morning."

Location matters a lot, too. Daniel Hynes, the founding brewer at Thunder Island (he then moved to Breakside), ran an experiment where he placed 1-gallon buckets of wort in Portland's Forest Park, a 5,200-acre plot dense with Douglas firs. It was a part of the Beers Made by Walking project, in which brewers use foraged ingredients to make beer. Hynes was out to forage wild yeast. It was winter, just following an ice storm. He scattered buckets around the forest for 24 hours, leaving them in different types of locations: next to a decomposing nurse log, by an old snag full of holes, in a patch of new growth, and three other spots.

He then pitched each bucket into larger volumes of wort, inoculating them with the bugs found in the forest. Despite the fact that all the beer came from the same forest, he made a surprising discovery. The old-growth and nurse-log worts produces the sweetest, most interesting worts and were richest in microorganisms. The worst-performing wort came from the newer growth. But more important, *they were all different.*

Maybe this isn't surprising. When I visited his brewery, the lambic maker Frank Boon shared his thoughts about where to find the best yeasts. "If your brewery is on the top of the hill, you will always have less wild yeast: temperatures in the night, difference of temperature in the night, and wind also. If you look at it from another side, the old English books will tell you if you're going to build a new brewery, put it on the top of a hill and make the opening of your cellars from the north. To keep the wild bugs *out*. So if you put it close to the river and put the openings to the south, you will have much more wild yeasts. If you count wild yeasts in the air, you will find much more wild yeasts near a river than at the top of a hill; if you count bacteria, it's about the same."

Aging the beer is another critical element. Spontaneous ales take a long time to develop, so each different species of yeast and bacteria has a chance to impart its own character. The importance of time and oxygen were discussed in the previous chapter, so I won't repeat it here, and different techniques to accomplish the aging will be discussed in Next Steps. The main thing to note is that these are slow beers, and you have to let them develop. In the recipe that follows, where you'll be inoculating with the yeast on the skins of fruit, the aging process is only a year long. But if you try a lambic-style spontaneous ferment, you'll notice changes up to three years later.

The final note has to do with temperament. If you wanted to boil the whole of modern brewing to a single goal, you would say that it involves trying to gain as much control over the biochemistry of the brewing process. This approach seems fundamentally contrary to brewing wild, which requires the embrace of randomness. When I visited Cantillon back in 2011, Van Roy — who is equal parts poet, philosopher, and brewer — put it this way. "It's never the same. Never. You never know what you will discover. That's why lambic is so fun."

> In French we have a saying, *Tout est dans tout*. If I translate it: everything is in everything. In this brewery, everything is playing a role in the final product. Everything.
>
> — JEAN VAN ROY, CANTILLON

This is not the approach of the modern brewer; it's something closer to an alchemist, which Kahler acknowledged. "It's kind of magical in my head. There's obviously hard science behind it, but I don't understand all that science, and I don't think you *have* to understand that science." He continued: "I don't worry too much about [it]. Getting back to philosophy: you have to get over your fear if you're going to try these beers. You can't lose sleep over something like this."

Remember Charlie Papazian's old maxim? "Relax. Don't worry. Have a home-brew." There's something of that approach in brewing wild. Put yourself in the right frame of mind, and just do it. The worst thing that can happen is you'll lose a few gallons of wort. On the other hand, you may make a batch of ambrosia.

In Jason Kahler's recipe, he calls for inoculation by fruit, an easy process that takes some of the guesswork out of natural fermentation. Discussion of spontaneous ferments follows in Next Steps.

MALT BILL

6.5 pounds German pilsner malt (87%)

12 ounces white wheat malt (10%)

4 ounces Carapils malt (3%)

0.5 pound acidulated malt (added to mash before lauter)

SINGLE-INFUSION MASH

154°F (68°C) for 1 hour

5-MINUTE BOIL

No hops added.

FERMENTATION AND CONDITIONING

Chill wort to 65°F (18°C) and add 10 pounds whole organic sour cherries, preferably straight from the tree or farmer. Fruit from a grocery store has been washed and handled; it's best if you can find a source with lots of yeast on the skins. Spontaneous ferments take longer to show visible signs of activity; don't panic if alcohol fermentation doesn't begin for 48 hours, and don't expect the quick, vigorous ferment of cultured yeast.

Keep in a dark place, and don't move the carboy around. It's best to keep it around 65°F (18°C), but this isn't absolutely critical. Kahler mentioned an experience he had. "I actually had a woodshed outside, and it would get up to the 100s in the summer, and it would freeze in the winter. I got a couple of years out of it before it went acetic."

Don't start tasting the beer until 9 months have gone by, and limit the number of times you sample it; 1 year should be enough time — meaning you can do these beers annually, with the fruit harvest. After a year the microorganisms will have fully consumed the fruit and left only the pits behind.

SPONTANEOUS ALE

JASON KAHLER

—

SOLERA

PACKAGE

Bottle-condition or keg.

- Expected OG: 13.5° P/1.055

- Expected TG: 1.5° P/1.006

- Expected ABV: 6.4%

- Expected bitterness: 0 IBU

Notes: The base beer recipe is flexible. If you want more color, substitute Vienna or Munich for a portion of the pilsner malt. Kahler's recipes generally fall within these parameters: 80 to 90 percent pilsner malt, 5 to 10 percent white wheat malt, 5 to 10 percent Carapils. He then adds up to 10 percent acidulated malt at lautering. This recipe will give you an initial OG of 11° P/1.044. You'll pick up the extra sugars when you add fruit, which accounts for the 13.5° P/1.055 values listed above. If you substitute other fruit for cherries, you will end up with a different gravity.

If you're worried about not using hops, you can use up to 10 IBUs of low-alpha varieties, and if you're using hops, boil for 1 hour. If you're *not* using hops, you can also just raise the wort to 180°F (82°C) and hold for 10 minutes, a practice Kahler uses. Use any fruit you like, but those that ripen on trees will have a longer time to collect yeast. Kahler is a fan of cherries and peaches. You may want to remove the pits of some fruits, such as peaches, before adding them.

NEXT STEPS

If you want to experiment with lambic-style spontaneous fermentation, both Jason Kahler and Daniel Hynes recommend starting with small amounts placed in multiple locations. They suggest that you start with a very basic recipe — just a simple wort of around 1.040 to 1.045 (10 or 11° P). Both even suggest starting with a quick batch made with dry malt extract. Many lambic makers create a dextrinous "turbid mash" to give *Brettanomyces* something to munch on, but for this stage of things, a simpler, easily fermented batch is fine. Start out with a regular 5-gallon batch; then divide the wort into equal portions, and place it in different locations you think might be rich in healthy yeast and bacteria (heeding Boon's advice above).

Climates vary widely, so follow these basic guidelines for season and temperature. You want it to be cool but not frozen. Overnight temperatures under 50°F (10°C) are a must, and it's better if the temperature is between freezing and 40°F (4°C). Hynes used sterilized plastic buckets, drilling holes in the lid to let in the microorganisms. Kahler uses open collectors protected by cheesecloth "to keep stuff from falling in there" (wise advice). The amount of liquid is so small that it will cool quickly, much more quickly than wort in Belgian coolships. As mentioned, because of the volume, Cantillon's beer ends up in the 60s F (16–21°C) by the morning, which will be far warmer than a gallon placed in your backyard. It doesn't seem to matter, though, so don't worry about the shape of the collector.

Place the wort samples in the evening, as the temperatures are falling, and retrieve them in the morning, putting them in sterilized carboys. Kahler waits until after the first freeze, which he thinks might help clear the air of a lot of the "crap" that inhabits it during the warmer months. (Europeans have long eschewed brewing in the summer for exactly this reason. In Belgium they called it the "taste of summer," which in this case was a very bad thing. One nineteenth-century source wrote, "The result strongly affected the taste and the more or less nauseating odor is the true character of this kind of ferment.")

You're going to have to let the samples ferment for some period of time to begin to guess what kind of bugs you found. You don't have to wait for months, though. If any of your ferments have gone badly wrong, you'll know in a few weeks. Let the worts go through primary fermentation, and then you can begin tasting to see if you're getting something promising. When you have a batch you think is doing well, create a wort using the ingredient and formulation Kahler provided above and blend it with the smaller portion of wild beer. You'll need to let that batch sit at least a year, during which time it may go through a "sick" stage when bacteria produce slimy ropes or form an unsightly fungal matting (called a pellicle). Both are totally normal, and the pellicle is actually beneficial development; it will protect the wort from oxygen.

THE ORIGIN OF THE SOLERA PROCESS

Modified solera programs are in use in a few breweries now, but they look a bit different from the original soleras that were developed in Portugal and Spain to age wine and sherry. In that system a solera is a network of oak barrels stacked in rows that are used to slowly age the wine. After the harvest an equal portion of wine (usually 25 to 50 percent) is taken from each barrel on the bottom row for bottling and sale. The same amount is removed from the barrels in the next row up and added to the older row beneath, and on down the line like that until the barrels in the top row have space for that year's wine. The process incorporates blending, so the finished product, though composed of many different vintages, will have a recognizable, complex flavor. In this way it's different from aged wine, which is particular to a given year's crop.

The Solera System

This process is so easy it seems like a cheat. The idea is to keep alive an ecosystem that has produced an especially tasty batch of wild ale. Kahler discovered it on his own as a way of preserving the serendipitous conditions that led to very good batches of spontaneous ales. He had been blending different batches of wild ales, leaving behind partly filled carboys. Rather than blend all the carboys out, he decided to top them off with fresh wort. "I thought, 'I like what this one's doing, and I'd like to have some of that in the future.' So I kept them going like that." Those living microorganisms fermented the wort, reproducing the original beer.

The advantages of this system are many. It's not only a way to replicate a great batch — something that's nearly impossible with spontaneous ferments — but it gives the avid wild-ale brewer a palette of different flavors for blending. Counterintuitively, this may mean keeping around one or two carboys that have flavors too strong or odd on their own — but that can add wonderful accents in a blend.

The first step is waiting until you have a batch you want to preserve. You can use this system with spontaneously fermented beer or with beer made by pitching wild cultures. In either case the yeast and bacteria will come into a natural harmony inside the carboy. This is the same process New Belgium uses in its expansive aging program. When I spoke to brewer Peter Bouckaert, he talked about each foeder as though it had a personality. "Foeder number two, that one we had to rebuild because it was leaky. We tried to rebuild it, and it worked, but that one produces a lot of the high acidic to lactic formations. Foeder number nine always produced lactic and ropiness." New Belgium has so many different foeders — each making a unique beer — that they have enormous flexibility in how a finished beer tastes.

It's good to give the first generation enough time to find this harmony; Kahler suggests a year to a year and a half. Once that generation is ready, you can pull off roughly two-thirds of the batch and top off with fresh wort. "It's all about care and feeding," he says. Subsequent generations are far speedier. "About three to four months later, I've found you have a beer that tastes like it's a year old."

An additional benefit of this system is that introducing fresh wort allows you to introduce oxygen into the carboy. Kahler has always maintained nonporous steel soleras, but adding fresh wort provides oxygen that would be available in staves in other aging systems. "I found no issues using stainless versus wood. When you're adding fresh wort to a solera, oxygenate it a little bit. Part of the endgame in doing that is you're making food; you're trying to keep these things alive and healthy." That's why you do it every four months: "a feeding period." With the solera system, you don't have to worry about wood aging to get that oxygen.

Finally, if you want to work with fruit after you've got soleras going, rack off the typical amount into a separate carboy, add fruit, and top off with fresh wort. If you're not inoculating with fruit, you don't have to buy organic produce straight from the farmer. The native yeasts will take care of things.

GLOSSARY

ACETIC. An aroma descriptor for a vinegar aroma caused by *Acetobacteria*. Common in sour, wood-aged beers.

ACID REST. A rest during mashing, usually between 90 and 120°F (32 and 49°C), used to drop the pH of a mash, particularly when making pale lagers. Not widely used anymore.

ALTBIER. A German beer made from top-fermenting yeast. Kölsch is an example.

AMYLASE REST. During mashing the main conversion of malt happens when two diastatic enzymes, alpha amylase and beta amylase, break down starches into sugars. Alpha amylase works optimally in a band of temperatures between 154 and 162°F (68 and 72°C); beta amylase in a band between 131 and 150°F (55 and 66°C). Together, they are sometimes referred to as a saccharification rest or starch conversion.

ATTEMPERATION. A process to control the temperature, usually by running water through pipes to cool hot wort.

ATTENUATION. The percentage of residual sugars that have been converted to alcohol and carbon dioxide during fermentation. The more sugars converted, the drier the beer and the more highly attenuated.

BARREL. The standard unit in commercial brewing. A US barrel is 31.5 gallons (119 L); a British barrel is 43.2 gallons (164 L).

BRETTANOMYCES. A genus of wild yeast used in brewing to produce barnyard (horsey), pineapple, and other aromas.

BURTONIZE. To add minerals to water to resemble the water profile of Burton upon Trent in England, long famous for pale ales.

CASK CONDITIONING. The British practice of fermenting beer a second time in a cask, with a second dose of yeast. Beer that has been cask-conditioned (cask ale) is sometimes referred to as "real ale."

CONDITIONING. The process of maturation of beer, whether in bottles or kegs. During this phase complex sugars are slowly fermented, carbon dioxide is dissolved, and yeast settles to the bottom.

COOLSHIP. A flat, panlike vessel used to cool hot wort. It may also be used to inoculate wort with wild yeast and bacteria.

COPPER. A British term for the brew kettle, so called because of its traditional material of construction.

DANK HOPS. "Dank" is a word that developed on the American West Coast to describe hops that have the aromatic and flavor quality of cannabis; sticky, resinous, and green are synonyms.

DECOCTION MASH. A mashing technique that involves removing a portion of the mash, heating it, and returning it to the main mash.

DOUGHING IN. A process of blending the grist with water between 95 and 110°F (35 and 43°C) so the grain can take in moisture and improve mash efficiency.

DRY-HOPPING. Adding hops directly to the tank or cask at the end of fermentation to increase hop aroma without adding bitterness.

DUNKEL. German word for "dark," as in dark beer. Usually refers to Munich dark style.

ESTERS. Compounds that are produced during warmer fermentation and are the main way ales are distinguished from lagers in character. Esters are typically described as "fruity," but they can read as sweet. Common esters include ethyl acetate (fruity in low concentrations, solventlike in higher), ethyl caproate (apple, anise), ethyl caprylate (apple), isoamyl acetate (banana or pear), isobutyl acetate (pineapple), and phenyl acetate (honey, rose).

FERULIC ACID REST. A mash step, at temperatures of between 104 and 113°F (40 and 45°C), employed by wheat beer makers that causes the barley to release ferulic acid necessary in the formation of spicy phenols in these beers.

FIRST RUNNINGS. The sugar-rich wort that drains off at the beginning of runoff. Used in former times to make a strong beer; nowadays blended in with the rest of the batch.

FLAMEOUT. *See* knockout.

FOEDER. A large wooden tun used to condition beer; Flemish for the word *fourdre*, used in French wine making.

GRANT. A vessel located beneath the lauter tun in a recessed pocket with an array of many swan-neck faucets. The attached valves were used to regulate the flow out of the lauter tun on the way to the kettle. Still used everywhere in the Czech Republic.

GRIST. The grain or combination of grains that have been milled and are ready for brewing.

HELLES. A pale lager similar to pilsner but emphasizing more soft maltiness.

HOP BACK. A vessel used to remove hop material before the wort is cooled for fermentation. Often used for post–kettle hopping.

HOT LIQUOR. *See* liquor.

IBU (INTERNATIONAL BITTERNESS UNIT). The accepted system for describing the hop bitterness of a beer.

INFUSION MASH. Mashing at a single temperature.

KETTLE. The vessel in which wort is boiled. *See also* copper.

KNOCKOUT. The moment when the flame is turned off the kettle (sometimes referred to as "flameout").

KRÄUSEN. The thick, foamy head on fermenting beer.

LACTOBACILLUS. A large genus of bacteria that convert sugar into lactic acid. Some brewers add *Lactobacillus* intentionally to create a sour flavor in certain styles of beer.

LAGERING. The process of storing bottom-fermenting beers at cold temperatures for maturation and clarification.

LAUTER TUN. A vessel used for lautering, the process of removing the sweet wort from the grains by straining.

LIQUOR. Hot water used for mashing and sparging.

MAILLARD REACTION. The natural browning that occurs between sugars and protein when food or wort is heated. This happens to roasting malt or beer brewed over an open flame.

MALT. Barley or other grain that has been allowed to sprout, then dried or roasted.

MASH. The process of steeping malted grain in warm water to convert starch to fermentable sugars.

MASH IN. The temperature at which warm water is added to the grist.

MASH OUT. The process of raising the temperature of the mash to the point (usually 167 to 172°F [75–78°C]) at which it will stop enzymatic activity and preserve the balance of residual to fermentable sugars in the mash.

MASH TUN. A vessel used for mashing, often including a perforated bottom so liquid can be strained out.

MELANOIDINS. A group of complex color compounds formed by heating sugars and starches in the presence of proteins. Created in brewing during grain roasting and wort boiling.

MOREISH. A British term that describes the quality of a beer that can be drunk over the course of a session of drinking.

MOUTHFEEL. Sensory qualities of a beverage other than flavor, such as body and carbonation.

ORIGINAL GRAVITY (OG). A measure of wort strength expressed as specific gravity; the weight of the wort relative to the weight of water. See also *specific gravity*.

PARTI-GYLE. A method of brewing in which the runnings from a mash are collected separately, boiled, and later blended to create multiple beers of different strengths.

PHENOLS. Flavor and aroma compounds that result from an interaction of the grain and yeast; they are spicy and may taste of clove, black pepper, or smoke.

PITCH YEAST. To add yeast to wort.

POST-KETTLE HOPPING. The process of removing the heat from the kettle after wort has been boiled and steeping hops in this sub-boiling liquid. In commercial breweries this usually happens in a hop back or in the whirlpool. Post–kettle hopping will extract some bitterness as well as hop aroma and flavor.

PROTEIN REST. A mash rest at 113 to 131°F (45–55°C) that is used to break down proteins in less modified malts.

RACK. To move the beer from one container to another. Unless otherwise noted, the goal is to separate beer from spent yeast.

RECIRCULATION. A process of filtering the wort of cloudy proteins and grain particles by running out wort and sprinkling it back on the grain bed.

REINHEITSGEBOT. The Bavarian law dating to 1516 that restricted the ingredients in beer to water, malted barley, and hops.

RUNNINGS. Wort that is drained from the mash during sparging. *See also* first runnings.

SACCHARIFICATION REST. *See* amylase rest.

SINGLE-INFUSION MASH. *See* infusion mash.

SPARGING. Sprinkling hot liquor on the grain bed of the mash to rinse out remaining sugars.

SPECIFIC GRAVITY. A measurement of the density of solid materials in the beer, compared to the density of water. Used in brewing to follow the course of fermentation.

STARCH CONVERSION. *See* amylase rest.

STEP MASH. A technique in which the brewer raises the mash temperature through two or more rests or steps to optimize enzymatic activity.

STRIKE WATER. The heated water added during mash in. Strike water is always warmer than the temperature of the first mash rest because the ambient temperature of the grain will lower it.

TERROIR. The unique soil, climate, and topography, among other characteristics, of a crop's geographic location, which affect the finished product. Often used in reference to wine and the grapes used to make it, but occasionally used in descriptions of hops and yeast or, more rarely, barley.

TORREFIED. Torrefication is the process of rapidly heating grain so it puffs up like popcorn. Commonly applied to barley and wheat. Often used in British pale ales.

TRUB. Coagulated protein and hop resin sludge that precipitates out of wort during boiling and again at chilling. (Pronounced *troob*.)

VINOUS. Characteristics that recall wine; typically refers to tart, dry, alcoholic notes or grapelike flavors.

VORLAUF. *See* recirculation.

WHIRLPOOL. A vessel used after boiling that removes solid particles by swirling the wort; the centripetal action of the wort causes the particles to form into a cone on the bottom of the vessel. It is sometimes used for post–kettle hopping.

WORT. Unfermented beer, the sugar-laden liquid obtained from the mash.

RECOMMENDED READING

Alworth, Jeff. *The Beer Bible*. Workman, 2015.

Beechum, Drew, and Denny Conn. *Experimental Homebrewing*. Voyageur Press, 2014.

Cornell, Martyn. *Amber, Gold, and Black*. The History Press, 2010.

Hieronymus, Stan. *Brew Like a Monk*. Brewers Publications, 2005.

Hieronymus, Stan. *Brewing with Wheat*. Brewers Publications, 2010.

Hieronymus, Stan. *For the Love of Hops*. Brewers Publications, 2012.

Jackson, Michael. *Beer Companion*. Running Press, 1997.

Mallett, John. *Malt: A Practical Guide from Field to Brewhouse*. Brewers Publications, 2014.

Mosher, Randy. *Radical Brewing*. Brewers Publications, 2004.

Palmer, John. *How to Brew*. Brewers Publications, 2006.

Palmer, John and Colin Kaminski. *Water: A Comprehensive Guide for Brewers*. Brewers Publications, 2013.

Pattinson, Ron. *The Home Brewer's Guide to Vintage Beer*. Quarry Books, 2014.

Wahl, Robert and Max Henius. *American Handy-Book of the Brewing, Malting, and Auxiliary Trades*. Wahl and Henius, 1902.

White, Chris and Jamil Zainasheff. *Yeast: The Practical Guide to Beer Fermentation*. Brewers Publications, 2010.

INDEX

ENRICH YOUR EFFERVESCENCE
with More Storey Books

THE BEER GEEK HANDBOOK
BY PATRICK DAWSON

Learn how to fully appreciate beer without becoming a snob! This fun-filled illustrated manual offers guidance on pulling off a beer tasting, tips for gracefully correcting an uninformed bartender, the Ten Beer Geek Commandments, and so much more.

CLONEBREWS
BY TESS AND MARK SZAMATULSKI

Brew your own beer that tastes just like premium commercial brands! These 200 recipes for popular ales, lagers, pilsners, porters, stouts, and specialty beers have been tested and tasted to deliver the perfect flavors.

THE HOMEBREWERS GARDEN
BY JOE FISHER AND DENNIS FISHER

From seed to suds, you can do it all with these easy instructions for growing your own hops, malt grains, and brewing herbs. The 29 specialty homebrew recipes will showcase your homegrown ingredients.

TASTING BEER
BY RANDY MOSHER

Uncap the secrets in every bottle of the world's greatest drink. Learn what makes each brew unique and how to identify the scents, colors, flavors, and mouthfeel of nearly 90 beer styles from around the globe.

Join the conversation. Share your experience with this book, learn more about Storey Publishing's authors, and read original essays and book excerpts at storey.com. Look for our books wherever quality books are sold or call 800-441-5700.